SMALL CHRISTIAN COMMUNITIES

James O'Halloran

Small Christian Communities
Vision and Practicalities

the columba press

First published, 2002, by
the columba press
55A Spruce Avenue, Stillorgan Industrial Park,
Blackrock, Co Dublin

Cover by Bill Bolger
Origination by The Columba Press
Printed in Ireland by Colour Books Ltd, Dublin

ISBN 1 85607 387 4

Contents

Introduction

This volume is in the lineage of *Living Cells, Signs of Hope,* and *Small Christian Communities: A Pastoral Companion.* It benefits, however, from six years of added experience in many parts of the world. Much of the writing is new, the spirituality more developed, and the theological, spiritual, and practical elements better integrated. In effect, I feel we are talking of a new book.

A glance at the table of contents will show that many helpful features are on offer. *I do not believe that there is a blueprint for small Christian communities.* What I share is a vision and practical suggestions that may help communities *to find their own path.* These insights are the result of thirty years experience with grassroot communities in all parts of the world, as member, coordinator, and promoter. What I invite readers to do is to look at the insights, reflect upon them, and, if they seem helpful, adapt them to their own environment. The small Christian community, like the gospel, must become flesh and blood where it is.

Over several years I have thought much and consulted with small Christian community members about the spirituality of the groups, and I believe I now give a more coherent account of it; also, as already mentioned, the spirituality, theology, and practicalities are presented in a more integrated fashion. *The spirituality that emerges could I feel be beneficial to every Christian; indeed it could prove thought-provoking for every person of goodwill.*

I am enthused by the historical profile, most of which is fresh. Those who contribute to it – Bishop Thomas Dabre, Ian Fraser, Roald Kverndal, José Marins, Paul O'Bryan, and Robert Pelton – are truly knowledgeable in the areas about which they write and, indeed, have had quite an involvement in the history with which

they deal. Their biographical details are given in the text. The North
American survey has the advantage of being backed up by a scientific study, owing to a generous grant from the Lilly Endowment
Inc.; the other writers have not had such support, but they know
their situations as well as anyone can at the moment. The result is a
worthwhile profile at the turn of the millennium. Many will probably be hearing about the fascinating history of Maritime Mission
and its communities for the first time. In fact the book as a totality
provides a fair snapshot of small Christian communities at the year
2002. The contributors do not pretend to know everything that is
happening in the tracts of the world that they cover, but they make
excellent attempts to give a picture. Their efforts will, hopefully, set
down signposts to facilitate the work of historians in the future.

The historical profile is Part IV of the book. People busily
engaged in pastoral activities do not rush to read the history.
However, if they don't do so, I think they are greatly impoverished.
I should perhaps also point out that the historical profile in this
volume's predecessor, *Small Christian Communities: A Pastoral Companion* (cf. bibliography), is not cancelled by the present one, rather
does it complement it.

I'd like to make a further point regarding the reading of this
work. It lends itself to a dipping-in approach, since it is purposely
practical in parts. But I would recommend that it be read once in its
entirety before the reader does this.

As in *Small Christian Communities: A Pastoral Companion*, I vary
the masculine and feminine forms, 'he' and 'she', throughout the
work.

I would like to thank the great host of people who contributed to
this book; in other words all those with whom I was privileged to
share on five continents over the past thirty years. To name them
would be to fill another volume, and, even then, some would probably be missed out. You are all in my heart and in my prayers. A
years's reflection at La Salle University, Philadelphia (Graduate
Religion) was of considerable help.

However, such was their support, there are two people whose
names I simply cannot omit: Monica von Ballestrem and Colleen

Fleischmann (RIP). As well as being valued friends, they were profound thinkers on the subject of small Christian communities.

There are a few organisations to whom I owe a debt of gratitude. Misereor (Germany), who have backed me, not only in this project, but in much of the work I have been doing over twenty years. I am grateful for the confidence they have always shown in me. At an earlier time Trócaire (Ireland) gave me valuable assistance. I thank my own Salesian Congregation too for having helped me in all sorts of ways, above all for having had the vision to allow me to work on the small Christian communities and youth groups project in the first place.

Finally, Christine Crotty, the artist who provided the illustrations for this work, points out that the picture on page 256 is a composite of the twelve preceding drawings, arranged horizontally in four groups of three. She invites the readers to see what they see.

PART I

The Vision

The essential elements of small Christian communities are:
- Bonding,
- Spirituality,
- Reality,
- Commitment,
- Communication.

Here in Part I, the theme of Bonding is found in chapters 1-4, but particularly in 1 ('The Church as Communion') and 2 ('The Kingdom of God'). The subject of Spirituality is also present in chapters 1-4, yet largely in 3 and 4 ('The Prayerful Dimension' and 'Permeated by Love'). Commitment, too, is treated of in chapter 1. These comprise the more visionary aspects of the subject. Reality and Communication are mainly dealt with in Part II of this volume, which concerns itself with the Practicalities of small Christian communities.

Before reading this book, I would recommend that the short introduction not be omitted; it gives the key for perusing the work.

CHAPTER 1

The Church as Communion

As already noted, I propose first of all to share on the visionary aspects of small Christian communities, and I begin with a story. In March 1994, I facilitated a workshop in Nairobi. At the beginning the participants were sharing experiences of such communities and I found the anecdote of a young woman called Sylvia of particular interest. 'When I left school,' she informed us, 'I would say that I had the faith. I lived on the outskirts of Nairobi and every Sunday travelled by bus to the centre of the city where I attended Mass at the Holy Family Basilica. But the basilica was very big and I didn't know anyone much. I felt alone. In the pulpit father talked about love and community, yet somehow I didn't understand. Then going home one Sunday and feeling a bit depressed, I said to myself, I don't have a spiritual friend in the whole world.'

This was the low point of Sylvia's narrative, and what she was saying was truly sad, because none of us goes to heaven alone. We are saved through relationships. The Bible says that it is not good for us to be alone (cf. Genesis 2:18). A person who cuts herself off from others is a human contradiction because, without one another, we could not even learn to be persons. Without the sunshine of love and the rain of acceptance, we cannot grow as persons. However, Sylvia went on to say: 'Soon afterwards I came across a small Christian community in my own area and became a member. With that all changed. In the community I didn't simply hear about love, as in the basilica, I actually experienced it, tasted the sweetness of togetherness. And little by little I grew spiritually, gained new ideas, made good friends, and was able to take part in work for my neighbourhood. I blossomed as a person. No longer am I that girl who travelled alone into Nairobi, was lost in the big church, and returned home downcast.'

What Sylvia was experiencing, by the power of the Holy Spirit people are experiencing in thousands of such groups on every continent. Furthermore the Spirit who is at work at the grassroots also blew strongly on this theme at Vatican Council II (1962-65). Paragraph 4 in the *Dogmatic Constitution on the Church* says: '... the universal church is seen to be "a people brought into unity from the unity of the Father, Son and the Holy Spirit".' These to me are among the lapidary words of the twentieth century with far-reaching consequences for the church and the world.

In effect we are asked in the church to be a community as the Trinity is community. This raises intriguing questions as to what kind of a community the Trinity is and how we make it present in the church. Just to choose a few challenging facts: the Trinity is a community where there is:

- intimate loving and sharing,
- full participation of the three members,
- absolute equality of persons, and
- outreach to the other.

How do we replicate this in the church? As we will see, the small Christian communities are one important way.

At this juncture I should like to make the point that the proposal of the church as communion in modern times has come from two sources, namely, the World Council of Churches in Geneva and Vatican Council II, as already noted. The World Council of Churches was in formation during the years of the Second World War and was finally founded in 1948. In the years following it did much research on the notion of the church as the 'People of God', a model that emphasised the role of the laity. This research was made available to the participants of Vatican II by a team of fifteen theologians from the World Council of Churches meeting with fifteen of their Roman Catholic counterparts, at the request of John XXIII. So, from two sources, Geneva and Rome, there flowed the model of church as communion in the image of the Trinity.

Community like the Trinity
We might take as our starting point the reality of the small Christian

community to seek answers to the questions we have just posed. In the group we find various members who strive through their loving and sharing to become *one*. The roots of this experience, I suggest, we find in no less exalted a place than among the *Blessed Trinity*. Here we have the Father, the Son, and the Holy Spirit who through their intimate loving and sharing *are one God, or one community*. As they say in Africa, 'There are three dancers but only one dance.'

Now we were created in God's image. In Genesis 1:26-27 we read how God created human beings 'in our own image, after our own likeness ... male and female ...' The statement that we were created male and female is significant. As already noted, we are not meant to live in isolation. From the beginning God's will was that we be *a community of brothers and sisters without divisions;* there can be differences that enrich, yes, divisions no. The message of scripture is clear: no barriers. This theme is taken up by Paul, who makes a creative theological leap in Galatians 3:28 to declare:

There is neither Jew nor Greek,

there is neither slave nor free,

there is neither male nor female,

for all are one in Christ Jesus.

So why must we be community? Quite simply because God is community, and we are created in God's image. It is true that God is within me and I reflect an aspect of God to the world that no one else can, and it is also true that I am uniquely a cell of the body of Christ. Nevertheless would it not be accurate to say that we are more fully like God and Jesus when we live in harmony?

Because of our abuse of God-given freedom, we sinned and brought division. We marred God's plan for creatures. In offending God, we did something that we could not of ourselves put right, God being infinite and we finite. The merciful answer of the Father was to send his only begotten son, Jesus, to be our Saviour. All human community is of course rooted in the Blessed Trinity, but Christian community, specifically, is *centred in Jesus.* It is characterised by belief in Christ who died and rose to redeem us and whose mystical body we are (1 Corinthians 12:27). We could put this another way and say that by the will of the Father, the power of the Holy Spirit, and the free consent of the Virgin Mary Jesus came to *restore community*. He is the one who reconciles us to ourselves, to God, to our brothers and sisters, and to creation round about us. If then the Christian community has its roots in the Trinity, it is the incarnate Jesus who mediates the infinite love of the Trinitarian community to the church and the world. The Jesus who cleansed the ten lepers, gave sight to the blind Bartimaeus, and forgave the woman taken in adultery made the Trinitarian God present in the world (cf. Matthew 1:23; John 14:8-14). In this latter text of John, for example, Philip says to Christ: 'Lord, show us the Father; that is all we need.' And the answer? 'Whoever has seen me has seen the Father.' He might also have added 'and the Spirit,' because Jesus is a human way of being divine and makes the loving God present in the world.

In the sacraments something that we can see makes present something that we cannot see. In baptism, for instance, the presence of the Christian community and the water which the minister pours can clearly be observed, making us aware of what is invisible, namely, the life of God flowing into the being of the one receiving the sacrament and her mystical integration into the community that surrounds her. So the historic Jesus, whom people could see, made the loving Trinity, whom they could not see, present. Christ was a sacrament of the Trinity, *the one who restored community*, restored God's image and likeness among us.

Christ is risen and no longer with us in the body as he was with his own people in those far off days. And yet he is still present through his church. Speaking to its members, Paul said, 'Now you are the body of Christ and individually members of it' (1 Corinthians 12:27). The church, therefore, is a sacrament of Christ. We can no longer see him in the flesh, but we can see him in the community. So the church makes Christ present in the world. Indeed as a community of brothers and sisters, who through their loving and sharing become one, it makes the Trinity present. And it is the church, activated of course by the Spirit, that must now carry on Christ's work of community-building, striving to reconcile us to ourselves, God, neighbour, and environment.

Much too big

The church, however, is a worldwide reality which is becoming increasingly hard to identify as a community of Christ's followers or as Christ's presence on earth. It is too big. The picture can begin to blur physically even at the parish stage. A place where the true nature of the church and its identity with Jesus become obvious is in the small Christian community. If to be church is to experience – and reflect – the intimate life of loving and sharing that characterises the Trinity, then this is *best achieved in small groups.* It is hard in a parish of thousands or for that matter even in a gathering of a hundred. How can intimate loving and sharing become apparent in such situations? Hence the importance of small Christian community. *Small Christian communities, though having their own relative autonomy, should be open to one another and can combine in a parish or wherever so as to form a communion of communities. In this manner a church in the image of the Trinity, as proposed in Vatican II, can be built up.*

This understanding of small community as a clear witness to the presence of Christ and the Trinity has considerable consequences for making Jesus known and passing on the faith. Although the small Christian communities are much more than evangelising groups, I believe that without their witness we are *severely handicapped* in communicating the gospel.

The following story may illustrate the point. I recall a bishop in Africa telling me that his diocese had an excellent catechetical programme for schools. Much of the effort expended, however, was like putting water into a bucket with a hole in it, because the family and the community were in disarray. The reason for this was that the menfolk, searching for work, migrated to the mining areas of nearby South Africa. Owing to the policy of apartheid, which still prevailed at the time, they could not bring their wives and children with them. Some never returned; others had families at home and in South Africa. Either way there was considerable social dislocation. Now what is the good of telling a child at school that God is *love,* if she does not *experience* love in family or small community? It remains a hollow word. The experiential, audio-visual aid of God is missing – the small community. Here again we have echoes of Sylvia's story.

The need to live Christ in a group is a refrain I have heard in
many parts, not least in my own small community in Dublin.

These examples pose searching questions for all Christians:

- Can we even begin to think seriously of announcing Christ
  (evangelisation) or explaining the faith (catechesis) without the
  witness of the small Christian community to Jesus and the
  Trinity?
- Isn't the small community an instrument without which we cannot function?

Even the Lord himself went about spreading the good news as part
of a travelling community. The love and sharing that he preached,
he practised.

Sharing

Sharing is obviously a key word for community; it involves participation in all aspects of our lives in common: faith, commitment,
worship, ideas, vision, good works, and material possessions. It is
an opening of mind, heart, and hand. In more formal terms we
might speak of a sharing that is spiritual, intellectual, intuitive,
emotional, and practical. Oftentimes when we talk of sharing, we
are thinking of food, money, or some such item. As we see, it is
much more than that.

It can of course be a matter of life's necessities. During a workshop in an African country that was undergoing a severe drought,
we were reflecting on Acts 4:32-37, the passage that speaks of the
early Christians as being 'one in mind and heart'. Starvation was
staring those people in the face, yet a poor farmer spoke up saying:
'This passage challenges me to go back home and share even the little that I have with others.' Here was love that cut deeply.

It is worth noting at this point that living in communion is not
just something which is pastorally necessary, but that equally,
according to experts in the field, is it a *deep psychological need* for
every human being. There is this hunger in all of us to belong,
despite a sinfulness that too often drags us towards division.

Commitment

From the realities that we share, as expressed above, we might perhaps single out commitment for special comment, because *it is the
heart and soul of community generally, and particularly of the small
Christian community.* By this, community will either stand or fall.
That it presupposes faith in Jesus the Saviour goes without saying.
There can be no question of Christian commitment without belief in
him, because *it calls for a persevering and total dedication to gospel values.* There has to be commitment on the part of each member and of
the community as a whole.

This also presupposes *conversion* – that the members have taken
seriously the responsibilities that come with baptism. At some
point in their lives they have made a U-turn away from evil and
towards God. But then the consequences of that conversion have to
be lived, so that every day they struggle to become a little less selfish, a little more generous. Faith isn't simply a matter of ideas in the
head, it translates into love in action. In other words, there is the
continuous effort, as Paul puts it, to grow to the full stature of
Christ (cf. Ephesians 4:13). There we find the life programme and
real challenge for every Christian: to become so Christlike that one
day she might be able to say with Paul '... it is no longer I who live,
but it is Christ who lives in me' (Galatians 2:20).

When sharing on conversion and commitment with groups, I
find it important to remind myself and those to whom I am speaking that this does not mean that small community is composed of
angels. It is made up of sinners who in their brokenness often fall
(cf. Proverbs 24:16), yet they steadfastly refuse to stay down. They
always rise again to seek reconciliation with God and neighbour.
Community is constantly being built up through continual reconciliation, and conversion needs frequent affirmation. St John Bosco
used to tell his young people that the tragedy lay not in falling, but
in failing to rise again. And Dom Helder Camara writes: 'At the
great judgment seat the Lord may say to someone: "How horrible!
You fell a million times!" But all is salvaged if that person can say:
"Yes, Lord, it really is frightful! But your grace helped me to get
back on my feet a million and one times".'[1]

This leads to my own understanding of commitment as *never ceasing to try*. And when I think about it, community members like Miguel often come to mind. From Monday to Saturday he spent long hours working in his South American factory for a paltry wage. He also spent long hours travelling to and fro on overcrowded buses. Yet on Sunday he laboured up the steep slopes of the Andes to share the good news of Jesus Christ with children. 'When Sunday comes,' he once told me, 'I often feel ill and not at all like going up the mountain. But how good the Lord is because, when I overcome my weariness and go, I always feel better.' Of such dedicated people surely is the kingdom of God.

We have seen, therefore, that all community, whether merely human or Christian, has its roots deep in the love of the Trinity. Furthermore Christian community is built on the incarnate Christ; indeed it is the body of Christ. He it is who mediates the infinite love of Father, Son, and Spirit to the church, and to the whole of creation. This of course would be a theological rather than a chronological progression. Above all the presence of the Trinity, the God who is love, and of Jesus Christ becomes palpable in small Christian communities, because their witness is so observable. They are clear sacraments of the Trinitarian community and of Jesus.

Summary
1) Through the power of the Holy Spirit, small Christian communities exist in thousands on every continent.
2) Vatican Council II says 'the universal church is seen to be "a people brought into unity from the unity of the Father, Son, and Holy Spirit".'
3) For members of the church this would entail intimate loving and sharing, full participation, equality, and mission.
4). How is this realised in practice?
5) Starting with the small Christian community, we find a group composed of separate persons who through their intimate loving and sharing become *one*.
6) The roots of this reality we find in the Trinity, where Father, Son and Spirit, though distinct persons, through their infinite loving and sharing are one God, or one community.

7) We were created as a community of brothers and sisters without divisions (cf. Genesis 1:26-27), but we sinned and marred community.

8) Jesus the Saviour came to restore community, to reconcile us to ourselves, God, brothers and sisters, and environment.

9) The historic Jesus was a sacrament of the Trinity in the world; he made the three persons present among us.

10) The church now continues the reconciling work of Christ and makes him present in the world (cf. 1 Corinthians 12:27).

11) The church, body of Christ, only becomes truly observable and tangible through reduced groups such as the small Christian communities.

12) Sharing all aspects of life – spiritual, intellectual, the work, and material possessions – is important for small Christian communities.

13) Commitment, or total dedication to Christ and gospel values, is the soul of small Christian community.

Questions

1) Have you any experience of being in a small group, religious or other, and what in the light of the foregoing chapter are your thoughts about it?
   Suggested Bible passage: Acts 4:32-37.

2) How does the Trinitarian model of church as communion relate to your own experience? Or does it relate at all?
   Suggested Bible passage: John 17:20-26.

3) Commitment is never ceasing to try. Do you agree?
   Suggested Bible passage: Mark 10:17-31.

CHAPTER 2

The Kingdom of God

As we have seen, the immense love of the Blessed Trinity is poured out in all creation. It is mediated to the church and the world by Christ the Saviour and becomes more defined in small Christian communities. That love, by the power of the Spirit, floods out beyond the confines of the church to the limits of the universe and time, reaching into eternity. This awesome domain we know as the kingdom of God. The kingdom, then, comprises an integral part of a Trinitarian, or communitarian, vision and spirituality.

The most important thing for Jesus in his ministry was the kingdom of God and its justice (cf. Matthew 6:33). The word 'church' is only used three times in the gospels (Matthew 16:18; 18:17) while Christ speaks frequently of *the kingdom*. Pope Paul VI describes the kingdom as 'the absolute good' to which everything else must defer (cf. *Evangelii Nuntiandi, The Evangelisation of Peoples*, no. 8). If, therefore, the kingdom is the priority for Jesus and if it is the absolute good, it is crucial that we consider the question: what exactly is the kingdom of God? A further query then would be: how does it relate to the church generally and, more specifically, to the small Christian communities?

I realise that there is a problem with the word *kingdom*. For some it would carry masculine connotations. However, the terms used to replace it so far seem to miss out somewhat on theological content, so we must wait upon experts to help us in this respect. Meanwhile I have opted to stay with the traditional expression.

There is a two-line poem by Hugh O'Donnell that has a teacher address a class so:
Attention!
Today, we will finish creation.[2]

That person was setting out to define the mystery. Where the kingdom of God is concerned, Jesus never defines it, precisely because it is a mystery. Nevertheless he says many things that shed light on this reality. But first of all let us turn to the Old Testament.

The kingdom in the Old Testament

The vision of the kingdom is deeply embedded in the scriptures commencing with the Old Testament.[3] Abraham sought out a new land (Genesis 1:1) and Moses 'a land flowing with milk and honey' (Exodus 3:8); so the earliest understanding of the kingdom was the rather basic one that it was *linked to territory*.

The prophets Isaiah and Jeremiah took this a step forward by declaring that in the promised land there would be *a privileged place for the poor*. Justice was not simply a matter of fasting while trampling on the little ones of the earth. Indeed such penance was worthless (cf. Isaiah 58:1-12). These prophets loudly sounded the note of justice.

In 587 BCE the Jews were taken captive to Babylon. This for them was a catastrophe because their land was the kingdom of God, and God dwelt in the Temple. Now they were cut off from both. Hence their lament:

How can we sing the Lord's song
in a foreign land? (Psalm 137)

God wasn't there to listen. During those awful times, when their dream had been shattered by exile, Isaiah encouraged his people to hope again (cf.42:1), and they began to get the idea that the vision of the kingdom was not just tied to territory, but was interior, an empire of the heart:

Thus says the Lord:
'Heaven is my throne
and earth is my footstool;
what is the house which you would
build for me,
and what is the place of my rest?'
(Isaiah 66:1-2).

In the centuries following the exile a powerful mood that the

end was near swept through the Middle East. And the notion that
the kingdom of God would not be fully achieved in this world
grew; it would stretch on into the *hereafter*. It was in this period too
that the actual expression 'kingdom of God' was used for the first
time (cf. Wisdom 10:10).

We see, therefore, how the understanding of the kingdom gradually developed in the Old Testament.

The kingdom in the New Testament
Jesus began his mission in Galilee with the clarion call: 'The time is
fulfilled, and the kingdom of God is at hand; repent and believe the
gospel' (Mark 1:15). The kingdom is the main theme of his mission,
the nub of the 'good news' he brings. Christ, as already noted, does
not define what he means by it because it is a mystery (cf. Matthew
13:11; Mark 4:11; Luke 8:10); however, we are told many things
about it in the New Testament. Here we give a selection of the
salient points. The kingdom:
- is the priority (cf. Matthew 6:33; Luke 12:31).
- lasts forever (cf. Luke 1:33; 2 Peter 1:11).
- is present in the world, yet is still to come (cf. 1 Corinthians
  15:12-28).
- means preaching the word (cf. Matthew 13:1-23; Mark 4:1-20;
  Luke 8:4-15).
- is near, 'within you' (cf. Luke 17:21).
- contains the good and the bad (cf. Matthew 13:24-30).
- grows from small beginnings (cf. Matthew 13:31-32; Luke 13:
  18-19).
- is a leaven (cf. Luke 13:20-21; Matthew 13:33).
- imposes obligations to love and forgive (cf. Matthew 18:23-35).
- welcomes all comers (cf. Matthew 20:1-16; Acts 5:34-39).
- is doing the will of God (cf. Matthew 6:10).
- means being always ready (cf. Matthew 25:1-13).
- calls on us to be bold and decisive (cf. Matthew 11:12; Luke 16:16).
- is 'where the blind see, the lame walk' (Luke 7:22) and where 'I
  was hungry and you fed me, thirsty and you gave me a drink'
  (Matthew 25:35).

Sometimes in the New Testament the kingdom seems to be identified with Jesus himself: Jesus is the kingdom (cf. Matthew 16:28;
19:29; 21:9; Mark 9:1; 10:29; 11:9-10; Luke 9:27; 18:29; 19:38; Acts
8:12; 28:31; Revelation 12:10).

John does not speak much of the kingdom. But again he would
appear to identify it with the person of Christ in all those 'I am'
statements that he makes in his gospel. 'You want to know what the
kingdom is like?' John would seem to say, 'Then look at Christ. It is
the mind, the heart, and the values of Christ.' The following would
be examples of this:

- I am the bread of life (John 6:35).
- I am the light of the world (John 8:12).
- I am not from this world (John 8:23).
- I am who I am, you cannot go where I am going (John 8:24).
- I am the gate for the sheep (John 10:7).
- I am the Good Shepherd (John 10:11).
- I am who I am (John 13:19).
- I am the way the truth and the life (John 14:6).
- I am the real vine (John 15:1).
- I am thirsty (John 19:28).

We have just said above that the kingdom welcomes all comers.
And that is true. Yet from the Beatitudes we gather that there is a
special place there for the poor, those who mourn, the meek, those
who hunger and thirst for justice, the merciful, the pure in heart, the
peacemakers, and those persecuted for righteousness (cf. Matthew
5:1-11). 'These,' to quote a friend of mine who put it rather graphically, 'are the "A" team in the kingdom of God.' If a worldly manager
were to select such an outfit, he would undoubtedly be summarily
fired!

Paul, of course, envisions the kingdom as 'a new creation,'
where neither circumcision nor uncircumcision counts for anything
(Galatians 6:15); and this is the same as John's understanding of it
as 'a new heaven and a new earth' (cf. Revelation 21:1) – a complete
transformation of old realities.

Looked at negatively, the kingdom is not simply about:
- money, as in the case of the rich young man (Mark 10:17-31),

- places of honour, which we learn from the rebuff of Jesus to the mother of James and John (Mark 10:35-45),
- earthly authority, gathered from Jesus reply to the question, 'By whose authority do you speak?' (Mark 11:28),
- worldly considerations such as taxes (Mark 12:13-17),
- buildings and structures: even the Temple is to be destroyed (Mark 13:1-2).

The spiritual dimension is supreme.

The foregoing provides a scriptural profile of the kingdom of God and, as we see, there is no attempt by Christ or anyone else to define this multi-faceted reality. We have to rely on symbols, and no matter how good these are they are dealing with something that is totally other. The kingdom is a matter of faith. Yet it is clearly something of infinite value, worth sacrificing everything to attain here and hereafter.

We might summarise this scriptural overview thus:

- 'a new creation' (Galatians 6:15; Revelations 21:1).
- the priority (Matthew 6:33; Luke 12:31).
- God's rule prevailing in the world.[4] (Psalm 103:19).
- the person of Jesus: his mind, heart, and values (cf. Matthew 16:28; 19:29; Mark 9:1; Luke 9:27; passim in the 'I am' statements in John's gospel).
- wherever there is harmony rooted in justice (Matthew 6:33; Luke 12:31).
- all that is good, gracious and, therefore, God-revealing – where 'the blind see, the lame walk' (Luke 7:21), and where 'I was hungry and you fed me, thirsty and you gave me a drink' (Matthew 25:35).
- openness and tolerance (Matthew 20:1-16; Acts 5:34-39).
- present and yet to come (1Corinthians 15:12-28).

Harmony would be the sustained note of God's kingdom, though in it we find some strange bedfellows indeed, as the beautiful images of Isaiah strikingly illustrate:

The wolf shall live with the lamb,
   the leopard shall lie down with
   the kid,

the calf and the lion and the
fatling together,
and a little child shall lead them.
Isaiah 11:6.

Two defining moments

There have been two great defining moments in the history of the
church. The first was when that pastoral genius, Paul, made the
breakthrough of realising that Christianity was not simply for the
Jews but for all peoples, and took the good news to the gentiles. He
understood too that, though the Christian religion grew out of
Judaism, it was something totally new (cf. 2 Corinthians 5:17;
Ephesians 4:4; Colossians 3:10-11). The second great moment has
occurred in our own times, when Vatican II and John XXIII flung
the windows of the church wide open and pointed to the kingdom
out there that needed continuous building up.

The church is part of the kingdom; it is not the whole of it. As we
said above, *wherever we find goodness* or *wherever there is harmony
rooted in justice*, the kingdom is there. It doesn't matter whether
those involved are Christians, Muslims, Jews, Hindus, or
Buddhists; we as a priority will support them. After all, if there is a
bridge to be built, there is no such thing as a Catholic, Methodist,
Muslim, or Hindu bridge. Bridges are ecumenical and permit all
sorts of people to cross over a river in safety. The idea of the kingdom is, therefore, a powerfully uniting force.

In December 1992, I had an experience that brought home to me
this universal nature of the kingdom. I had the privilege of visiting
some Buddhist communities in Thailand. One of them, the
Tamkaenjan group, was situated on the banks of the River Kwai,
just below the famous bridge. What I noticed particularly about the
members of this community was their deep reverence for God's
creation. 'Look here,' said Paiboon, an animator of the group, 'some
undergrowth was cleared away from this area so that we could
replant it, and immediately this profusion of grass sprang up to
prevent erosion. The more I see of creation the more I become
aware of the greatness of the Creator.'

As you would expect, the community farmed in a fashion that was friendly to the environment; it also had eight of its members going throughout Thailand on bicycles, sensitising people on the subject of the rain forest. These latter made their listeners acutely aware of what a terrible loss the destruction of this facility would be. It could mean the disappearance forever of natural and medicinal resources that human beings acutely need. Cures maybe for cancer, AIDS, and ebola. Who could tell? Many secrets of the rain forest still remained to be unearthed.

In addition to these activities there was a school for poor boys, some of them Cambodian refugees who had fled the killing fields, to whom the group was communicating the noblest of ideals.

There was a flock of geese that belonged to the group cavorting on the river. In fact two ganders fought a pitched battle in the vivid moonlight over some likely goose while I was there, and had to be quarantined in the interests of nocturnal tranquillity. However, the community did not eat the geese or the fish that abounded in the River Kwai, because they were strictly vegetarian. The flock was there purely so that they could rejoice in God's creation.

Most enlightening of all, however, were my conversations with Paiboon. Right from the start we found we had a lot in common. Neither of us was locked into his own position and we were eager to learn. I told him that the most important thing for Christ was the kingdom of God. I tried to shed some light on what this entailed for Christians, explaining how it meant upholding goodness and working to build a world where there was harmony rooted in justice. In short we were talking about the creation of *a civilisation of love.*

He had no problem in relating to all this. Actually the core Buddhist teaching is:
- not to do evil,
- to cultivate goodness,
- and to purify one's mind.

'How can you know God,' he asked me on one occasion, 'since God cannot be known?'

'Well, God cannot be known,' I fumbled, somewhat surprised

by the question, 'in the sense that no matter how much we know there is no end to what we still have to learn. But it doesn't mean that we cannot know anything at all about God. Creation speaks of God, as you yourself have shown so clearly, and *our* Bible tells us that God, who has given us this wonderful world, is a God of love. In fact it says God *is* love. So we can know God through other people, for when we experience love from our fellow human beings, we are experiencing God. Now if we *experience* something, that is truly knowing. The best road towards knowing God is through living community, as you are doing.'

There was a long silence. 'What do you think of what I've just said, Paiboon?' I asked.

'It's all very new to me,' he replied.

Quite out of the blue the next day he volunteered the following: 'I've been thinking of what you said. Now I believe that God is compassionate. That's just another name for love, so what you said makes sense.'

At that moment I could imagine Christ looking at him and saying with wonder, 'You are not far from the kingdom of God' (Mark 12:34).

I was not able to stay with the group as long a I would have wished. What I saw, however, led me to believe that, although the Tamkaenjan Community was not Christian (and I do not intend this to be disparaging), it certainly could, from our point of view, be described as a kingdom group. Their priority was Christ's priority. Here was goodness, openness, and harmony rooted in justice. It patently showed the kingdom flourishing beyond the confines of Christianity, and brought home to me the need to be ecumenical in the broadest sense by linking up with all people of goodwill to build a better world.

A personal vision of kingdom

Besides the commonly held perceptions of the kingdom, we all have our personal vision, or vocation. It may consist simply in someone doing an ordinary task and struggling to bring up a family as good Christians and honest citizens. There is much that passes for ordinary that is quite extraordinary. I feel that legions of great saints have led hidden lives, sanctifying themselves by doing a whole array of minute chores thoroughly and with love over a lifetime. Few get the chance to live high-profile lives. A doctor I know has quietly given her whole life, sacrificing the possibility of marriage and family, to the service of the African people. Our private aspirations we of course integrate with the wider panorama of the kingdom of God.

Our doctor no doubt suffered, and that too is an integral part of our destiny (John 12:24). To gain the kingdom we will have to die and rise again with Christ. While hanging on the cross, Jesus felt desolate and abandoned, though in reality the Father never abandoned him. Through Jesus, God entered history and endured the pain of the cross, because Jesus is a human way of being divine. The astonishing truth, then, is that the Almighty shared in our human lot of suffering – so much for the myth of a God that is distant and uncaring. In the desolation of Christ, the Father risked failure, but Jesus did not fail. Even as he cried out, 'My God, my God, why have you forsaken me?' (Matthew 27:46) and passed painfully through the gap of death, he clung with his fingernails to hope. He trusted in his Abba and in the promise of the kingdom – the kingdom that he had so convincingly preached and borne witness to, in the course of his ministry. And God vindicated his trust and the whole purpose of his life by raising him from the dead. The cross is what we did to Jesus; the resurrection what the Father did. Along this path, sooner or later, all of us must follow Christ. And we too will have to hang on with our fingernails, hoping and trusting, as we give our final answer to the great question of love.

As well as having our own personal vision of the kingdom of God, we can have our own particular examples and images of it too. Those that come to my mind relate to the women of the world; to begin with those of my own family. After those there were the laundry women in South American *barrios* who sweated over the clothes of the rich so that their families might survive. And the mothers of Soweto, who during the bus boycotts in the struggle against apartheid, arose in the dark and walked for long hours to their

domestic tasks in the luxurious homes of white South Africans in
Johannesburg. And, then, at the end of the long trek home in the
evening, there was supper to cook. These were the unsung heroes
of the freedom struggle. Also, there were the women of famine-
stricken Mozambique, who trudged across the border with
Zimbabwe, bearing enormous loads of grass for animal fodder.
These they sold to buy bread for their starving children. Great sacrifices entwined with the thousands of seemingly lesser sacrifices of
cooking, cleaning, and caring that help to keep this world on
course. Up to this, women have largely borne the burden of life. It is
now time for all to fully join the struggle. Justice must be done.

Justice
Justice is to the kingdom what oxygen is to life. They have to go
together. Jesus does not merely say, 'Seek first the kingdom,' but
adds significantly, 'and its *justice*...' (Matthew 6:33); we cannot
have the harmony without the righteousness.

Justice, according to the Bible and the documents of the church,
means having right relationships with:
- self,
- God,
- neighbour, and
- environment.

It is total in its approach to unity. And isn't the expression *right relationships* merely another way of saying community or kingdom?
These realities are closely interwoven.

Oftentimes, when we speak of justice, we are thinking only of
economic justice: fair returns for our work, proper conditions in
industrial plants, and so on. Justice, however, is much more than
that because it touches all aspects of our existence.

I once heard a woman of African origin say at a meeting in a São
Paulo *favela*, or deprived district: 'I am oppressed three times over.
I'm oppressed because I am poor; I'm oppressed because I am a
woman; and I'm oppressed because I am black.' I was somewhat
surprised to hear her say, for example, that she was oppressed
because she was a woman. The men in the district, after all, were

passionately involved in issues of justice. And yet this woman, and others as it turned out, felt oppressed because of their gender. So, apparently, the menfolk still lacked a clear understanding of the full nature of justice.

If relations with persons and, consequently, with the Creator are marred by discrimination, justice suffers.

Respect for the environment is also an integral part of justice. There is the divine community of the Trinity, the human community, and the community of creation – all intimately bound together, all to be reverenced.

A poem called *Stupidity Street* by Ralph Hodgson,[5] shows how the things of nature are so precariously linked together. The poem is all the more remarkable because it was written early in the twentieth century, when the public was certainly not as environmentally conscious as it is today. It says:

I saw with open eyes
Singing birds sweet
Sold in the shops,
For people to eat,
Sold in the shops of
Stupidity Street.

I saw in a vision
The worm in the wheat,
And in the shops nothing
For people to eat;
Nothing for sale
In Stupidity Street.

In her fine book, *The Cry of the People*, Penny Lernoux makes the same point, showing the havoc that reigns when multinational corporations are allowed to rape the rain forests. She writes as follows:

But perhaps the worst example of the multinationals' slash-and-burn methods in the Amazon is provided by the Italian conglomerate Liquigas, which purchased 1.4 million acres in the heart of Xavante Indians' territory. Sixty Indians died when the military forced them to move from their land, and now only a few charred stumps remain of the forests where the Xavantes once hunted, the land having been seeded in grass. Like most Amazon cattle ranches, the Liquigas project produces only for the export market, using an airstrip big enough to accommodate chartered 707s that fly direct to Italy with the meat packaged in supermarket cuts and the price stamped in lire.[6]

A final point about our description of justice, given above, is necessary. It might seem presumptuous to put right relationships with self before right relationships with God. But the reasoning behind it is that, unless we can relate properly to ourselves in the first place, we are severely hindered in relating to God, neighbour, or environment. *Community and kingdom begin in my own heart.*

Now what we do, as opposed to what we say, about justice is of tremendous importance when we come to proclaim the gospel. The Synod of Bishops meeting in Rome, 1971, had this to say:

Action on behalf of justice and a participation in the transform-ation of the world appear to us as *a constitutive dimension* of preaching the gospel, or, in other words, of the church's mission for the redemption of the human race and its liberation from every oppressive situation (italics mine).[7]

So in the matter of passing on the faith, as in ecumenism, the query is never, will we, or will we not, do something about justice? The only question to be asked is *what exactly* are we going to do? What is the best course of action in our circumstances? During the days of apartheid in South Africa, for example, when an individual mis-sionary stood up in a pulpit and condemned the system, expelling that person from the country was an easy matter. But when an epis-copal conference spoke out as a body, how could the authorities possibly counter that? This was to prove a most effective strategy.

Action for justice is not solely a matter of shaping national events. Quite the contrary. In fact it is unlikely that people will eventually immerse themselves in these more difficult, and some-times dangerous, issues, if they are not doing the work of justice in more humble ways. The places to begin are in the home and neigh-bourhood. If relationships in these areas are not right, with what credibility can we operate further afield.

Option with the poor

In the 'kingdom of justice and peace,' which the preface speaks about in the Eucharist on the feast of Christ the King, an option with the poor is a given. The Roman Catholic Church made an option with the poor at Puebla, Mexico, 1979. In doing so it was simply following Christ whose own choice it clearly was:

The Spirit of the Lord is upon me,

because he has anointed me to preach

good news to the poor.

He has sent me to proclaim release to captives

and recovery of sight to the blind,

to set at liberty those who are oppressed,

to proclaim the acceptable year of the Lord (Luke 4:18-19).

It has been common to speak of an option *for* the poor, yet many economically deprived folk prefer the expression option *with* the poor. It seems to them less condescending. Besides, *with* the poor is where everyone belongs in any case, and it is the *haves* who benefit from solidarity with the *have nots* rather than the reverse. The poor proclaim the good news to the rich, recall them to a true sense of values, and disabuse them of the spurious notion that diamonds are forever.

Jesus was one with the poor, stood solidly with them in their just cause, loved them, shared with them, and lived simply himself. Well, was he not born in a stable? Did he not die stripped of all on the cross? And during his arduous ministry, unlike the birds of the air and the foxes of the field, was he not often without a place to lay his head at night? His simple lifestyle is a challenge to every Christian. The evils of the world exist precisely because people fail to love, share, and live simply. The Irish development agency, Trócaire, had a large poster some years ago that boldly proclaimed: *Live simply so that others can simply live*. That gets to the nub of the issue. On this planet of ours, the greed of the minority deprives the many of life; the misguided few mistakenly think that they can create an oasis of happiness in a desert of discontent. Above all, if we want to have an authentic vision of the world, we must view it through the eyes of the poor as Christ did.

I find from experience that the option with the poor and what it means is a stumbling-block for many, and in discussion it can die the death of a thousand rationalisations. Who are the poor anyway? It is a question often asked, never, ironically, by the poor themselves. I once heard a student remark that, instead of talking endlessly about this problem, one would do far better to go live and work with the deprived and learn from experience, which was what he had done himself. I am sure he was right. However, it is not surprising if we find this option with the poor bitter medicine. So too did the apostles. Mark tells us:

And they were exceedingly astonished,
and said to him,
'Then who can be saved?'
Jesus looked at them and said,
'With mortals it is impossible,
but not with God;
for all things are possible with God.'
(Mark 10:26-27)

Jesus, I think, is not saying that we can hang on happily to our riches and expect salvation, rather is he telling us that by the grace of God we can simplify our lives and make an option with the poor however difficult it may appear.

Obviously, though, when we come to consider who the poor are, *the materially poor* first spring to mind; the vast majority of the world's population who do not know where their next meal is coming from. Then in the Old Testament the Hebrew terms for poverty (*ani* and *dal* in particular) convey a notion of powerlessness. So the poor are *the powerless ones*. The state of powerlessness, of course, usually goes with material want. And, finally, they belong to the little ones of the earth, or *anawim*, who opt with the poor and adopt a simple lifestyle. Incidentally when we talk about poverty, or simplicity of living, we are not referring to misery. We would want every human being to have sufficient means to procure a home, food, and clothing; to be able to educate his children and provide for legitimate recreation. There is no virtue in degradation and filth. Jesus proclaimed that he came so that we might all have life and have it abundantly (cf. John 10:10).

In the light of the foregoing, I am often baffled by references to what is called the middle-class church. I understand, of course, that this may be a convenient sociological rather than a theological description. But looked at theologically there is no such church. There is only the church of the poor (the materially poor and those who identify with them), a community of the faithful, all equal through baptism. So we should not lightly use the expression *middle-class church*. Surely classism is as abhorrent to the Christian as racism or sexism, and the feminist movement has made us all aware of the importance of being sensitive in the language we use.

In the foregoing we have shared some thoughts as to what is meant by our Christian priority, the kingdom of God and its justice. At the outset we also posed the further question regarding how the kingdom related to the church generally and, more specifically, to the small Christian communities. We will now consider this query.

The kingdom and the small Christian communities
The church is called upon to be salt and light in the world, or an agent for the fostering of goodness (cf. Matthew 5:13-14). Because of this, it ought to be a *powerful expression* of the kingdom on earth and *an effective instrument* for promoting it , but it is not of course the whole of the Lord's domain, as already noted. This stretches to the farthest reaches of creation and beyond into everlasting life. The kingdom of God was there before the historic church, and it will still be there when it is no more.

A point we made in the previous chapter again becomes relevant. In terms of witness where can we put our finger on the church? Where can it be clearly seen? In a parish of thousands? Even in a group of a hundred? No. The church is most obviously discernible in small Christian communities; in practice it is these that are at the cutting edge of testimony and action. *The small Christian communities are the most effective agents for building the kingdom of God and its justice*. They witness palpably to it. They forge it. In the course of this book, we cite numerous examples that bear this out.

The examples also show the relevance of the groups to the justice issue. They are down-to-earth and not floating about in an other-worldly haze. If justice is about right relationships, they give witness to, and are fine instruments for, promoting it in society.

Other names for small Christian community is *basic* Christian community or basic ecclesial communities. These mean that the group is:

- of the poor.
- involved in actions from the grassroots.
- a place that invites fuller participation by all, for example, women, youth, and children.
- immersed in real life issues.

In short the community is context and instrument for justice.

Elsewhere we referred to the small community as context and instrument for evangelisation and catechesis. If we were to explore the possibility, we would also find that it is context and instrument for communication, participation, inculturation and morality. Are these not all about relating to people effectively and properly? The small Christian community is not simply another pastoral strategy; it really is at the core of everything we aspire to in life.

The kingdom of God, then, pertains to the visionary context of the church. Therefore it pertains equally to the visionary context of small Christian communities, each of which is a cell of the church and truly of its essence. Paul VI said as much in *The Evangelisation of Peoples*, paragraph 58, and John Paul II repeated this in his *Address to the Brazilian Basic Ecclesial Communities*, 1980.[8] This cell contains in itself all the characteristics of the universal church: it is *in* and *from* the universal church, just as the universal church is *in* and *from* the cell. The worldwide church is not a federation of local churches. The cell and the universal entity interpenetrate each other; ultimately we are dealing with mystery. In *Redemptoris Missio* , no. 51, John Paul II also says that the communities are 'a sign of vitality within the church, an instrument for formation and evangelisation, and a solid starting point for a new society built on a civilisation of love.'

Knowledge of the visionary, or Trinitarian, context of small Christian communities is of the utmost importance for their members. Let me yield the last word on this matter to Peter, a coordinator of a small Christian community in Sunyani, Ghana. At the conclusion of a workshop, he commented: 'We were like ants in our small Christian communities. We saw our own little patch of ground but not the wider landscape. Now we have a vision. We see where we fit into the church and the kingdom and can go forward feeling more confident. I feel very happy.'

Summary
1) The immense love of the Trinity flows out into the church and all creation, mediated by the incarnate Christ.
2) This timeless, awesome domain we call the kingdom of God.
3) The kingdom of God (and its justice) is the priority for Christ and his followers.
4) What is the kingdom ? And how does it relate to the church and the small Christian communities?
5) The kingdom is scriptural (ample references provided from the Old and New Testaments).
6) From the scriptural overview we might summarise by saying that the kingdom is:
- 'a new creation' (Galatians 6:15).
- the priority.
- God's rule prevailing in the world.
- the person of Jesus, his mind, heart, and values.
- wherever there is harmony rooted in justice.
- all that is good, gracious and, therefore, God-revealing.
- openness and tolerance.
- present and yet to come.
7) We can have our own particular vision of the kingdom, which ties in with our calling, and our own special images of it too.
8) The kingdom and justice are inseparable.
9) Justice is right relationships with self, God, neighbour, and environment.
10) Action for justice is an essential element of preaching the gospel
11) The church is not the total expression of the kingdom of God, but can be a potent expression of it. It should give powerful wit-

ness to that kingdom and its justice and be an effective instrument for promoting this ideal.

12) Because the church is geographically and numerically extensive, these roles of witness and instrument are more concretely and efficiently realised in small Christian communities.

Questions

1) What do you understand by the expression kingdom of God? How does your understanding fit in with your experience? Suggested Bible passage: Matthew 6:25-34.

2) What does the kingdom mean for you personally? Any relevant images or examples? Suggested Bible passage: Matthew 13:1-23; or Matthew 13:24-43; or Matthew 13:44-51.

3) From your experience what is your understanding of justice? Suggested Bible passage: Isaiah 58:1-12; or Matthew 25:31-40.

4) What can small Christian communities and groups do about justice in your area? Suggested Bible passage: Luke 1:46-55.

5) How do you feel about the option with the poor? Suggested Bible passage: Luke 4:16-21; or Mark 10:17-31.

CHAPTER 3

The Prayerful Dimension

While reflecting on the themes of the church as communion and the kingdom of God, we cannot have failed to notice how vital the scriptural or, if you wish, the prayerful dimension was. And this too is part of the vision of small Christian communities that we need to address. In this dimension we include *the word of God, prayer, the eucharist, reflection, and reconciliation.*

In the autumn of 1994, I was involved in giving a workshop in a Dublin parish which was hoping to launch small communities. During the sessions it became obvious that the parish was a most apostolic one. There was an activity group to meet virtually every human need: the elderly, sick, handicapped, youth, deprived … And yet the participants felt that something crucial was missing. They identified it as being a contemplative dimension; their action needed a more intense spiritual backing. The routine activity made them feel like 'squeezed-out lemons'.

Similarly, in 1992, a priest who was a chaplain to Young Christian Workers and Students in Canberra, Australia, said, 'We have been very justice conscious, but we have been missing out somewhat on the prayer dimension.'

The word of God
Regarding the word it is important to realise that it does not take precedence over the life experience of the members of a community. They must first look at their own lives and try to make sense of them in the light of the scripture, or Christ-event, just as the early Christians did. The Spirit of Christ is not only found in scripture but also in the Christian community of every era. As Carlos Mesters, a Dutch scholar and missionary working in Brazil, puts it: 'The word

of God is not just the Bible. The word of God is within reality and it can be discovered there with the help of the Bible.'[9] So ideally to use the scriptures effectively, a community should meet around the word, yet relate the realities of their own lives to the text. 'Their struggle becomes part of the picture.'[10]

Yet another point on the use of scripture. According to some experts, the best way to deal with the Bible is to ask how the passage under consideration helps or challenges me. What issues does it raise for me? I may then share my insights with other members of a group without trying to force my point of view upon them. We express our thoughts in a spirit of 'this is how this passage challenges me' or 'this is what it says to me ... maybe it helps you, maybe not'. It is a question of I, me, we, us rather than you and they. And we do not argue. We respect what the members say and do not set them right. There is a difference between a Bible discussion, when we strive to thresh things out together, and a quiet, meditative Bible-sharing.

In 1991, I was conducting sessions in Sierra Leone, on small Christian community as usual. The following is an entry in my journal for March 15th:

Today we had an intensive, day-long workshop in the village of Benduma, towards the south-east of the country. It took place in a chapel made of slats and covered with a thatched roof. It was quite an experience. The whole Christian community was present, including the children. The village chief, a Muslim, complete with flowing garment and fez, also attended to show respect for those of his people who were Christians. In addition to the children within, all the remaining youngsters of the village were jostling outside in an effort to peer through the slats to see what was going on.

Every so often an adult would shoo them all away, yet they would be right back like bees to a honey pot. And there was the buzz too. The catechist was reading ponderously from the Bible. Beneath the lectern a boy was carrying on, just a little. In reality the children were well behaved. Anyway, the catechist snapped the Bible shut and gently, but firmly, cracked the lad on the head with the word of God. After this momentary episode the reading proceeded with all due decorum. It's amazing what happens when one is struck by the word of God!

I tell this story to make what seems to me an important point. We must not use the word of God to beat other people over the head with and take bits out of context to prove our arguments. Scripture was not intended for this purpose. It is there to question, strengthen, and affirm us while we travel as pilgrims along the arduous, yet exciting, road of life. And we must never lose sight of the total context.

An interesting phenomenon of our times is that the Bible is to be found back in the hands of the laity. It is no longer the sole preserve of the cleric or the scholar. This is a wholesome development because it was written by ordinary people for ordinary people in the first place. Such folk can often be more at home than intellectuals with the stories, myths, symbols, songs, poems, dramas, and powerful word pictures that are the very stuff of which the scriptures are made. They can be utterly fascinated by it all. In this context I recall the story of a venerable African lady who loved reading. Above all she devoted herself to the scriptures. As she sat with her Bible one day, a neighbour asked why she didn't give more time to other literature. To which she replied: 'Other books I read, but this book reads me.' I have seen a learned article of about twenty pages that made the same point. Not as memorably.

I do not wish to downgrade the contribution of scholars in Bible reflection. Far from it. They do the invaluable work of giving us the historical and social context of the text. But that is not the only purpose of Bible study. Still more important is what Christians are saying about scripture as they relate it to their present lives. Ideally, of course, the two contributions should be brought together because they complement each other.

Sometimes there is a person in a small Christian community who has a good knowledge of the Bible. How can she best help the group? One thing is certain: she must beware of taking over the meeting and turning it into a Bible lesson, thereby stifling the spontaneity and participation of the members. She could help, however, by briefly providing something of the historical and social back-ground of the passage being shared.

We see Ernesto Cardenal do this skilfully with the peasants of Solentiname in Nicaragua. The community is about to discuss Matthew 6:7-15, which deals with the Lord's Prayer. Taking the words:

And in prayer.

do not heap up empty phrases,

Ernesto goes on to explain, 'The translation is rather, "Don't go blah-blah-blah-blah." The Greek word that Matthew uses is *battalo-gein*, which is like saying blah-blah-blah-blah.' Then, dealing with the expression:

Our Father who art in heaven,

he further elaborates: 'Jesus didn't really use the word "Father". He said in Aramaic *Abba*, which is "papa" and that was probably always the word he used in speaking of God.'[11] Indeed even the intimate 'papa' hardly conveys the warmth of *Abba*. With Ernesto's instruction, the stage is set for a most absorbing reflection by the participants.

Regarding the power of the word of God, I had a striking experi-ence in Zimbabwe. We had been reflecting in community on John 17, and afterwards a little sister approached me. 'Jim,' she began, 'I was really impressed by those words of Jesus, "I pray not only for them, but also for those who believe in me because of their message." Here was Jesus going out to die, and I realised that he was thinking of me at that moment. The poor soul, he prayed for me. I felt like crying. I work as a chaplain in the mission hospital. Many people there are dying of AIDS ... young people ... some of them relatives ... and they fear death. Now I'm going to be able to say to them, Don't be afraid. Look here in the gospel; Jesus prayed for you! There's no need to be afraid.'

Prayer

Flowing naturally from a life-connected reflection on the word of God in small communities is a healthy discipline of prayer. The most common form of prayer practised in the groups is *spontaneous*, that is, *comes straight from the heart*. And since it follows upon the word, it is usually broken by long pauses for silent meditation. Spontaneity in this case certainly does not mean a thoughtless blurting out of sentiments; the term means that no set or formal prayers are necessarily used.

Following a reflection on Matthew 25:31-40 ('I was hungry and you gave me food, I was thirsty and you gave me drink ...'), for example, someone might pray like this:

Almighty God, help us to realise the dignity of every human being. Jesus considers as done to himself whatever we do to the least of our sisters and brothers. Help us, Lord, to treat all your people with respect. May we assist them when they are in need. Lord, hear us.

At a meeting of a Dublin community, basing his intervention on the words of Jesus, 'Strive to enter by the narrow door; for many, I tell you, will seek to enter and will not be able' (Luke 13:24), a young man prayed thus:

Lord, the scripture asks us to enter heaven by the narrow door, asks us to be counter cultural, to go against the tide, not to seek the way of easy popularity. Help us, Lord, to be narrow-door people insofar as we are just, not sold on material goods, and use the things of earth well. Help us also to lead others through the narrow door, the way of simplicity of lifestyle, of gentleness, of compassion, love, and of selflessness. Lord, hear us.

Many of the prayers quite rightly centre on the concerns of life: the recovery of a sick relative, work for the unemployed, success in an examination, freedom from hunger, disease, and oppression. And always these prayers are accompanied by the knowledge that something has to be done about them.

The more simple the context, the more skilful folk can be at composing their own prayers. In economically deprived countries, the people are quite often at home with spontaneous prayer. By contrast, the affluent nations are conditioned by instant tea, instant coffee, microwave ovens, and slick computers. The instant society can fail to understand that a facility for spontaneous prayer cannot be acquired overnight.

An example will help us to understand that there is a process involved. It is taken from a group in Ireland. When they first started, this group, which was rather youthful, discussed problems a great deal. They tended to shy away from anything religious. Since they had been formed as a small Christian community, however, the coordinators would read some passage of scripture related to the problem under consideration. The reading at that stage was not an integral part of the meeting, but something of an afterthought that could at a pinch be discarded. And that was how matters stood at the beginning.

After some sessions the animators began to invite all to recite the Lord's Prayer to finish off the meeting.

Almost imperceptibly, some spontaneous prayer crept in. Usually it was the animators who did it. But gradually others began to imitate them and acquire the skill. The word of God also became a more integral part of the proceedings. Nowadays that same group can dim the lights, place some votive lamps on the floor, and pray for an hour or more.

Private prayer

Small Christian community members, in addition to their prayer life in common, usually feel a deep need for private prayer. There is no one way of doing this. The important thing is to focus on God, and the method we use seems to be secondary. Whether it be silent or oral is a matter of choice. Commenting on Matthew's phrase, 'In your prayers do not babble as the pagans do' (6:7), Charles de Faucauld says:

> In this counsel you [the Lord] are telling us that for mental prayer words are not necessary: it is enough to kneel there lovingly at your feet, contemplating your majesty with every admiration, every desire for your glory, consolation, and love, in short with every movement of our hearts that love prompts us to. Prayer, as St Theresa tells us, consists in not speaking a lot, but in *loving a lot*.[12]

So prayer is above all a matter of relationship. It means being an intimate friend of God. Charles de Faucauld's understanding of it might be described as *thinking of God with affection*.

This description is not too unlike 'the methodless prayer' of Jane de Chantal the *anam chara*, or soul friend, of Francis de Sales. Jane is quoted as saying the following:

The great method of prayer is to have no method at all. When the Holy Spirit has taken possession of the person who prays, it does as it pleases without any more need for rules and methods. The soul must be in God's hands like clay in the hands of a potter so that God might fashion all sorts of parts. Or the soul must be like soft wax to receive the seal's impression, or like a blank tablet upon which the Holy Spirit can write the divine will.

And she goes on to say:

If going to prayer, one can become pure capacity for receiving the Spirit of God, that will suffice for any method. Prayer must happen by grace and not by any artfulness. Go to prayer in faith, remain there in hope and go out only by charity which requires simply that one act and suffer.[13]

Prayer is *a simple waiting before God*. Sometimes in our busy lives we are so weary that the efforts to marshal our thoughts proves even too much. This should not disturb us. We can remain affectionately in the presence of God. If we think about it, being affectionately in the presence of God is something that is possible at every moment of our lives. Whether or not we advert to it consciously, we are inevitably in the presence of God. Jesus tells his followers of 'their need to pray always' (Luke 18:1). This is made possible, even when we are not consciously thinking of the Lord as in formal prayer, by holding the truth of God's presence at the back of our minds and sending little shafts of love God's way in those seconds when it becomes overt, on a bus, in the factory, or at home watching television.

On the subject of prayer, Jane de Chantal also remarks, quite rightly, that it is a grace, and we cannot give it to ourselves. All we can do is to dispose ourselves for it and leave the rest to the Lord. It is helpful also to recall the words of Paul who reminds us that, when we fail, the Spirit within us can act on our behalf:

Likewise the Spirit helps us in our weakness; for we do not know how to pray as we ought, but that very Spirit intercedes

with sighs too deep for words. And God, who searches the heart, knows what is in the mind of the Spirit, because the Spirit intercedes for the saints according to the will of God.
(Romans 8:26-27).

There are those who find it helpful to pray by reciting a mantra such as *Maranatha* (Come, Lord Jesus) over and over again, as a means of focusing the attention on God. They usually do this sitting in an upright position, breathing easily and with eyes closed. However, psychologists tell us that the human attention span is 20 minutes maximum, so we must not be surprised if distractions keep on intruding. Personally I feel that the phrase *a continual fight with distractions* would sum up the story of my own prayer life. But I place myself in the presence of God, I want to be there, and I struggle. I wonder if the distractions matter all that much in the end.

Thérèse of Lisieux was not overly worried by distractions and showed a great freedom in her attitude to prayer; indeed her understanding of it was ingenious and profound. She expresses it as follows:

I just do what children have to do before they've learnt to read; I tell God what I want quite simply, without any splendid turns of phrase, and somehow God always manages to understand me. For me, prayer means launching out of the heart towards God; it means lifting up one's eyes, quite simply, to heaven, a cry of grateful love, from the crest of joy or the trough of despair; it's a vast supernatural force which opens out my heart, and binds me close to Jesus.[14]

The Eucharist

The word *eucharist* means 'thanksgiving'. Above all it is *thanksgiving for*, and *a celebration of, unity*; of the efforts we make in families and small communities to be one. When the presiding minister raises the host, we are powerfully challenged to be body of Christ. 'Though we are many, we all become one, for we share in the one bread and the one cup' (1 Corinthians 10:16-17). How can we possibly partake of these mysteries and fail to be united? If people riven by class division celebrate the sacrament, it becomes an empty gesture. With the Christians in Corinth who are falling into this error, Paul is blunt: 'It is not the Lord's supper you are celebrating' (1 Corinthians 11:20).

The eucharist, then, is a clarion call to Christians to be the body of Christ, and to the whole world to be a community of brothers and sisters in the image of the Trinity. Like the mystery of the Trinity, the eucharist demands a world where there is universal collaboration and equality among people. It is, therefore, intimately linked not just to purely spiritual issues, but also to political, social, and economic ones. The justice element here is obvious. Christ generously breaks bread with the whole world, and we are challenged to do the same, especially with the 40 million who die of hunger or hunger related diseases every year; *a number that corresponds to the combined populations of Belgium, Canada, and Australia.* And this catastrophe is befalling people in a world of hoarded meat and corn, butter mountains and wine lakes. As often happens, also, most of the victims are children. Indeed countless little ones are denied the right to be born at all. Never in this life will they be able to rejoice with the psalmist in saying, 'I thank you Lord for the wonder of my being' (Psalm 139:13-14). When we talk of breaking bread, we are not simply referring to real bread; we are speaking too of breaking the bread of unity and fairness with all.

While I was working on this book, my brother passed away, and I had the consolation of giving him Holy Communion for the last time. When I arrived at his bedside on the afternoon before he died, he whispered to me insistently, 'Communion, Jim, ... Holy Communion.' Although I thought the hospital chaplain must already have given it to him, I decided to administer the sacrament. However, I later learned that because his mouth and throat were so sore from chemotherapy, it was felt he could not have swallowed the host. He had not received; hence his agitation. I gave him a tiny portion of the bread with a little water. He smarted at the touch of the water, but managed to receive in the presence of his family. I will never forget the peace that then descended upon him. I began to see a little more clearly what Jesus meant when he declared, 'I am the bread of life' (John 6:35).

If we conclude from the foregoing that the proper place to celebrate the eucharist is in community, no one will be surprised. And yet I feel that too often, particularly in the affluent world, the assembly is composed of an amalgam of individuals – well-meaning individuals – but individuals nonetheless. This was brought home to me clearly by an incident that happened in Ireland. I was giving a retreat to some university students and was removing the vestments after celebrating the eucharist, when a young man approached and spoke to me. 'I haven't been to Mass for a long time,' he informed me, 'and I have a difficulty with the eucharist. I'm only here because my friends pretty well dragged me here. But the Mass we had today was different from anything I have experienced before in my life. It really moved me.' I have to say I was somewhat surprised by his words. Quite honestly, the celebration was nothing out of the ordinary. As I pondered what he had said later, however, I concluded that the whole experience was transformed for him by the fact he was celebrating with his intimate friends. It was truly a celebration of community, in community.

One of the things that most preoccupy me about modern youth is that many of them separate spirituality from the church. They have a spirituality, and thank God for that. They will fast and collect money for the hungry, because they have a keen sense of justice, and that too is good. They are admirers of Jesus Christ and believe they can have him without being practising Christians. However, Jesus is not disembodied; he is in the church. Paul tells the Christian community in Corinth '... you are the body of Christ' (1 Corinthians 12:27). Jesus himself says, 'Very truly, I tell you, unless you eat the flesh of the the Son of Man and drink his blood, you have no life in you' (John 6:53). Christ is inextricably linked to life and practice. We cannot have one without the other. A disembodied spirituality is one in grave danger of withering.

But the church too must examine itself. Are our liturgies alive? Can people fully participate in the church's life, particularly in decision-making? Are we clerics struggling to preserve a type of control that we have no right to in the first place? And so forth.

Finally, I should like to add that not only does the eucharist challenge us to live in harmony; it also helps us to do so. It is food for the weak as we journey through this hazardous world. During his life there was nothing Christ liked to do more than sit down and have a meal with his friends and tell stories, or parables. It was one way that this person-for-others gave himself to his neighbour. On the night before he died that was exactly what he did, sat down and had a meal with his disciples, while his enemies plotted his down-fall out in the darkness. This, however, became a very special meal in which he gave us his flesh to eat and his blood to drink, so that we might have life, and asks us to go on as long as time lasts doing this in his memory (cf. 1 Corinthians 11:23-26). The next day he was going to shed that blood to the last drop for us on the cross. And that is why the *meal* and the *sacrifice* are always so linked together in the Christian memory. The eucharist and the cross are one, the place where true lovers meet, and a powerful source of grace which irrevocably joins people together in life and death.

Reflection
Naturally this quality is important to the prayer dimension. By reflection we are of course referring to meditative prayer, but it goes further than that. The spirit of reflection must permeate the whole life of the group. In a small Christian community the mem-bers should reflect on, and evaluate, all aspects of their life in com-mon: worship, faith-sharing, commitment, vision, exchange of ideas, friendship, outreach, and participation in material resources. Many small communities, including those of religious, have come to a standstill because they got themselves on to a treadmill of activ-ity, yet ceased to reflect on what they were doing. We cannot stress enough the importance of reflection for our communities. Without it, there is no way forward. And, of course, as individual members of community, each one of us must be a reflective person.

Reconciliation
This quality is also vital for the groups. It is built upon forgiveness, but I see a distinction. No matter how bad or angry I feel, I can make an act of the will and forgive. Indeed we learn from the gospel that

there must be no limit to the number of times we forgive (Luke 17:4). We are all a mixture of saint and sinner and, because it is so, we offend one another, sometimes without even meaning to. And conflict, as we will see later, is inevitable in community. So we have to be ready to forgive. But reconciliation involves the healing of psychological wounds and that takes time and must happen from the inside out; there is a process to it. I can forgive with my will – which is the important thing – but I may have to be patient with my scarred feelings. They may not be able to keep pace with my will, even though I am well disposed for reconciliation. Maybe peaceful coexistence is the first step, and then the offended parties can begin the painstaking work of building bridges of reconciliation. As I write this, the North of Ireland is very much in my mind.

Also in my mind was an experience I had at Stanstead Airport. I was checking in on Ryanair 285 from London to Dublin. Directly in line behind me were two Dublin girls, and I could not but overhear their conversation. They were just returning from a weekend in London.

'Darren said he loved me,' said one.

'Dat weirdo,' replied the other. 'Yer not havin' anthin' to do with him ever again, are ye, ye headbanger?'

'Ah I dunno. He asked me to forgive him.'

'Janey, after all dat he done, yer not goin' to, are ye?'

'If ye love someone, ye have to forgive him every time he asks. Ye know wha' I mean? Ye can't be f ... ... countin'.'

The language might have been rough, but the sentiment was straight from the gospel.

Finally, there was Susan whom I met recently in South Africa. In 1967, during the struggle against apartheid, her husband was slowly and brutally murdered. As if this weren't tragedy enough for one lifetime, her two sons and a nephew were shot in the students' uprising, Soweto, 1976. She herself suffered exile in Cuba and Tanzania and, in the course of this exile, had to battle tuberculosis. Gnawing homesickness eventually drove her back to South Africa and the graves of her loved ones. She was bitter. And who would deny that she had ample reason to be so? But one day she sat down and took stock. 'This hatred is a poison that is consuming me,' she thought. 'And the fathers and sisters have been so good to me. Not all white people are bad. I can't go on like this. I must forgive.' And she forgave from her heart. Yet the wounds are still healing, slowly. Not only are there hidden psychological scars to mend; there are also the evident physical scars resulting from torture on her body. Ironically the man who killed her husband endured a lingering agonising death himself, from AIDS. Susan did not gloat; for him she had only prayers and compassion.

Summary
1) The prayerful dimension is a vital element of the vision of small Christian communities.
2) It includes the word of God, prayer, the eucharist, reflection, and reconciliation.
3) The word of God must be life related; it is within reality and it can be discovered with the help of the Bible.
4) The most effective way to use the Bible is to ask how it questions, or what it says, to me.
5) There should be no badgering or putting down of others with the scriptures.
6) In communal sharing me and we and us are used rather than you and they.
7) A resource person can help a small community in its Bible-sharing by briefly (no long lectures!) filling in for the members something of the historical and cultural background of a scripture passage.
8) The most common form of prayer in a small community is shared and spontaneous.
9) Some people may have to grow into such prayer, particularly in the affluent world.
10) Private prayer is also important for group members.
11) Any method that puts one in contact with God is valid, whether or not words are used.
12) Methodless prayer, or a simple waiting on God, is another possibility.

13) The Spirit too pleads on our behalf and it is good to remember this (cf. Romans 8:26-27).

14) The eucharist, meal and sacrifice, celebrates and creates community.

15) The eucharist is a clarion call to unity.

16) It is also a call to break the bread of justice with the whole world.

17) Meditation and meditative reflection on all aspects of the group's life in common are vital.

18) A ready forgiveness, which disposes to the healing process of reconciliation, is crucial.

Questions

1) Does your group give due importance to the prayer dimension of spirituality?
   Suggested Bible passage: Luke 6:12-16; or Luke 18:1-8.

2) What does the eucharist mean to your community?
   Suggested Bible passage: John 6:41-58; or 1 Corinthians 10:16-17; or 1 Corinthians 11:17-22.

3) Does your group relate the word of God to life and life to the word of God?
   Suggested Bible passage: John 1:1-14; or James 1:22-25.

4) How does your small Christian community pray?
   Suggested Bible passage: Matthew 6:5-15.

5) Does your group meditate? And does it reflect frequently on all aspects of your life in common (faith, commitment, worship, ideas, vision, creativity, friendship, good works, and material possessions)?
   Suggested passage: Acts 15:1-41, the disciples evaluate.

6) From your experience would you say that forgiveness and reconciliation are important elements of your community?
   Suggested Bible passages Psalm 129(130); Luke 7:36-50 (forgiveness); Luke 15:11-32 (reconciliation); Luke 17:1-4; Luke 18:9-14; Luke 19:1-10 (reconciliation); Luke 23:33-43; 1 Corinthians 13:1-7; 2 Corinthians 12:5-10.

CHAPTER 4

Permeated by Love

In the previous chapters we have been considering the vision that informs small Christian communities. We will have seen that there are theological and spiritual elements to that vision. In other words there are aspects which relate to theology and others to spirituality. Though both of these have their autonomy, it is obvious they are closely related and impossible to separate in pastoral practice. Spirituality is theology with a glow upon it, a glow that makes us aware we are entering the realm of the Holy Spirit, whose ways often utterly baffle human logic. *The major spiritual insight to emerge clearly from the vision is that we creatures are totally permeated by the love of the Blessed Trinity, so the core of the spirituality is Trinitarian.*

God loves us. Even before we were born or could begin to love God, God loved us. John puts it tellingly: 'Love one another, because God has loved you first' (15:12). Henri Nouwen eloquently reminds us of what scripture has to say on this matter: 'I have loved you with an everlasting love. I have written your name in the palm of my hand from all eternity. I have moulded you in the depths of the earth and knitted you in your mother's womb. I love you. I embrace you. You are mine and I am yours and you belong to me.'[15]

This love of God is unconditional. The Almighty does not say: 'I will love you, but only if you are good.' Whether we are good or bad, God still loves us. God *is* love and cannot do otherwise.

All our lives many of us will have known of this love. Parents and teachers will have told us about it. But do we really know this truth? Oftentimes we know things in the head, but we are not convinced of them in our hearts. The journey from the head to the heart is the longest in the world. Yet it is in the heart or, if you like, the gut that we must be convinced of God's love for us.

If I am thus convinced, it can change the whole way in which I see the world. Take human love, for example. I will begin to understand it for the exquisite reality it is: something shot through with the infinite love of God. Only God can fill our hearts, of course, and we will not expect humans to be God for us. However, we will be in awe at the wonder of love among our fellows. And we will grasp that, if we could see them with the eyes of God, they would shine with the brilliance of the sun.

Thérèse of Lisieux regarded love as the greatest gift. Enclosed in a cloister as she was, she knew that many possibilities were not open to her. She could not become a pastor, for example, and it was unlikely that she would ever be a martyr. Her vocation, she concluded, was purely to love, yet love was the greatest vocation, the heartbeat of all. Without it, apostles, martyrs, prophets, and pastors would cease to exist. All sin was consumed in its white heat. For Thérèse relationships were charged with the love of God, a love to which she was completely open, a love that she mediated for others. She was in fact profoundly challenged by Jesus' command that we love one another *as he loved us*. On reflection she became aware that this was impossible. The love of Jesus was divine while ours was merely human. She comes up with the ingenious solution that Jesus must 'loan' us his love, and that each of us should channel that love to others. What an incomprehensible privilege! If we do this, we cannot but love sensitively and well.[16] Although devotion to Thérèse has been overly personalised and privatised, she was nothing if not communitarian.

On the subject of God's love for us and the relevance of our relationships to this love, the insights of Francis de Sales, Jane de Chantal, and Aelred of Rievaulx are bold and imaginative. Quite simply, according to them, we come to share the divine love *by befriending each other in God*.[17] Come to think of it this phrase could serve as a graphic expression of the entire spirituality we are considering. In the warmth, even the passion, of our human friendships, we find the loving God. God is love, and in providing an experience of love for one another we provide an experience of God. Francis and Jane had a tender love for each other, but that love was rooted in the Lord. On one occasion, Jane was on retreat and

Francis quite ill; instead of concentrating on her spiritual exercises, Jane was constantly worrying about him. Reflecting on this, she realised that it was not in order and wrote to Francis to say so. He agreed with her. Tender though their love might be, it nevertheless required a degree of detachment. *In the end, it was God who mattered.*[18] Furthermore their friendship was forged in the Spirit and, as such, could not be conceived 'apart from the wider community of friends.'[19] This obviously resonates with the subject matter of our present volume. *If it is true that no one person is an island,*[20] *it is equally true that no two can be.*

Am I afraid? Well, a further consequence of heartfelt love of God is the unshakeable conviction that love drives out fear (1 John 3:18). One of the things that Jesus urges most in the gospel is that we be not afraid (Matthew 14:27; Mark 6:50; John 6:20). So why should I be afraid? I am in good hands.

Knowing in the depths of our being how the Almighty loves us, can also help us to cope with the rejections that inevitably come our way in life. *After all, if God loves me, what else matters?* Here lies the key to peace in 'the deep heart's core'.

Regarding my own story, I have come to be overwhelmed by the thought that in a sense I have always existed and been loved by God. Previously I did not look further back than my mother's womb, and that was where it all began physically. However, from all eternity I was known to God. I was there in the loving womb of God's mind.

Loving the Lord in return is the issue. Our brothers and sisters we see, God we do not see. If we could see God face to face, love for God would overwhelm us. Until we enter eternity, there has to be a huge element of faith and anticipation in our relationship. It's not easy to *feel* the love. Something that a monk friend told me I find consoling. According to him, St Bernard said that wanting to love God is the same as doing so.

A lived experience

I once heard spirituality described as a 'lived experience of faith' and the expression impressed me. It is difficult to sit down and work out in theory what my spirituality is. But, if I look back on the highs and lows of my life's journey, the chief features of my spirituality can emerge. What were those elements that motivated me in my relationships with self, God, brothers and sisters, and all creation?

Regarding small Christian communities this is a question I have pondered a great deal. I have also got members of the communities to think back over their experience in an effort to identify the important factors of their spirituality. Here are my findings:

- *Their motivation is above all Trinitarian.* This we have already seen. Not all express it as imaginatively as East African Christians. In Tanzania they are fascinated by the Three Dancers, whereas there is only one dance. Actually this is an interesting way of explaining the source of our bonding, and not without a historical foundation. The Greeks in the early church used the word *choreuein* (to dance) in an effort to describe how the persons of the Trinity related to one another. It is from *choreuein* that we get the English word 'choreography', that is, the arranging or designing of ballet or stage dance. Can we visualise the Trinity as a dynamic trio dancing gracefully through eternity, luring all of us, their fellow dancers, to follow? And, like them, though we are various dancers, are we not all engaged in one dance?

- The infinite love of Father, Son, and Spirit is mediated to the church and the world by the incarnate Christ who redeemed us by dying and rising again. As we have seen, the Christian community is centred in the redeeming Christ, is indeed the body of Christ (1 Corinthians 12:27). Belief in him is essential. He it was who restored community by reconciling us to ourselves, God, brothers and sisters, and to the environment. And the cross is an eloquent symbol of God's immense love for us. This much we have also seen. However, there is a unique quality to the relationship of small Christian communities with Jesus. It is a vital relationship with Christ. I am at a loss to find words to describe the warmth of this bond. Jesus is a deeply loved friend and palpable presence; his is the extra chair at the table. The mind, the heart, and the values of Christ are the lodestar of their lives. This is most opportune, because at the beginning of the new millennium it is crucial that we put Christ firmly at the heart of the Christian message once more. So often we seem to be caught up in many questions which, though important, are not the heart of the good news. The core of the gospel is:

For God so loved the world

that he gave his only Son,

so that whoever believes in him shall not perish

But have eternal life (John 3:16).

- Such was the *sensitivity* of the early Christians *to the Spirit*, the Acts of the Apostles could just as easily be termed the Acts of the Holy Spirit. (cf. Acts 15:28). With the help of the Spirit, the early followers of Christ discerned their every important move. In the small Christian communities around the world one detects the same sensitivity and mode of operation. Spirit-consciousness is extraordinarily high. The Spirit is the vitality between Father and Son and activates Trinitarian love among peoples.

  The core experience of small Christian communities,therefore, is of the intense love of the Trinitarian God for creatures. This fundamental Trinitarian impulse then goes on to express itself in some quiet definite ways, which we now go on to explore.

- Clearly, spirituality is not a purely individual exercise; it inevitably has to take Sipho McChang and Maria Rarotonga into consideration. It is not simply about being kind to me, but equally about being kind to them. Nevertheless a Christian spirituality deeply respects the person, and in this it differs greatly from those ideologies for whom the collectivity is all. I knew a Marxist in South America who was told by his party that he could not marry, but must sacrifice himself for the cause of the masses. Participants in small Christian communities, while reverencing the individual, also know that the person is a social being who can only fully realise himself in relation to others. These two factors have to exist in creative tension.

- Another notable feature of the communities is the integration of faith and life. This need to express faith in action was not always appreciated. Faith was separated from life, religion from practice. There is a verse in Ireland that brings out this fact graphically:

Paddy Murphy went to Mass,

Never missed a Sunday.

But Paddy Murphy went to hell

for what he did on Monday.

A story of a novice from my own seminary days in England illustrates this mentality. On entering the novitiate at that time, he would have been told that he was leaving the world. He fell ill in the course of the year and the doctor was summoned. The medic was a big bluff man who professed no religion. I suppose he was agnostic. He enquired of the novice if he had ever had the illness before. To which the youth replied that he had had 'a touch of it' when he was in the world. There was a long baffled silence as the doctor tried to come to terms with this novices-peak. Then he asked casually, 'As a matter of interest, where the devil do you think you are now?'

Paddy Murphy and the novice failed to make the connection between faith and practice with consequences that were not so pleasant for Paddy, while the neophyte was left looking rather foolish.

- Just to note again that a prayerful dimension is an indispensable feature of the spirituality of small communities. Here we are talking of the word of God, prayer, the eucharist, reflection, and reconciliation. These we dealt with adequately in the previous chapter.

- It is also true that a new person is emerging in the communities. People tend to be more committed. Many times and in different parts of the world I have heard someone, reflecting on their experience in the groups, say something like: 'Before becoming a member of the small Christian community, I was a Sunday Christian. But now I realise that being a Christian is a fulltime task.'

Folk are no longer seen in terms of gender, race, age, social condition, or colour, but rather as human persons, children of

God, and brothers and sisters in Christ. These are the realities that give individuals their inalienable dignity and they are to be found in a handicapped child, begging on the street of some teeming city in the developing world, as surely as in the President within her palace. In this the members are beginning to make real the vision of Paul:

There is neither Jew nor Greek,

there is neither slave nor free,

there is neither male nor female,

for you are all one in Christ Jesus (Galatians 3:28).

So the task is clear and Paul enunciates it well: '… clothe yourselves in the new self, created according to the likeness of God in true righteousness and holiness' (Ephesians 4:24; cf. Colossians 3:10). The challenge is a matter of growing 'to the measure of the full stature of Christ' (Ephesians 4:13), so that one day we might be able to say with Paul, '… it is no longer I who live, but it is Christ who lives in me' (Galatians 2:20). On that day we will have reached, not only our full Christian potential, but also our full human possibility, for Christ shows us what a complete human being is capable of. Nietzsche believed life to be meaningless and was no lover of Christians. Nevertheless he was – amazingly – a great admirer of Jesus Christ whom he considered a person who was integrally human, one who lived life to the full and loved the earth and its creatures. Practically he imposed meaning on the meaningless. What the atheistic philosopher would not hold, of course, was that there was any religious significance in this.[21]

- Another important aspect of the groups is that they tend to be culturally relevant. Not only do they promote the dignity of every person, as noted earlier, they also attend well to what may be distinctive by fostering cultural awareness.

Cultures are dynamic. They encompass the present and future as they do the past. However, this does not mean that the myths, stories, dramas, proverbs, poems, songs, dances – in a word folklore – of a people are allowed to slip into oblivion.

In a Kenyan group the members were sharing on their experience of small Christian community. One man commenced by telling a story. 'Long, long ago,' he began in the ritual fashion, 'a tribe of people lived in our land called the Jumas. These Jumas had very large heads. So large that, when they fell over, they could not get up. Like a beetle that gets turned on its back and then threshes the air with its spindly legs and goes nowhere. If another Juma didn't come along and lift up the fallen one, it would mean death for the unlucky person – the same as the beetle. Sometimes, when Jumas fell over, there was no one to lift them up, so they died. The result was that they began to get less and less in number and decided to go underground – I suppose they couldn't fall over down there – and our people, the Kikuyus, came to live on their land.'

The narrator went on to say that he had heard this story from his mother. 'I learned about community at my mother's knee before ever hearing of Christian community,' he continued. 'Even as a little fellow I knew the importance of lending a hand, so that we might all survive. What small Christian community has taught me is that I must be ready to help not just my friend, but also my enemy. This is a big lesson.'

I found the tale a most effective use of folklore to make a Christian point. A case of the culture nurturing Christianity and Christianity the culture. The story was from the past, yet applied imaginatively to the present, and contained a challenge for the future.

- Needless to say, the kingdom of God and its justice is a priority for the groups. On this subject we need not elaborate further, having dealt with it in chapter 2.

- A characteristic of small grassroot communities that has impressed me is their spirit of perseverance through good and bad times. It always brings to mind the word of the gospel, '...the one who perseveres to the end will be saved' (Matthew 24:13). Life has its trials and only our faith can carry us through to the end successfully. A group that is truly community tends to be long-term; the one in which I am a member in Dublin has now been going for twenty years. It started with a little band of

school-leavers various of whom are now married and have children. We have had our difficulties, yet we are still here. For
many years the group successfully followed a youth model, but
as they married and had family it began to prove inadequate.
That was a painful time and the Spirit seemed to leave us floun-
dering for quite a while. Now we are finding new ways that
include the children and permit the parents to continue.

One of these means is a children friendly eucharist once a
month followed by tea and a treat for the little ones, who show
much enthusiasm for this arrangement. Paradoxically, it is the
children who are driving their parents to Mass!

Another form that the continuity has been taking for some
years now is that the members go away for weekends together
once a quarter for a course, retreat, or prayerful relaxation. This
supports the participants in their Christian and family lives, so
necessary in times that seem to grow increasingly individualis-
tic and materialistic.

Small communities, then, must never allow themselves to
become cosy, and must be prepared to die should they discern
this is what the Lord wants. After all, death for Christian communities is never a question of extinction. They die only to give
birth to something new. As John's gospel says so beautifully:

Truly, truly, I say to you,

unless a grain of wheat falls into the ground and dies,

it remains alone; but if it dies, it bears much fruit (John 12:24).
When some of the believers were scattered by persecution following the death of Stephen in the Acts, the church spread to
Antioch and elsewhere. Indeed it was at Antioch that the followers of Christ were first called 'Christians' (cf. Acts 11:19-30).

• The small Christian communities tend to be low profile. This is
  so in terms of what they are and what they do. Their style is not
  flambouyant; they are ordinary people who can hopefully be a
  leaven that helps to transform society. Often, more especially in
  their beginnings, before some sort of linkage takes place, they
  can be quite hidden. In Bathurst, Australia, I met two communities that were situated within a few streets of each other and still

unaware of one another's existence. In Ireland, according to a recent survey, there are many disconnected faith-sharing groups. Part of the explanation for the reticence is that they enjoy a new-found breathing space in the church and fight shy of being seized upon and dragooned by some over-zealous individual or organisation. Networking and structure have their place, yet these developments have to be organic and come from the grassroots and, of course, never take precedence over relationships or deprive small Christian communities of their legitimate freedom.

On the other hand, I had an encounter with a group of young adults in Dublin who were surprised by the influence they were having on some of their peer group. These latter were taking keen notice when they did not appear to be. The groups are not clandestine but, while they do not publicise themselves, neither are they able to hide their light.

Small Christian communities are also ordinary in the things they do. It is a question of the members striving to be Christian at home, in the factory, or in the school; a matter of visiting the sick, burying the dead, working with youth, the elderly, or the handicapped. There can, of course, be the heroic deeds too. I have had the privilege of working with five people in Africa who were subsequently martyred. I think of the humble catechist, James, in Sierra Leone, killed by the rebels because he refused to take part in their violent plans. Besides, he told them, he was the only support for his elderly mother. Yet no mercy was shown him. Mostly, however, it is not a case of heroics. It is a question of doing little things well and with love over a long time.

• A hunger for knowledge of God would be another characteristic of the groups. The dynamic of the communities appears to lead inevitably to this. The members become acutely aware that there is so much to learn that they want to explore areas such as the truths of faith, the word of God, social doctrine of the church. In our Dublin community, for example, various of the members, male and female, have taken night courses in theology. This they did at the beginning of their working lives at considerable cost to themselves in time and money. Such was their hunger to know more about Christ and his message. And the hunger continues.

• Last, but by no means unimportant, joy is integral to the spirituality of small communities. Fundamentally it is a joy in the Spirit that surpasses all understanding. Even in the normal meetings there is a lot of *craic* – the Gaelic for 'fun', pronounced 'crack', though it has nothing to do with the prohibited substance of the same name! Then there is much social toing and froing: engagements, weddings, newly-born babies, holidays, outings, parties, picnics, pilgrimages, casual encounters for a coffee and a chat. One of the great joys of the extended Dublin community has been the arrival of so many babies. In a previous book, I gave an extended list. This time I refrain from doing so, in order not to compete in length with *Gone with the Wind*. Actually, while reflecting on our experience in the Dublin group, one girl said that the first thing that came to mind was all the fun we had had together. Not indeed that we did not have our moments of crisis too.

The foregoing were the major points made by small Christian communities, when they reflected on their life experiences. They sum up their lived experience of faith , or spirituality. Above all, it is a spirituality of the heart; it is about relationships. There is the implicit understanding that, though the world may be plagued by myriad problems, when we practise genuine love, we are living the solutions.

Literary allusions

That love and relationships are of the essence is sometimes expressed more vitally by secular rather than spiritual writers. Hilaire Belloc divines the mystery when he writes:

> From quiet homes and first beginning,
> Out to the undiscovered ends,
> There's nothing worth the wear of winning,
> But laughter and the love of friends. [22]
> (Dedicatory Ode)

Raymond Carver too, while dying young after a difficult life – a life in which he experienced love at the end – penned these poignant lines:

And did you get what
You wanted from this life even so?
I did.
And what did you want?
to call myself beloved, to feel myself
Beloved on the earth.[23]

Only if we have loved, have we lived. Laughter and the love of friends, to feel myself beloved, tasting the sweetness of togetherness – these are the seeming trivia of every day life. Only they are not trivia. Their origins are to be found deep within the core of the Blessed Trinity. They are an expression of 'the burthen of the mystery'.[24]

Summary
1) The vision that informs the small Christian communities has elements of theology and spirituality.
2) The major spiritual insight to emerge from the vision is that we human beings are totally permeated by the love of the Blessed Trinity.
3) Spirituality is best described as a lived experience of faith and, when we reflect on our life's path, its main features become apparent.
4) Reflecting on the experiences of small Christian communities, the following are some points that stand out about the groups:
• They are motivated by the love and unity of the Trinity.
• By the power of the Spirit and the free consent of the Virgin Mary, this love is mediated to the church and the world by the incarnate Saviour, Jesus Christ; he is palpably a friend in the communities, which are centred in him and whose body they are.
• The groups are sensitive to the workings of the Holy Spirit; the level of Spirit-consciousness is high.
• In them faith and life become integrated.

- They have a strong prayerful dimension embracing: the word of God, prayer, the eucharist, reflection, and reconciliation.
- A new person is emerging in the communities (cf. Ephesians 4:24).
- The groups are culturally relevant.
- Their priority is the kingdom and its justice (cf. Matthew 6:33).
- There is a spirit of perseverance.
- The communities are low profile; theirs is 'the little way'.
- Theirs also is a hunger for knowledge of God.
- And, finally, they are characterised by great joy.
5) Secular authors often perceive and express the mysticism of human relationships better even than spiritual writers.

Questions
1) What does the word 'spirituality' mean for you? Is it relevant to your life?.
2) From your own experience of intimate relationships what would you add to, or subtract from, the points made above regarding the spirituality of small Christian communities?

   Suggested readings: Genesis 1 (or a suitable extract therefrom); 1 John 4:7-12; Galatians 2:20-21; Galatians 3:26-29; Micah 6:8; Vatican II, *Dogmatic Constitution on the Church*, no.4.

PART II

The Practicalities

We recall here that the essential elements of small Christian communities are:

- Bonding,
- Spirituality,
- Reality,
- Commitment,
- Communication.

The visionary features of Bonding, Spirituality, and Commitment have already been largely covered; we now turn to Reality, which is dealt with mainly in chapters 5 ('Organisation'), 6 ('Meetings'), 7 ('Pastoral Planning'), 8 ('Common Issues').

CHAPTER 5

Organisation

We must not in the least underestimate the importance of reality and communication, or the practicalities, of small Christian communities. *They are a working out in the marketplace of that love whose seeds are found hidden in the mystery of the Trinity, and flow seamlessly from the vision.* We have often heard the saying that the devil is in the detail. Whatever about that, God is certainly in the detail. Vatican II in its *Dogmatic Constitution on Divine Revelation* makes the amazing point that the self-revelation of God is not simply a matter of the Almighty speaking, but of God *acting* in creation. Revelation is always being made. The document puts it well: '… as the centuries go by, the church is always advancing toward the plenitude of divine truth, until eventually the words of God are fulfilled in her' (no. 8). The story continues, then, in the mighty events of history, but more importantly, perhaps, in the fall of a sparrow. In effect, the bread-and-butter details that we turn to now can be as significant as the visionary elements that we have described.

In turning to the practicalities we must deal with items such as: organisation and action, communication, meetings, pastoral planning, and common issues. In the current chapter we treat of organisation, action, and communication, while those items remaining will need chapters to themselves.

In short a small Christian community is a group:
- consisting of about eight members, give or take a couple.
- usually related to a specific neighbourhood, though members sometimes come from different areas, but is also found in schools, universities, on the high seas – the emphasis is on people rather than place.
- which links up with similar groupings to form a communion of communities.

- whose members believe in, and are committed to Christ – in whom Christian community is centred – and strive to share all aspects of their lives, such as, faith, commitment, worship, ideas, intuitions, friendship, material possessions, and good works; the sharing is holistic: spiritual, intellectual, intuitive, emotional, and practical.
- who relate deeply to one another, giving witness in their unity to the harmony of the Trinity, being, in fact, body of Christ; he being the one who mediates the love of Father, Son, and Spirit to the church and the world.
- for whom Christ is a palpable friend and the Spirit a motivator.
- that are anchored in the eucharist, word of God, prayer, reconciliation, and reflection.
- for whom leadership, seen as ministry, is a matter of animation, coordination, facilitation, enablement, not domination, and whose decisions are made through dialogue and consensus – discernment.
- who are a leaven humbly at work among the people.
- who reach out from the reality of their unity to further the kingdom of God and its justice through mission – action – in the world.
- who make an option with the poor and live simply, as Jesus did. Obviously we are going to have keep on unpacking all of this.

Some people imagine that small Christian communities are composed of members who, like religious, live under the same roof. Not so. There *are* residential groups. However, the vast majority are made up of people who live in their own homes, but gather together on occasions in a house or some other appropriate place to form community.

From the outset there is one fundamental point that has to be made regarding the ordering of small Christian community. *The organisation is for people, not people for the organisation.* By this we mean that if the structures employed by a group do not help the participants in their efforts to relate to one another, they must be looked at seriously and, when necessary, changed. Persons must come first.

Where do we start?

When we come to the issue of organising the small communities, how to start becomes a problem. A good way to do so is to begin with fervent prayer, so as to recommend the process to God. Then there must obviously be a person or persons interested in the idea. This person or these persons can be lay, religious, or clerical. It is not enough, however, for someone to be an enthusiast if she doesn't win the people at the grassroots to her cause. Where the initiative comes from is of no great consequence. What is important is that the people make it their own. In Africa, as in most of Asia, the original inspiration seems to have come from the bishops, but it found fertile ground among the people. Currently in Ireland I believe the initiative is coming more from the common people.

The next principle is that *we must start from where we are.* This means that local circumstances must be carefully taken into account. If, for instance, I am trying to get groups going in Africa, I can count on a strong sense of community and family among ordinary folk. The ground is prepared and I can start directly with the work of launching the communities. This I actually saw happening in many an African situation.

In the West it can be an entirely different matter. Very often people feel alienated and family and community are weakened. In Dublin during recent decades many residents were uprooted from communities with a long and rich tradition in the inner city to be moved to featureless suburbs, where they were surrounded by strangers. The nuclear family was left to flounder without the support of gran and grandad, uncles and aunts, cousins and neighbours. This was a traumatic experience. The first task in a situation like this has to be a fostering of basic human relationships. So one would strive to bring people together on whatever basis: recreational, social, or political. At the beginning it might be just a chat and cup of coffee, and it might progress to groups getting together to obtain those amenities that sometimes are forgotten in the rush to put up more and more houses.

In Perth, Australia, Exodus, a residential small Christian community in a populous area, engaged in the task of bringing more cohesion to their district in the hope of getting neighbourhood groups going. They knew it could not be done overnight. Gradually they were making social contact with their neighbours and involving them in such activities as arts and crafts. As I remember, they also did some Bible sharing and prayer. Even in South America, where the residents in the *barrios*, or humble urban situations, are quite community-minded, I found formative courses in a variety of areas – spiritual, educational, and technical – a good means of triggering small communities.

No matter where we happen to be, when we come to the point of starting a group, the first thing required is *information*. Those who might be interested need to know something about small Christian communities, and this often leads to a course or workshop on the subject. During the workshop the animating team can share guidelines regarding the practical workings of the communities and the vision that accompanies them. But as mentioned in our introduction, there is no neat package to unwrap; no blueprint. There are only ideas and down-to-earth suggestions that can help groups move in the right general direction. And, most importantly, everything said on a workshop has to be examined by the participants in the light of their own experience, because they have to make it flesh and blood in their own situation. The communities relate closely to the areas in which they find themselves. They cannot be transplanted unchanged from one situation to another.

Incidentally, the workshop has to be well publicised for some weeks before, I would suggest. Means to do so would be homilies, parish bulletins, local radio, house visits, even targetting some persons whom the organisers feel would be keen. The course should be open to all who might be interested in the subject, which is briefly explained. However, it could be mentioned that people already in any kind of group, religious or secular, could find it particularly helpful. If we wish to get a reasonable response to an invitation, we must be ready to do the preparatory work.

If those doing the course decide they want to implement small Christian communities, they must be urged to be practical. Vague intentions are of no use at this point. What is called for are about four or five really concrete steps that will help to launch the groups. So the participants are urged to discern these through dialogue and the guidance of the Holy Spirit.

In the autumn of 1994 I was involved with a workshop in a Dublin parish. It ran for about two hours each Thursday over six weeks. Thoughts regarding the vision and practicalities were duly shared and the participants examined them in the light of their own reality. Most of those who had taken part were eager to establish communities. But now there came the task of belling the cat. How were they going to establish them? They divided up into groups and discussed, discerned – allowing the Bible to shed its light – and prayed. On coming together they put forward these functional points:

- First of all they would build on existing groups trying to enrich them, so that they might become small Christian communities and not remain simply groups.
- Those who were not members of any group would start their own with a view to becoming a community.
- They would emphasise the whole area of spirituality; there was an activity group to cater for every need in the parish, but they felt the spiritual backing was insufficient.
- Those excluded from economic well-being, travellers for example, should be of special concern, they resolved.
- Lastly, they decided that each group would have a contact person for keeping in touch with the various communities and that there would be an overall contact person to bring them all together on occasions. This to avoid groups becoming isolated.

Although we have been using the word 'group' while referring to 'community' to avoid repetition, strictly speaking there is a considerable sociological difference between the two. In fact, to move from being a group to becoming a community demands something of a seachange. The divergences are as follows:

- A group has a *specific purpose* (e.g. to study the Bible or save the whales), whereas a community has *broad interests* (e.g. worship, passing on the faith, peace and justice, environment, youth, and so on).

- The members of a group are usually of *the same age, specialisation, or sex* (e.g. youth, married couples, or women); in a community on the other hand *people differ* in age, social condition, race, sex, and even religious practice – in the case of an ecumenical community.
- The group is *temporary*, assembles for a purpose, and disbands when its objective is achieved; but a community of its nature tends to be *long-term*.
- The most profound distinction is that in a group the members do not necessarily have the intention of *relating in depth*, yet in a community they do have such an intention.
- A group is not generally *a priority* for its members, whereas a community most certainly is.

We do not point to these differences through a lack of appreciation for groups. Indeed, as a matter of urgency, we ought to encourage constructive groupings of all kinds, whether religious or secular. It is simply a case of pointing to the divergences that sociologists indicate

My own aspiration would be that small Christian communities promote other small Christian communities, but also groups of all kinds, whether religious or secular, that are doing anything to build a better world. Further, they would urge them to network with one another. An aegis for Christian groups of all kinds would, of course, be provided by mother church, a fact that could assure a certain cohesion.

A further suggestion for starting small Christian communities would be *to build on existing groups*, so that they are transformed into communities. The reader will remember that this was what the participants in the Dublin workshop, mentioned above, decided upon, with some success from what I have heard. One could think of a number of interest groups that could lend themselves to such a change:

- Bible study gatherings,
- Bible reflection groups,
- RENEW groups,
- prayer, charismatic, liturgical, choral, and catechetical groupings,

- graduating classes,
- small congregations at house Masses,
- those involved in discussion or problem-solving forums,
- groups engaged in some struggle, or cause,
- participants at a workshop, programme (e.g. RCIA, Marriage Encounter. RENEW), or practical task,
- fellow-workers,
- fellow students,
- ship-mates,
- close neighbours,
- persons of the same ethnic background – provided they remain entirely open to those of other ethnic origins.

In Africa it has often been:
- a core of the extended family,
- a group of the newly baptised,
- a nucleus of compound, village, or outstation.

Finally, it is essential that the whole process of starting small Christian communities be accompanied by fervent prayer.

Incidentally, launching one community may at times be the best we can do. It is more satisfactory, however, to begin with at least two. This makes interaction and sharing of experiences possible. Sometimes, though, persons who have been through a course or workshop form a pilot group to begin with, and learn by doing. When eventually they feel confident about running the meetings and facilitating the group, they start in their own neighbourhoods. They act as resource people. But when the neighbours are comfortable with the process, the resource person, or planned leader, allows their own animators to emerge. Indeed the major concern of the resource person should be the enabling of all the members of the community.

The issue of groups sharing experiences is also of the utmost importance. The early Christians met in homes (cf. Acts 12:12; 16:3-5, 11, 14-15), yet the small communities that met there came together in the Temple area or at Solomon's Portico (cf. Luke 24:52-53; Acts 5:12) to form *a communion of communities*. So obviously those Christians felt they needed a dual approach: that of the intimate group on the one hand, and of the larger gathering on the other. And I feel that, if we can combine these two ways, we are getting a complete experience of church. We need the life of the *intimate community*, yet equally we require *the wider network*, so as not to wither and die.

The small Christian communities are autonomous, but not absolutely so. Occasions should therefore be sought to bring groups together in a variety of ways: for meetings, courses, liturgical and social celebrations. In Africa, diocesan and parish small Christian community days are proving helpful.

The leader's role

I was once attending a group in Southern Africa that was discussing leadership. They were critically examining the word *chairman* which is a title frequently used for the leader of a small community in that region. One person present was quite emphatic: 'To speak of the *chairman* of a small community is a contradiction in terms!' The consensus was for some new title that would respond better to what was required. 'I suggest that we use the word *servant* in our own language,' said a woman. 'That is what a leader is supposed to be.' The trouble with *chairman* or *chairperson* would be that historically they carry the meaning of a dominating, top-down brand of leadership. The attempt to invest the words with a new meaning would be like trying to pour new wine into the old wine-skin of the chairperson. So the group concluded amid laughter. It happened to be the *marula* wine season!

Does the problem exist to the same extent for the term *leader* itself? I feel it may. However, one thing is certain. What the woman said about leadership being for service is pure gospel. The leader's role is *one of animation, coordination, facilitation, enablement, not of domination* (cf. Matthew 20:20-28; Mark 10:35-45; Luke 22:24-27 and John 13:1-20).

In our Dublin small community we speak of *coordinators* rather than leaders. And instead of having one coordinator, there is a *team* of three. There are both practical and theological reasons for this. Because of work, it may on occasions be impossible for a particular coordinator to be present, so the others continue. One of our coordinators at the moment is a nurse and her working hours are of course irregular, which means that sometimes she is unavoidably absent, or delayed. A solitary coordinator may also grow possessive of the group and begin to speak of 'my community,' whereas the group is of all. Theologically, if there is a team of animators rather than a solitary one, the principle of community is maintained even in the leadership. The motor of the community is itself a little community. And, after all, isn't the universe facilitated by a team of Three? Furthermore it is highly desirable that both male and female be represented on the coordinating group.

It is the community which is the priority and the coordinating team is there to help it function and make decisions. I have come across some groups which rotate the leadership from week to week. They said it worked for them. I would wonder if it might not cause confusion at times. In any case the leadership in a community is usually renewed with regularity and, if there is a team, not all the leaders are changed together. This facilitates renewal, yet at the same time assures continuity. A maximum of two years service would be common enough.

Coordinators should be chosen with care. In our community we usually devote a few meetings to the process. We dialogue so as to identify the qualities required in our animators at the time the choice is being made. We bring the word of God and prayer to bear on the issue. And then we choose. Usually with us a few names are floated and we say, 'Annette, would you mind?' or 'Andrew, how about it?' The members have been generous in accepting and nearly everyone has been a coordinator at some time or other down the years. Indeed some have been called on more than once. In other places the members agree to go the road of a secret ballot.

Considering the qualities needed in the coordinator at a particular time is important. For the past couple of years we have had a number of new members join our group, so we felt it would be good that one of the animators should be a person with a gift for making people feel at home. *If even one new member joins a group, it is no longer the same.* Welcoming the new recruit and acquainting her with the story of the community are of the utmost importance.

A final point on the choice of coordinators. If a group is beginning, it is a mistake to choose them too soon. The members must be
given a chance to get to know each other. Usually the resource person, or planned leader, who helped to establish the community in
the first place, assists the group in getting well off the ground
before facilitators are chosen. Leaders must be given time to
emerge.

In order for a group to work smoothly there are *vital inter-personal
skills* that coordinators must strive to cultivate both in themselves
and in the membership.[25] These would be:

- empathy (the ability of listening to, and walking with, another),
- personal disclosure (an openness to the other),
- confrontation (challenge that is responsible and non-menacing),
- non-defensive exploration (a readiness to examine a situation,
  when challenged, without feeling we have to defend ourselves).

The coordinators must also help the group to deal with conflict,
which is an inescapable part of the life of any community, and especially of the small Christian community where relationships are
deep. Conflict does not mean the end of the world. It is more often a
sign of health than a symptom of disease. We must be prepared to
accept feelings of anger in ourselves and others and show respect
for people even when we disagree with them. When we argue
strongly over issues that really matter to us, we engage at deeper
levels than usual. Not to care either way destroys a community
much more speedily than conflict. To differ sharply can be a first
step towards resolving a problem through constructive confrontation. This, for example, should be a case of inviting a member to
examine some aspect of behaviour objectively rather than attacking
her in a harsh judgmental way. *If we sincerely focus our attention on
issues and not on persons, we can indeed avoid a great deal of tension.*

We must always deal promptly with conflict. Problems do not
get better by leaving them; usually they get worse. There are skills
for dealing with one another in a group that help us to overcome
conflict. They are as follows:

- *clarification* (to be clear as to what exactly the problem is),
- *negotiation* (dialogue to resolve the difficulty),

- *imagination* (to seek out fresh ways of dealing with the issue),
- *celebration* (to employ liturgical and social occasions to bring about healing).

Allowing for diversity can also relieve tension within communities. After each one of us was created, the Lord broke the mould. We are unique, reflecting God to the world in our own special way and, if we don't do it, no one else can. Of course it is not only humans who are different; we also find diversity in God, ministry, and belief, so the ability to rejoice in diversity is crucial. It would be an intolerable world if everything and everybody were the same. So the animators of groups must urge the members to live with diversity. Jesus sets the example. There is that wonderful little episode in the gospel where John comes up to him and says:

Teacher, we saw a man

casting out demons in your name,

and we forbade him,

because he was not following us.

To which the Lord replied:

Do not forbid him;

for no one who does a mighty work in my name

will be able soon to speak evil of me.

For the one that is not against us is for us.

(Mark 9:38-40; cf.also Luke 9:49-50)

Other vital tasks for the coordinators would be involving each and every member in the life and activities of the community. A judicious sharing of chores is called for here, so that some are not left free-wheeling. Special attention is of course paid to relating people to one another and fostering commitment. Liturgical and social celebration can play a great part in achieving these objectives. This we have already mentioned. The eucharist may be central, yet a birthday should not be forgotten either.

Symbols too are important. In our Dublin community we were discussing whether religion had anything to do with nature. Dolores, the animator, had put flowers, a candle scented with eucalyptus, a book containing the story of Humpty Dumpty belonging to her little daughter Niamh, and a banana on a small table in the

centre: all to remind us that the world round about us is the sacrament, or presence of God. God is the light, little children at play,
trees and flowers swaying in the wind, the food on our table ... And
somehow, through employing these earthly symbols, our sharing
reached depths of content and intimacy that we had rarely achieved
before. Jesus anointing the eyes of the blind man with spittle sud-
denly took on a whole new dimension (cf. Mark 8:23). 'I feel that I
have been moved on in my spiritual search by this meeting,' said
Annette. 'Maybe we have all moved on.' I'm sure she was right.

Much happens in the meetings of small Christian communities
and coordinators must have the ability to facilitate them. It does not
mean that they have to conduct the sessions every time; they can
delegate the work. But for whoever does it these hints may be of
help:

- Try to get people to sit together and in as near to a circle as feasi-
  ble.
- Ensure that eye contact between participants is possible.
- Encourage all to get involved, yet try to avoid lecturing, advice
  giving, and badgering.
- Attend to body language – if people look confused, ask the
  speaker to clarify the point.
- Make sure the participants keep to the topic.
- Allow for diverse opinions, urging persons to consider views
  other than their own.
- Stress the importance of listening.

The fact that we discuss the role of the coordinators in communities should not distract us from the fact that it is not they, but the
community as a whole, that is the priority. The leaders are there to
serve the body. It is most difficult to free ourselves of the mindset
which sees leadership in terms of domination. The coordinator
offers a ministry of animation to the community. Another member
might have a gift for working with young people; yet another a talent for music or liturgy. Through baptism we are a community of
equals and the various members will have their areas of competence, or spheres of influence, with which to embellish their group.
So overall coordination, or leadership in the gospel sense, would be

an area of competence no greater or no less than a gift for the youth apostolate. Both build up the body of Christ. We are all part of a royal priesthood, all fundamentally equal through baptism. We are a church of leaders; put another way, we are a church of servants. Is not the operative word *ministry* rather than *leadership*?

In our own community I, an ordained priest, am not on the coordinating team at present. I seem to be emerging as a friend, counsellor, resource person, and unifier for the community. They do not regard me as being above or below them, which is fine. I see it as important to help link the members to each other, to neighbouring groups, to the parish, diocese, church, and world at large. I do not want to control proceedings. And I believe that, because the lay members are fully exercising their role, I am seeing my priestly identity more clearly. With the understanding of leadership that I have tried to outline, I do not feel threatened. I am a leader. We are all leaders. In fact I feel that I may have a more wholesome influence now than when I played the traditional role of priest. This, I am convinced, is a way forward for the whole church.

Historically, the day of the top-down institution, whether religious or secular, is ended. That model is the old Ford car that no longer fits on our headlong motorways. The call is for structures that are lighter, where all stand side by side and play our full part in humbly serving the church and the world.

Decision-making
Decision-making in a small community is done through dialogue and consensus with the coordinator facilitating this process. The members sit down together in a prayerful atmosphere and calmly talk matters out so that they come to an agreement as to what to do. Decisions are normally made in line with this agreement, or consensus.

This manner of ordering affairs is achieved through conscientious, open dialogue. Force, manipulation, and unsavoury horse-trading are studiously avoided. It is characterised by a genuine desire to discern the will of God with the guidance of the Holy Spirit; the word and prayer are brought to bear on the process. Paul

VI says that it is through trustful dialogue in community that the will of God is discovered for a community (cf. *Evangelica Testificatio: Witness to the Gospel*, no. 25).[26] So we see the vital importance of the community meeting and of the dialogue which takes place there. In the church we really must commence listening carefully to, and deeply respecting, what its members are saying; even when we don't like what we are hearing.

Dialogue is not simply a matter of speaking, even more so it is about diligent listening. It demands that we stand in the shoes of the other person. Such an ability to listen will help to prevent the members from stubbornly persisting in flawed, entrenched positions and will foster a mature spirit of give-and-take.

Nor is consensus majority rule. All the members of a group must come to an agreement. But suppose there are a couple of people who have deep reservations about some proposed course of action. Should they remain silent? These owe it to the Holy Spirit, the community, and themselves to voice their opinions. Indeed assemblies have been turned right round by timely or prophetic interventions. Yet if the group, having duly considered their viewpoint, still feel that the proposed course ought to be followed, then the persons concerned must be sensitive to the direction in which the Spirit is moving the consensus.

As an example of a prophetic intervention, I would like to recall an incident that happened in West Africa. The coordinator for a community was being elected, and a man on the verge of being chosen. One of the members then remarked that the group had been speaking a lot about truly valuing its womenfolk and proposed that they elect a woman. This entailed quite a departure from normal practice in the locality. So voting began anew, and a woman was speedily elected!

The Holy Spirit has a way of surprising us. Some years ago I was requested to facilitate a weekend meeting for a group here in Ireland. There were some tensions among the members and it looked as if the body might be about to break up. My great hope was that it would not come to this and that unity would prevail. Before we got down to discuss, we celebrated a eucharist, reflected on the word of God, and prayed. Then we had a lengthy sharing after which we went to lunch. Everything was going according to plan. The plan, that is, as I envisaged it.

When we returned in the afternoon, events took a dramatic turn. It became clear that there were two equally valid but irreconcilable visions among the participants and that the Spirit seemed to be asking them to go their separate ways. This they did without acrimony and with a tinge of sadness. I have to admit that the Holy Spirit left me a little breathless that day.

I should like to refer to one part of the dynamic of that session which was to my mind crucial. It was the whole prayerful preparation consisting in this case of eucharist, the word, and prayer. In my experience a prayerful environment can transform the situation in such meetings and lead to a tranquil and constructive exchange. Somewhere in the prayer there comes the awareness that it is God's business we are about and not just our own.

So that is how decisions are arrived at in small Christian communities. We talk. And if there is no outcome, we talk some more. It may not seem as efficient as having cut-and-dried decisions handed down from on high, but in fact it is. Any progress made will tend to be irreversible, whereas with an authoritarian approach sooner or later we are prone to end up back where we started.

What we are searching for in discernment is of course the will of God. Where is it to be found? Is it existing out there somewhere waiting for us to come across it? Or does God so respect us that the Almighty is with us in the discernment? Are we, in other words, active partners in the process of forming God's will? In discerning we must also bear in mind that the Spirit of Jesus is in the whole community (1 Corinthians 12:27) and, consequently, it is essential to tap into the wisdom of all.

The church is not a democracy is a refrain that is often used. Unthinkingly I feel. In a democracy 150 votes beats 149, which leaves quite a number of dissatisfied people. This would be completely unacceptable in a community where dialogue and consensus operates. To say, then, that the church is not a democracy is true, because it ought to be much more democratic than a democracy. *The church is a community* , and there are no outsiders.

Finally, let me say that I have a simple litmus test to discover whether or not a group is motivated by the communitarian vision of Vatican II. I look at how they make their decisions. Do they, in the spirit of the Council, employ the process of dialogue and consensus, or not? Are matters worked out together, or is there someone with a direct line to the Holy Spirit telling everyone what to do? For any individual to speak on behalf of God is foolhardy in the extreme.

Diligent listening ... prayerfully seeking the will of God together ... striving to stand in the shoes of the other – what we were dealing with in this last section was of course *effective communication*. And this we have already singled out as one of the main features of small Christian communities. Without communication that is honest and open, we cannot build community. There is no place for equivocation, ambiguity, deceit, or the hidden agenda.

Ongoing formation

After they had survived their various high and low points for a quite a number of years, I once asked a group with whom I worked in South America what it was that kept them going. The response was unanimous. It was the formation they had received and were receiving.

The word *formation* can have overtones of manipulation by others. But so too can *training, education*, or *instruction*. It is what actually happens that matters. The formation that we are talking about here is ultimately auto-formation, or formation that comes largely from within oneself. In other words the subject desires and participates actively and critically in the educational process; it is a question of self-enrichment.

Since formation in this sense can be so helpful, we must necessarily dwell on the topic. Formation begins with the establishment of a small Christian community and continues as long as the group lasts. It should be formation in the fullest sense: spiritual, intellectual, intuitive, human, practical, and so forth.

Most formation comes through dialogue at meetings and casual conversation with friends. This means the small Christian community is itself an excellent school of formation. A sister in Zimbabwe told me of those mothers from Mozambique, already referred to, who during times of famine came over the Zimbabwean border carrying crushing loads of grass for animal fodder. These they sold to buy bread for their starving children back home and then set out on the long, wearying return journey. This moving scene is rivetted in my mind together with the lesson of love and sacrifice that it communicates. No lecture or treatise could have succeeded half so well as the image of those modern-day Christs, bearing their crosses with agonised and famished faces while they trod those eternal miles. Thus the good people with whom we meet and converse in our communities, and indeed elsewhere, are our greatest educators. The scripture says as much:

For out of the abundance of the heart the mouth speaks.

The good person brings good things out of a good treasure (Matthew 12:34).

Formation, therefore, comes through normal interaction; or to use a more formal term, most formation is relational. But with time the members of a community usually request a more organised approach as well. The dynamic of the group, as already mentioned, itself creates a longing for knowledge. Sometimes as a result of encounters and discussions in their places of work or study they may, for example, realise their deficiencies regarding the Bible or religious knowledge and ask for a solid grounding in either the one or the other. This provides the opportunity for a competent person – lay, cleric, or religious – to step in and meet a vital need.

Among the means for meeting such needs are:

* courses,
* workshops,
* sharing experiences with other small communities,
* retreats,
* talks,
* audio-visuals, and
* literature …

Formation can be provided in such areas as small Christian community itself, Bible, basic theology, justice and peace, catechetics, animation skills, group dynamics, counselling, and so on.

There are often pastoral centres where people can go for such courses and we also find resource persons who move about giving input to groups. There is a need for both approaches. One advantage of taking courses to the people is that entire small Christian communities can benefit from them, which is useful since the coordinating role circulates in communities. Normally individuals are selected to go to pastoral centres. These persons, however, should do courses with a view to going back and sharing all that they have learned with their groups. And it would be much better if a team of two or more were to go rather than just one person. They support each other when they return home.

Action/Reflection

One of the most formative dynamics in a small community is an ongoing action/reflection process which penetrates ever more deeply into the problem situation. The members do not simply do things mindlessly; they continually reflect on their action and then go out to perform better. In this action/reflection approach consists the so-called process of conscientisation. Conscientisation raises our awareness not simply for the sake of raising our awareness, but with a view to our doing something to change the world.

An example may help to explain what conscientisation means. A community in a South American *barrio* decided to give the poorest of the poor children a little present for a festive occasion.

Reflecting on this action at their weekly meeting, the members were happy with the way it went. But, after some discussion, one person remarked on the reaction of the parents. They had stood by with rather grim faces. The ingratitude of it!

None too quickly it dawned on them that maybe the parents were mortified because they themselves were not giving their own children the gifts. So the next time there was the occasion to distribute presents, the group secretly supplied them to the mothers and fathers, who then went on to give them to the children.

In the following meeting the community agreed that this proved much more successful. However, someone then wondered why it was that those parents couldn't afford even a small gift for their children. By dint of reflection and action the community was getting to the core of the social problem.

I often feel that the process of conscientisation – action/reflection – is the planet's best university, for it certainly takes one far. Some of the most educated people regarding the world and how it functions in religious, political, social, and economic terms, whom I have met, have been poor *campesinos* – peasants – in Ecuador and factory workers on the outskirts of São Paulo, Brazil. In a real sense they were far more educated, thanks to conscientisation, than even some professional people whom I have encountered elsewhere. These latter could be most proficient in their calling, yet quite limited, for example, in their knowledge of the workings of society. Or their religious awareness might have been arrested in childhood.

Implicit in action/reflection, of course, there is a sense of process, or gradualness; a realisation that growth does not happen overnight, but is the work of years. Such a realisation is important for the members of small communities. True progress is neither unduly rushed nor unduly delayed. It proceeds at a proper pace.

Practically this means that the group:

* takes people where they are,
* challenges them to grow,
* and strives to create the environment of love and acceptance that alone makes personal and community growth possible.

When we proceed in this way, we are only imitating the manner in which God deals with all of us. The Almighty accepts and loves us as we are, challenges us through the gospel to grow, and wills for us a loving Christian family and community to help us in our endeavours. So God is most respectful of the person and we must be the same. Without acceptance and love we cannot mature as human beings.

In the Western world of computers and instant everything, we can easily lose our sense of process. Ours is in fact an instant society. Efficiency is at a premium: 'We have no time to stand and stare' (Davies). It is not so in the economically less well off nations. I recall visiting a chief in Zambia who, it transpired, had lost his eldest son to a crocodile in the dark river near his compound only three weeks before. Grieving though he was, he insisted on seeing me. We of course talked about his terrible loss, but then he went on to enquire about my work. I told him that I was trying to promote small communities among Christians. He himself was not a Christian, yet politely asked how it was all going. Very slowly, I told him. He was silent for a long while, and then cited a proverb of his people: *When God cooks, there is no smoke.*

Instant coffee there may be. But there are no instant communities. We must begin humbly at the grassroots, even with one or – better – two communities, and see where the Spirit takes the experience. This patience is not easy. I have worked in situations where folk wanted to launch small Christian communities and started well. However, their expectations were too high and, when groups didn't spread rapidly, they got discouraged. We are talking leaven groups here, not mass movement. Indeed we are considering the very nature of the church. Is it a mass movement in the world or a leaven to promote the kingdom of God?

A simple Rule of Life
Some small Christian communities have a simple Rule of Life. As an example I should like to quote that of the Little Gidding group in England. This is a residential community, Anglican in its origins, but now ecumenical in its membership. This Rule asks the members:
- to pray together once a day,
- celebrate communion and, if possible, share a meal with other community members at least once a week,
- to commit time and resources to God's service,
- and aim to live peaceably with God and others.[27]

These items are simple undertakings, not vows. And they are not meant to be cast-iron, but flexible. This flexibility is indicated by the words 'if possible'and 'for those who are able,' which are often on the lips of the group members. The flexibility does not mean of course that commitments are to be taken casually.

Membership of a community involves certain things, such as:
- being together,
- worshipping together,

- sharing lives and goods,
- and reaching out to others (especially to those in society who are pushed aside or totally excluded) on behalf of, and inspired by, the community.

The participants do their best about these requirements in accordance with circumstances.

Most communities that I meet do not have an expressed rule like Little Gidding. My home-based Dublin group does not have one. Implicitly there are shared understandings and the essential bonding, spirituality, reality, commitment, and communication. These, however, have not been formalised into a set of stated commitments. This would be the case with most neighbourhood groups around the world. We are talking about a human, relational thing. I do not see, though, how having four or five broad-based undertakings could do anything but good. It would provide focus. I will certainly be taking the matter up with my community – I did so later but they decided to carry on as they were.

Action

A small Christian community must be involved in action. But what action? First of all the members, simply by being what they are ought to bring gospel values, which are merely basic human values, to those places where their daily activities take them: the teacher to the school, the nurse to the hospital, the young person to the youth club, the politician to parliament, the factory worker to the factory, the business person to the shop. For many this is a whole new perspective on action, which they would tend to see as something over and above the normal things they do. Yet in *Populorum Progressio* (*Fostering the Development of Peoples*) Paul VI calls on Roman Catholics the world over, 'without waiting passively for orders or directives, to take the initiative freely and to infuse a Christian spirit into the mentality, customs, laws and structures of the community in which they live.'[28] This amounts to an excellent strategy for building the kingdom of God in the world.

Not only will the members of small Christian communities witness to gospel values in their own places of study, work, or residence, but they will also take their skills back to their homes and neighbourhoods. If someone is a nurse and a neighbour's child is ill, he will call to see if something can't be done. In reality members get involved in a whole welter of activity: providing religious education, working with young people, conducting courses, visiting the sick and those with problems, comforting those stricken with AIDS, engaging in development work, being active on behalf of the little people whom society pushes aside or excludes as being of no account.

I think it is helpful if a group has a plan of action. Certainly the members ought to do something in the name of the community, and be accountable for what they do. The purpose of this is not that the group may be able to check on its members, rather is it a matter of providing an opportunity for affirming and supporting them. When they can talk about their difficulties and are upheld by the prayers and concern – even the active assistance – of their friends, it is of enormous help.

I should like to make the point here that persons should never become so involved in community work that their marriage or families suffer. The family, or domestic church,[29] is the priority for them. So the demands of community and family have to be kept in creative tension. One of the pleasing aspects of my own Dublin community is how faithful the young marrieds are to their families. Could it be that, at certain phases of life, commitment to the family is the totality of what some members can do as action on behalf of their small Christian community?

If it be possible for the members of small communities to work in teams and not just as individuals, so much the better. Jesus sent out his apostles on mission two by two, not alone. 'For,' as he says in Matthew's gospel, 'where two or three are gathered in my name, there am I in the midst of them' (18:20; cf. also Matthew 10:5-15; Luke 10:1-20).

In the complicated world of today it is not usually possible for the members of a community to be engaged in the same task. If on occasions, however, they can all join together in doing something, it is a marvellous help towards developing community. From time to time, our group is called upon by the parish to help with a bucket collection for some worthy cause. A warm atmosphere always pre-vails and it is a wonderful chance for bonding. Indeed all the work done in the name of the grouping, whether by teams or individuals, contributes greatly to creating a community spirit.

In the beginning a community will respond to some obvious needs round about it. With time, as it grows in maturity, the mem-bers may become more thoroughgoing in their approach. This could entail making an analysis of their area in an effort to get at the problems as seen by the ordinary people of the place. We are now talking serious pastoral planning, which is an issue we will deal with in chapter 7.

Action of course is buttressed by prayer. The spirituality of the small Christian community is an integral one that combines prayer and outreach – indeed some would see prayer as a form of out-reach. Neither aspect is neglected and this is important, because a spirituality that tries to function either on the basis of prayer or action alone is a spirituality trying to fly on one wing. Sooner or later it will splutter and crash. In a lecture in the United States I once heard Daniel Berrigan say that prayer which did not issue in action was spurious. And Teresa of Avila used to declare, 'The Lord walks among the pots and pans.'[30] And finally, although a monk, Thomas Merton was one of the first to sense that there was some-thing awfully wrong with the Vietnam War, and condemn it. He wrote:

> But 'no man is an island.' A purely individualistic inner life unconcerned with the sufferings of others, is unreal. Therefore my meditation on love and peace must be realistically and inti-mately related to the fury of war, bloodshed, burning, destruc-tion, killing that takes place on the other side of the earth.[31]

These people are mystics. We might have a vision of them as being somewhat other-worldly. Not so. Indeed their words show that the step from mysticism to social concern is a short one. They were truly in touch with reality.

Reality, or practicalities, is what we have been about in this chapter – reality in terms of the organisation of small Christian communities and also in terms of their outreach to channel the love of the Trinity to, and build God's kingdom in, this troubled world of ours. As we pointed out at the beginning, these practicalities, however minute, are the stuff of God's action, or revelation, on earth.

Summary

1) We now consider the practicalities – reality – of small Christian communities which work out in creation the effects of the love of Father, Son, and Spirit, and are palpably Trinitarian presences and body of Christ.
2) These practicalities consist of organisation and action, meetings, pastoral planning, and common issues; the current chapter deals with organisation and action.
3) Confer (p. 73-74) for a brief description of small Christian community.
4) Organisation is not more important than people.
5) Small community starts:
- backed by prayer
- with an interested person or persons,
- from where we are,
- with the necessary information,
- possibly by building on existing groups.
6) The experience of the intimate group is necessary, yet equally that of networking, or being a communion of communities.
7) Leadership is for service (cf. Matthew 20:20-28; Mark 10:35-45; Luke 22:24-27; John 13:1-20).
8) The leader's role is one of animation, coordination, facilitation, enablement, not domination; best viewed as one of many equally important forms of ministry.
9) Better a team (of three?) coordinators rather than one, for practical and theological – Trinitarian – reasons.
10) The entire community, not the coordinating team, is the priority; it proposes and disposes facilitated by the coordinators.
11) There are interpersonal skills vital for the running of community: empathy (ability to listen), personal disclosure (openness), con-

frontation (responsible challenge), non-defensive exploration (examining issues without fear).

12) To deal with inevitable conflict the following are needed: clarification (to be clear where the problem lies), negotiation (dialogue), imagination (fresh ways of proceeding), celebration (liturgical and social).

13) Allowing for diversity also relieves tension.

14) Coordinators should involve members in the activities of the group and foster relationships by using celebrations (e.g. eucharist, birthdays) and symbols (e.g. a garland or bunch of flowers to show appreciation).

15) The priest or pastor in a small Christian community is a friend, counsellor, resource person, and unifier; not into control.

16) The will of God for a community is discovered through 'trustful dialogue' (discernment) in the group (Paul VI, *Evangelica Testificatio: Evangelical Witness*, no. 25); decisions are arrived at through dialogue and consensus, and all members must be listened to carefully and with respect; this is relevant to open and honest communication – one of the main ingredients of small Christian communities.

17) There should be initial and ongoing formation (understood as auto-education, or self enrichment) in the small community; formation in the fullest sense: spiritual, intellectual, intuitive, human.

18) One of the most enriching factors in the group is the action/ reflection procedure that it adopts – the process of conscientisation.

19) A small Christian community must develop a sense of process – the awareness that growth is gradual and can neither be unduly rushed nor unduly delayed; it involves taking people where they are, challenging them to grow, and striving to create the environment of love and acceptance that makes growth possible.

20) A simple Rule of Life, or four or five broad-based commitments, may be of help to a community.

21) The spirituality of small Christian community is integral; it has two facets, prayer and action.

22) Having a plan of action can be of assistance.

Questions

1) Taking your own situation into account, have you any ideas as to what practical steps you might take to go about starting small Christian communities?

   Suggested Bible passage: Mark 1:14-28.

2) What does leadership mean for you and your group?

   Suggested Bible passage: Matthew 20:20-28; or John 13:1-20.

3) How are decisions made in your community?

   Suggested reading: Luke 2:41-52; Paul VI. *Evangelica Testificatio (Evangelical Witness)*, no. 25 (cf. Vatican II, Flannery, 1980, fifth printing, p.692).

4) Is formation a concern for your community?

   Suggested Bible passage: Ephesians 4:7-16.

5) What action does your group take?

   Suggested Bible passage: Isaiah 29:12-14; or James 2:14-26.

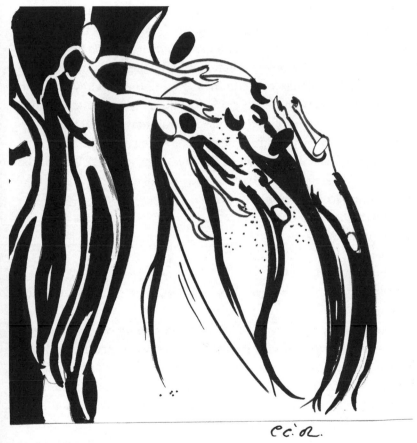

CHAPTER 6

Meetings

I once saw an intriguing poster which was completely filled with the heads of turkeys looking expectantly in all directions. The caption underneath read: *Now that we're organised, what do we do?* This reminds me of a problem often posed by people who hope to launch small Christian communities. 'Right,' they say, 'we want to start a small community. We come together. Now what do we do? What are the meetings like?' Let us say straightaway that there is no cut-and-dried answer to this question. No fixed agenda.

The essential components of the meetings, as of the life, of the communities are those we have already alluded to:

- bonding (communion)
- spirituality
- commitment
- reality
- communication.

Whatever order or form they come in, they should always be present.

The meeting of the small Christian community ought to be relevant – respond to needs. At the moment in my country, Ireland, one of the burning issues is the peace process in the North. This, of course, should figure in sessions. In fact a young couple from our Dublin group travelled on a peace train to Belfast, taking their baby girl with them, in the tense days proceeding the process. Stones were thrown at the train, yet the politicians achieved a ceasefire which still holds.

Before the execution of Ken Saro-Wiwa and his companions, our meeting took the form of a candle-light vigil outside the Nigerian Embassy in Dublin, demanding that their lives be spared.

Shamefully, the plea fell on deaf ears. But the session was relevant. It might be that a group needs to plan something, and the meeting is devoted to this. Or they might feel the desire, as our group often does, for a spiritual fillip and devote an entire meeting to prayer or the eucharist. Needs decide the agenda; there ought to be no rigid pattern. This doesn't mean that sessions are unplanned. Quite the contrary. In fact the preparation has to be more thorough than when there is a regular format. Generally at the end of a meeting the participants decide the coordinator and subject for the next session.

A group of course may want to have an ongoing theme for those moments when nothing of urgency presents itself. To go systematically through a book like this one, dealing with the questions provided, could be a help in such a situation. Or it might be a document of Vatican II such as *Apostolicam Actuositatem, Decree on the Apostolate of the Lay People.*

When a group clings to some fixed methodology, it can lose out on relevance. There are suggested methods for reflecting on the Bible – one is provided in the course of this chapter – which need careful handling. The members can spend so much time on the method that they do not get round to talking about life or its problems at all. And this despite the fact that most methods rightly insist that the word of God must be related to life and put into practice, providing for this in their procedures. If this recommendation is ignored, then communities can become simply Bible-discussion and prayer groups.

There is also a practice, which is common enough, of reflecting week by week on the gospel of the following Sunday. This has the advantage that the faithful have already thought of the reading in advance and can, therefore, derive more fruit from the homily at Mass. Or, in situations where there is a shared homily, they can readily contribute. Most times this can be relevant, but not always. A Sunday gospel may have little to say to Wednesday's rioting. In which case a passage that is more to the point should be used. It is important to be flexible and adapt. The watchwords then are relevance, flexibility, and adaptability.

An event that happened in King William's Town, South Africa, will bear out the foregoing. On the night when the news of Steve Biko's murder came through, the African townships surrounding this city were ablaze in protest. Biko came from one of those very townships. That same night some Christian groups were meeting for a course that had been going on for some time. An excellent course, but the agenda and scripture passage on that occasion had little relevance to the mayhem in the townships. One of the participants told me that there was a terrible sense of unreality about the proceedings.

When we think of meetings, formal gatherings usually come to mind. Yet our lives are made up of rather more casual encounters: relaxed meetings at work, running into friends on the street, a game of cards or chess, study groups, meetings to prepare or celebrate the sacraments, cultural or religious functions, outings, holidays, and pilgrimages. All these can help considerably in forming community. We should be aware of this. Indeed when members reflect on factors that keep them together over long periods, apart from spiritual considerations, purely social encounters are very much to the fore. But, then, Christ himself loved to sit and eat and chat with people. And he provided the drinks for what must have been one of the earliest recorded cocktail parties!

Before I proceed to give some models for meetings of small communities, let me say that there are no great difficulties involved. All over the world today quite simple people will:

- sit down together,
- pause for a moment to recall they are in the presence of God,
- perhaps say a short opening prayer,
- share the joys and problems of life,
- see what light the word of God sheds on their situation,
- consider what can be done in the circumstances,
- and pray with one another.

    If we analyse this, the basic dynamic is:

1) life
2) the word
3) life / action
4) prayer

This is an ordinary format that anyone could use. I must admit I have a fondness for sessions that begin with life issues and then bring the word to bear upon these issues, though I would not want to close off other possibilities. Actually, within this broad framework there is ample room for variety. Relationships deepen, issues and circumstances change, life moves on. In our Dublin community I have never found that any of the many meetings run along these lines palled. However, the sample meetings that follow offer a wide range of possibilities.

Sample meetings
Despite having stressed the importance of flexibility, I am aware that the organising of sessions can present some difficulty for groups, especially in their early stages. I now give a sampling of some 23 gatherings that may be of help to communities. The intention is that they may serve as examples, or paradigms, to spark off possibilities in the mind of the group facilitator, not that they be adhered to exactly. Various of them deal with topics that are important for an understanding of small Christian community, such as, unity, commitment, kingdom, contemplation, dialogue, leadership, communication, planning, evaluation. They are in note form and largely derived from meetings that have actually taken place.

Incidentally, I notice that Meetings 1-10 touch on the vital subjects of community, spirituality, and commitment, while reality is part of all of them. So beginners might like to model their early gatherings on these.

Meeting 1: An Exercise
Theme: Relationships/Community
The basis of this meeting takes the form of an exercise, or group dynamic, to help the members of a community relate to one another. I have had extremely good feedback on this session. It is especially good when a group is in its initial phase, and efforts are being made at bonding.

Before launching into this dynamic, there are some points that I should like to make about sharing in general where small Christian communities are concerned. No pressure is ever exercised in small communities to get people to reveal themselves. While openness is desirable, it is completely up to people to reveal as much or as little of themselves as they wish. We must remember that persons differ greatly in this respect, and no one should say or do anything with which he feels uncomfortable. It would be a mistake for one to wear his heart on his sleeve early in the life of a group, before it has co-alesced as a community. If members are going to open their hearts, they need the support of a community that they can trust. This trust grows slowly with time.

In my own community we can share quite deeply now, and there is absolutely no problem about it. At no time in fact has it been an issue. We know one another well; are like an intimate family. Still, after 20 years, some are better than others at sharing about themselves. Anyway, mostly we talk about community topics. And the community is not our spiritual director. There are very personal matters that I do not feel I have to talk to my community about, though I will speak to a director or perhaps a close friend – *anam chara* – within the community. What I'm trying to say is that it would be a mistake for someone to shy away from becoming a member of a small community through a fear of sharing, because this issue is dealt with in such a sensitive way.

(1) The Exercise

(a) The animator of the meeting asks all present to think about the question: *Who am I?* (10-15 minutes).

(b) Each member is asked to seek out a person whom he does not know or would like to know better. The pair introduce, and chat with each other about themselves. They will, it is hoped, reveal something of their *feelings*. When we say how we feel about some-thing, people get to know us better: our feelings are our own, our thoughts may be those of Aristotle. Interesting details can add spice. I once talked to a girl in her teens who had done a parachute jump for charity. I'd think twice before jumping off a three-foot wall. The two also discuss what they would like to gain from being in community (10-15 mins).

(c) The leader calls upon the twosomes to join other pairs so as to make groups of four. The participants introduce and chat not about themselves this time, but regarding their partners of the previous step. Points of interest about persons are noted, and they are asked to decide as a group what their expectations of small community are (15-20 mins).

(d) The groups of four now combine to form groups, or a group, of eight. They choose a name for this grouping, a person to animate proceedings, and a secretary to take notes. The introductions are repeated in this larger group. Again the participants present their partner of step (b), noting any interesting detail. They share the expectations of community as decided upon in the gatherings of four, and they choose four expectations which they consider the most important.

(e) All now join in a general forum but the groups of eight stay together. The secretary gives the name of the grouping, introduces its members, noting interesting points, and says what their four chosen expectations are. These are written up on a blackboard or on a flip-chart and discussed (15-20 mins).

(2) Suggested Bible passage: Acts 4:32-37.

Having seen how the scripture might shed light on the discussion, the assembly decides on some very practical outcome from their session – something concrete, however small, that will help in community-building.

(3) There is now spontaneous prayer, or prayer that comes straight from the heart, using one's own words (may include hymns, chanting and music; a guitar may prove useful, or recordings).

Note: The above exercise follows the pattern of human relationships. First we are alone. Then we open to another (mother), to a limited group (the family) and finally to the whole community. Exercises, or group dynamics, can be a fruitful source for meetings.

* * *

Meeting 2: Simple Exercise
Theme: Community / Sharing
(1) The members place themselves in the presence of God (pause in silence).
(2) Each relates some happy event from his life, saying something of how he *felt*.
(3) Suggested Bible passage: Luke 2:1-20.
Does this passage shed any light on your sharing?
(4) What *action* might the group take as a result of sharing experiences and the word of God?
(5) Shared Prayer (cf. Meeting 1, 3).

* * *

Meeting 3: Simple Exercise
Theme: Community / Sharing
(1) The members place themselves in the presence of God (pause in silence).
(2) Each one relates some sad event from his life, saying something about how he *felt*.
(3) Suggested Bible passage: Matthew 11:28-30.
Does this passage shed any light on the sharing?
(4) What *action* might the group take as a result of sharing experiences and the word of God?
(5) Shared prayer (cf. Meeting 1, 3).

* * *

Meeting 4: Simple Exercise (dynamic)
Theme: Unity
(1) Check-in: The group may wish to share briefly with one another regarding how things have gone for them since their last meeting. (This is a possibility for opening most sessions. The check-in may sometimes develop into an entire meeting and the community may decide to do this.)
(2) The animator produces a bundle of twigs bound together and

invites various members to break them. If there are enough of them this is impossible (Be careful! I met one who succeeded in doing the impossible!). The facilitator then unties the bundle and asks the participants to try breaking them individually. This proves a very easy task.

(3) The members then discuss the exercise and its relevance to their lives.

(4) Suggested Bible passage: Matthew 12:22-28.

Does this passage shed light on the discussion?

(5) The group decides on some *action* resulting from their sharing.

(6) Shared prayer (cf. Meeting 1, 3).

* * *

Meeting 5: Worship/Bible Reflection

Theme: Community

N.B. This session is devoted entirely to a Bible reflection and a six-point method for doing this is provided. The Bible passage under consideration: John 17:20-26.

(1) Invite those present to place themselves in the presence of God (pause in silence).

(2) Ask for a volunteer to read the passage and leave a couple of minutes for the members to think about it. Do not fear the silence; it gives the Spirit a chance to speak.

(3) Read the extract a second time (different reader) and pause once more for three to five minutes.

(4) Invite the participants to share regarding what the passage says to them, paying particular attention to the challenges it raises for their lives. Bearing in mind what was said about sharing the word of God in chapter 3 should prove useful.

(5) Determine the *practical application* of the passage for the lives of the participants. What *action* are they going to take? It may not always be a question of doing something new, but of intensifying some action already being taken. Maybe they are enriched as persons and become aware that this can have practical repercussions. Identify these.

(6) Shared prayer (cf. Meeting 1, 3).

Note: This method can be applied to any scripture passage.

Meeting 6: Worship

Theme: Need for prayer / reflection

(This session is taken from notes that I made of an encounter in our Dublin community some years ago.)

(1) Check-in (cf. Meeting 4, 1).

(2) The animator announced that the bulk of the meeting would be devoted to personal reflection and prayer. A selection of stimulating reading was placed on a table. A letter supposedly from Jesus Christ was set up in one corner of the room with a few colourful votive candles near it. In the letter Christ reminded the reader of the personal friendship between them and wondered if in the hurly-burly of life he found time to talk with his Saviour. The members were free just to sit and meditate, browse through the material provided, go read the letter, or visit a nearby oratory.

(3) After about 45 minutes the members were asked if they would like to share something with the community. One participant said that in the course of the meditation she thought of the people she loved and of those who loved her. Often in daily dealings with them she became overly aware of their faults; the meditation restored a proper perspective, so that she saw the goodness more clearly. A second member said that she felt relaxed and happy. A third informed us that he had spent the whole of the previous evening discussing God with friends. On reflection, however, he realised that the only one whose words were not considered in the dialogue was in fact God. Again he said that the meeting put things in perspective. And so it went.

(4) The scripture reading was from Ecclesiastes 3:1-9 ('For everything there is a season...'). The members reflected that in the welter of activities that went to make up their daily lives they would have to be careful not to forget their Friend, God / Jesus. There must be the restoring moments in order to go to the mountain top or desert place and get a true perspective on what is truly important in life. The session gradually wound to a close in a mixture of reflection and prayer.

* * *

Meeting 7: Worship/Eucharist

When a group devotes a session to the celebration of the eucharist, the important thing is the preparation. If this is done thoroughly, the celebration usually goes well. Items to be prepared:

- the place of celebration
- music and hymns
- things to be celebrated; the members may be asked to be ready to announce at the beginning of the eucharist items which they wish to celebrate (e.g. 'I would like to celebrate the friendship that I find in this group')
- readings and bidding prayers and who are going to do them
- thoughts for the shared homily
- offertory procession (including what symbols?)
- mime at the offertory (?)
- communion reflection

Afterwards there may be a sharing of food. This should always be kept simple, mindful that in certain parts of the world Christians are so poor that they have no other choice. We should be sensitive too of putting financial burdens on people, or embarrassing them.

* * *

Meeting 8: Worship

Theme: Reconciliation

(1) Check-in (cf. Meeting 4, 1).

(2) Participants place themselves in the presence of God (silent pause).

(3) Examination of Conscience:

- Do I love my neighbour without laying down conditions for my love?
- Do I pay attention to my spiritual life?
- Am I just (i.e. are my relationships right) at home, in the community, and with people in general?
- Do I make an option with the poor and am I compassionate towards the disadvantaged?
- Am I open to to others?

- Am I open to change?
- Do I put the word of God into practice?
- Do I strive to live at peace with others overcoming all obstacles in the way of doing so?
- Do I really listen to people?
- Does failure worry me, or do I see it as a possible step towards a new beginning?

(4) Suggested Bible passage: John 8:1-11.

Does this reading shed any light on the reconciliation process?

(5) Act of sorrow recited in common.

(If a priest is present, some may wish to confess privately at this point.)

(6) The members make a private resolution of amendment and are encouraged to keep it as down-to-earth as possible; it should not be vague. The group may wish to make a purpose of amendment on some point as a community (?).

(7) As a symbol of conversion, the members might want to write down their faults secretly on a piece of paper and then proceed to burn them in some safe container (I have seen some hazardous burning of sins!).

(8) Shared prayer (cf. Meeting 1, 3).

(9) A sign of peace is shared by all.

Hymn: *Peace is flowing like a river* .

* * *

Meeting 9: Ordinary format (cf. pp. 102-3 for details)

Theme: Commitment

(1) Check-in (cf. Meeting 4, 1).

(2) The members are asked to share on what commitment, or total dedication to Christ and gospel values, means to them in their lives.

(3) Suggested Bible passage: Luke 9:57-62.

Does this reading shed any light on the discussion?

(4) The group decides on the *action* it will take.

(5) Shared prayer, (cf. Meeting 1, 3).

* * *

Meeting 10: Worship
Theme: Commitment
Follow the same method for Bible-sharing given in Meeting 5, cf p 107, reflecting on the following passage: Mark 10:17-31.

* * *

Meeting 11: Ordinary format (cf.pp. 102-3)
Theme : The Kingdom of God
(1) The members place themselves in the presence of God (silent pause).
(2) Check-in (cf. Meeting 4, 1).
(3) Suggested Bible passages: Matthew 6:33; Matthew 13:1-33.
What do these extracts tell us about the kingdom of God and its members?
(4) What does each participant personally consider the kingdom of God to be?
(5) What practical impact can our understanding have on our lives and outreach to others?
(6) Shared prayer (cf. Meeting 1, 3).

* * *

Meeting 12: Simple exercise
Theme: The Kingdom of God
(1) The participants place themselves in the presence of God (silent pause).
(2) Check-in (cf. Meeting 4, 1).
(3) Take the understanding of the kingdom as being wherever we find harmony rooted in justice. Then ask the participants to think of experiences, incidents, or stories from their own lives that would illustrate this.
(4) Suggested Bible passage: Matthew 18:23-35.
What light does this shed on the sharing?
(5) The group decides on some practical outcome to their sharing.
(6) Shared prayer (Meeting 1, 3).

Meeting 13: Group Dynamic
Theme: Animation/Leadership
(1) The members place themselves in the presence of God (silent pause).
(2) Check-in (cf. Meeting 4, 1).
(3) The dynamic is as follows:
- The participants are are invited to stand in V formation with the animator of the session at the point of the V.
- All hold hands.
- The animator/leader proceeds to move while trailing everybody else after her.
- Next the group is assembled in a huddle and the leader endeavours to push them all forward.
- Lastly they assemble in a line and, encouraged by the leader/animator, move forward on their own steam side by side.

(4) The members are now asked to decode, or explain, the exercise. Are there any implications for leadership?
(5) Suggested Bible passage Matthew 20:20-28.
Does the passage shed light on the discussion?
(6) Some action to be decided upon, resulting from the foregoing reflections.
(7) Shared prayer (cf. Meeting 1, 3).

* * *

Meeting 14: Group Dynamic
Theme: Coordination/Leadership
(1) The members place themselves in the presence of God (silent pause).
(2) Check-in (cf. Meeting 4, 1).
(3) Here I would suggest a washing of the feet ceremony as happens on Holy Thursday, while some appropriate hymn is being sung; the facilitator of the meeting to do the washing – play the role of Christ.
(4) The members are asked to comment on the significance of the exercise.
(5) Suggested Bible passage: John 13:1-11.

Does the passage speak to the issue on which the group is sharing?
(6) What action can be taken in the light of the reflections?
(7) Shared prayer (cf. Meeting 1, 3).

* * *

Meeting 15: Ecumenical
Theme: Ecumenical Outreach
The following is an account of a session which I had with a small Buddhist community in a boathouse on the River Kwai just below the historic bridge.
(1) First of all as a guest I shared a simple vegetarian meal with the community. Indeed it seemed to me that simplicity of lifestyle was for them essential to holiness. I could only guess as to what they thought of the affluent West.
(2) After the meal we sat together exchanging ideas and experiences. I learned about their reverence and concern for creation, peace and justice, a wholesome education, a world that would not be plagued by consumerism and all its attendant ills. They were interested in what I had to say about small Christian communities (I was just returning from having worked in Australia). I told them that their concerns were also concerns for the Christian communities. I assured them that Christians respected all religions and upheld freedom of conscience. A thing that struck me was the genuine respect of the young people present for their elders. It is something precious that has been undermined in the West with dire consequences. As a young mother in our Dublin community once put it, 'If respect goes, everything goes.' This value needs recapturing, urgently. However, the opposite is also true; if adults are to receive respect from the youth, they must merit it. Furthermore they themselves must be careful to reverence the young.
(3) We talked long over these issues as a burnished moon rolled out a glittering carpet across the River Kwai.
(4) Afterwards we sat for a considerable time in silent meditation together. I prayed to God that all their endeavours to build a better world would be blessed.

(5) Finally we dispersed and I settled down on the deck of the boathouse to sleep. They made sure to provide me with a mosquito net so that I could have an undisturbed night's rest.

* * *

Meeting 16: Ecumenical
Theme: Strength in weakness
This session took place in a retirement home in Toronto. There were eight members present (an Anglican, Baptist, Greek Orthodox, Lutheran, Pentecostal, Presbyterian, and two Roman Catholics).
(1) Coordinator: May the grace of Our Lord Jesus Christ, the love of God, and the fellowship of the Holy Spirit be with you all, now and forevermore.
All: Amen.
(2) Check-in: They all relate how they have been since their last weekly meeting. A check-in is normally brief, yet in the context of the retirement home it proved somewhat lengthy. The opportunity to be listened to seemed deeply valued.
(3) The previous week a lady had pointed out how hard she found it to be charitable to an irritating neighbour. This led to the choice of the theme, Strength in weakness, for the current session.
(4) Bible extract chosen: 2 Corinthians 12:5-10.
The members shared experiences of weakness and how God helped them in their debility. There was a great deal of scriptural reminiscing, a Finnish lady fondly recalling Sunday school back in her homeland when she was a little girl.
(5) They resolved to strive to be patient and kind despite their infirmities.
(6) Shared prayer. The participants concluded by praying for the chaplain, care staff, and patients, especially for Marjorie who was at death's door. They thanked God for a variety of things: the lovely Sunday service they had had, the arts and crafts class, the singalong … Then Mabel declared: 'It's wonderful how all of us, though of different denominations, can discuss and worship so marvellously together. This meeting is the highlight of my week.'

Meeting 17: Prophetic (i.e. deals with a justice issue. The prophets were greatly involved with justice issues).

Theme: This session took place in an African group. The issue was a poorly maintained road in a township.

(1) The participants said a short prayer invoking the help of the Holy Spirit in their sharing.

(2) The problem of the road was hotly debated. It seemed that its condition was so appalling that a small child nearly drowned in one of the potholes.

(3) Bible passage chosen: Luke 3:1-6.

This passage speaks about the 'rough ways being made smooth'. If the way for Jesus is to be properly prepared, the paths must be straight. There must be no crookedness, a member said. Justice was required.

(4) *Action:* They decided to protest by going in a delegation to the municipal council, bringing a list of signatures with them from the residents of the area.

(5) The shared prayer had a scriptural ring about it making use of expressions like 'making the rough ways smooth'.

* * *

Meeting 18: Prophetic/Miscellaneous: a meeting can be built on a poem, song, reading from any source etc.,

Theme: Justice (Environment)

(I was walking in a neighbouring park with a friend when I came across a sight that greatly distressed me. There was this shapely ash tree that must have been growing for thirty years or more, and in a matter of minutes some vandals had cut a circle of bark from it, assuring it of a slow, wilting death. My friend and I were outraged at the wantonness of this. As a result I thought up the following meeting.)

(1) The members place themselves in the presence of God (silent pause).

(2) Check-in (cf. Meeting 4, 1).

(3) The following poem, entitled *Stupidity Street,* to be distributed

and the participants asked to ponder it for some minutes, even commit it to memory:

> I saw with open eyes
> Singing birds sweet
> Sold in the shops,
> For people to eat,
> Sold in the shops of
> Stupidity Street.

> I saw in a vision
> The worm in the wheat,
> And in the shops nothing
> For people to eat
> Nothing for sale in Stupidity Street.

(4) The group then discusses the incident referred to above, together with the poem, and tease out their implications.

(5) Suggested Bible passages to choose from: Genesis 1:1-31 ('And God saw that it was good.'); Matthew 6:28-29 ('Consider the lilies of the field...').

(6) What *action* can be taken as a result of the reflections that might protect the environment and bring home to the perpetrators the harm they are doing? The thought occurred to me that we should start a little project to clean up the park and plant some trees, and we could involve the youth and children of the area in doing this. If a child were to plant a tree, it would surely make a difference.

(7) Shared prayer (cf. Meeting 1, 3). As part of this prayer, Joyce Kilmer's *Trees* could be read.

* * *

Meeting 19: Planning
Theme: Justice
A big fiesta is approaching, and the members of a small Christian community in a populous South American barrio want to do something to make it a memorable occasion.

(1) The members say a few short introductory prayers.

(2) Many ideas are put forward as to what they might do for the feast. Eventually they decide that they are going to give a small gift to the poorest of the poor children of the *barrio* (deprived area in a city). Then some members volunteer to seek sponsors so as to raise funds to purchase the gifts; others undertake to wrap them and decide who are to receive them; and finally there are those who promise to present the children with the packets in their homes.

(3) Bible passage chosen: Acts 20:32-35 ('more blessed to give than receive').

It certainly spoke to the situation.

(4) Shared prayer (cf. Meeting 3, 1). Hymn: *Caridad y comprensión (Love and understanding)*.

* * *

Meeting 20: Evaluation

Theme: Justice

(After the fiesta the community evaluates its action)

(1) Jorge plays the guitar and the members sing *Santa Maria del Camino:*

> While you journey through life
> You are never alone.
> With you on the road
> Mary goes.
> Although your footsteps
> Seem useless,
> You forge a path as you go;
> Now others will follow on …

(2) The community evaluated the whole episode of giving the gifts to the children. They felt it had gone well. It was satisfying to help the little ones, and a delight to see them so happy. All well worthwhile. Then someone sounded a discordant note. The parents didn't seem so elated. In fact many of them stood by with morose faces. After all the efforts, you would expect a little gratitude. Then a woman pointed out that maybe the parents were sad because they had to stand by and watch others give their children a gift for the

fiesta. Ah yes, that was true. Obvious now that they thought of it. What parent wouldn't feel sad in those circumstances? Next time they repeated this gesture, they would secretly pass the presents along to the parents and let them give them to their own offspring. All agreed this would be much better.

(3) Bible passage chosen: Amos 5:21-24. A passage on justice that really shed light on the situation.

(4) Shared prayer (cf. Meeting 1, 3). The prayers were very related to the Bible reflections.

* * *

Meeting 21: Evaluation
The following are a list of questions that might help a small community to evaluate its life and action. The work can be spread over maybe three sessions, or a day (once a year?) be devoted to this rather complete assessment.

(1) The community places itself in the presence of God (silent pause).

(2) Check-in (cf. 4, 1).

(3) Bible reflection: Acts 15:1-35 (the apostles plan and evaluate). Does this passage shed any light on the evaluation exercise?

Other possible readings to choose from should the task go to more than one session: Acts 6:1-7 (the apostles plan and evaluate); *Evangelica Testificatio (Evangelical Witness)*, Paul VI, no. 25 (cf. *Vatican Council II*, Flannery, Fifth Printing 1980, p. 692).

(4) Questions for evaluation exercise:

• Do we have a spirituality?
• What are the chief facets of our spirituality?
• Do we imitate the Blessed Trinity in our efforts to love and share?
• Is our community centred in Christ whose body we are, Christ being the person who mediates the love of the Father, Son, and Spirit to the church and the world?
• Have we a keen Spirit-consciousness?
• Do we value the eucharist, prayer, the word of God, forgive-

ness/reconciliation, and reflection?
- Is our use of the Bible life-related?
- Do we always reflect on what we do and act on our reflection?
- Have we, as a small community, been able to maintain a relative autonomy within our mainstream church while at the same time preserving links and a cooperative relationship?
- Is working for a society where there is goodness and harmony rooted in justice (the kingdom) a priority for us?
- Have we made an option with the poor?
- Are women, youth, children and all who are disadvantaged and excluded given a voice and the opportunity to make their contribution?
- Are we open to others and prepared to change?
- Are we prepared to die like the grain of wheat?
- What are we growing into?
- Are our decisions truly arrived at through dialogue and consensus?
- Do we face up to and resolve conflict?

(5) What *action(s)* is to be taken as a result of the evaluation? (*prioritise* four or five for immediate attention and keep the others in mind for consideration, when it becomes possible).

(6) Shared prayer (cf. Meeting 1, 3).

* * *

Meeting 22: Exercise/Group Dynamic
Theme: Communication.
Reactions to this meeting are usually good, and the opening exercise gives it a good-humoured start.

(1) Check-in (cf. Meeting 4, 1).

(2) Exercise:

a) The participants are seated in a semi-circle.

b) The facilitator composes a sentence in secret and writes it down, but must not let anyone see it. It need not be complicated.

c) The facilitator whispers the sentence in the ear of the one seated on either edge of the semi-circle, taking care that others do not hear (they will probably be laughing anyway). The facilitator makes it clear that the sentence will only be uttered once and will not be repeated.

d) The first person who receives the sentence will then pass it on to her neighbour, taking care not to repeat.

e) This procedure is repeated exactly until the message reaches the end of the semi-circle.

f) Then the facilitator reveals what she had communicated at the beginning.

The differences are usually marked!

(3) The participants then discuss the implications of the exercise.

(4) Scripture reading: James 3:1-12. What light does this passage shed on their discussion?

(5) What *action* might the community take as a result of their reflections?

(6) Spontaneous.prayer.

* * *

Meeting 23: Exercise/Group Dynamic
Theme: Self-confidence
This session is taken from notes that I made of an encounter in our Dublin community. It is probably better suited to a youthful group.

(1) Check-in (cf. Meeting 4, 1).

(2) There were musical chairs to enliven the proceedings. I hasten to add that the participants were young on the whole, so there were no sprained ankles!

(3) Soap-box activity: each member was seated on a central chair in turn and asked to speak spontaneously on a topic that was picked out of a hat. There were such items as: sliced bread, socks, ashtray, orange, curtains, giraffe. I got this last subject! It stretches you. The group proved quite inventive and articulate in addressing these topics. The animator pointed out that the subjects were trivial and caused a lot of mirth. However, if people could speak on these they could speak on anything. Another member observed that it was good to have been put on the spot, because spontaneity helps self-confidence.

(4) There followed a more thorough debriefing in which these items were noticed:

- the need for people to affirm one another,
- the importance of paying attention,
- how necessary it is to have a certain inner toughness and not be overly sensitive,
- the need to believe in oneself,
- and how important family and community are for all of us.

(5) A selection of mottoes were then read out. Each member was asked to reflect on them and select one that appealed to her. Here are some examples:

- Let us be grateful for every single moment of this wonderful day!
- An optimist is someone who takes the cold water thrown upon an idea, heats it with enthusiasm, and then uses the steam to push ahead.
- Help me, Lord, to remember that there isn't anything that can happen today that you and I can't handle.

(6) Bible Reflection: Matthew 6:25-34.

This is the beautiful passage that tells us how God looks after the birds of the air and the flowers of the field. Much more so, then, will that God look after all of us. And there in brief is the ultimate reason why we face the joys and sorrows of life with self-confidence. Motivated by this thought, the members of the community determined to bring a sense of self-confidence to everything they did.

(7) The facilitator played a recording of Julie Andrew's animated version of 'I Have Confidence' from *The Sound of Music*.

(8) Shared prayer (cf. Meeting 1, 3). At the end all hold hands and recite the Lord's Prayer.

Memorable Sessions

A couple of meetings that I experienced in the course of my travels so impressed me that I wrote about them. I think it may prove helpful to quote them here. The first comes from West Africa:

Fr Emiliano and myself bumped along the deeply-rutted dirt road in a jeep through the African bush. It was night. Occasionally the headlights would pick out the bejewelled eyes of some creature in the undergrowth, transfixed by the lights. We came to a halt near a cluster of huts. Emiliano got out and started to walk through the darkness. I followed in his wake, fearful that a snake might be slithering around at my feet. It's best to carry a lamp.

We entered a thatched hut made of slats that was dimly lit by a storm lantern hanging from one corner. A small Christian community had assembled for its weekly meeting, the children seated on the floor in the middle and the adults on forms round the sides.

We were welcomed somewhat formally and the meeting began with a lively hymn to the accompaniment of drums. This was followed by a reading from Matthew 25 ('I was hungry and you fed me, thirsty and you gave me a drink etc.'). The members of the community then shared their insights on the passage; the exchange was truly impressive. The sharing over, the surrounding bush again echoed to the sound of enthusiastic singing and drumming that are features of African communities.

Then the crunch came. What were they going to do about the word of God which they had read? Actually, it emerged that they were already doing their share. River blindness is a hazard in Sierra Leone, the country in question. People go searching for diamonds in the sediment of rivers and are bitten by a tiny organism in the waters. As a result they go blind unless treated, so, not surprisingly, Sierra Leone seems to have more blind people than usual. This small Christian community was taking care of some such persons and one of them was actually present at the meeting. They felt, therefore, that they were trying to do something about the word of God which they had heard, but decided to look more diligently to see if there were other folk, not necessarily blind, who might be in need of support.

More drumming and singing and then a call for prayer.

Heads bowed reverently. There was profound silence. A mosquito whirred at my ear and I became aware of the chafing of cicadas in the surrounding bush. The prayers began to flow freely from individuals at various points of the assembly. Moving prayers. Heartfelt prayers.

There was a boisterous final hymn followed by warm farewells as people melted away to their huts in the darkness. A young boy led the blind man by the hand. He lived in a world of darkness that was nevertheless filled with much light.

One of the things that impressed me about this meeting was the local flavouring of it all: the singing, the drumming, the setting, the issues, and so forth. It was so different and yet had much in common with meetings elsewhere.

* * *

The second encounter took place in Perth, Australia. My short account went like this:

There was a significant session in the house of Peter and Marya Stewart in Perth. Having tried to play a little football with a group of lively children, I went into the house to get my thoughts together for the eucharist. The participation was striking. There were about ten adults (parents) and twenty children present. What moved me was the involvement of the children. After the grown-ups had shared for some time on the gospel, someone asked: 'And what do the children think of the reading? Do they have anything to say?' Did they have anything to say? They had plenty to talk about and it made lots of sense.

During the Mass the children vied with one another to hold baby Eugene, who with great wondering eyes remained placid and hiccupping as he was passed around the assembly like snuff at a wake, as we say in Ireland. Those little ones who had not yet made their First Communion and, therefore, could not receive were given blessed bread, so that they didn't feel left out of the celebration.

Afterwards we shared a pot-luck meal. Care was taken to feed the young ones first. Then a video was put on for them and I got a chance to chat separately with the adults. These good people were interested in a wide variety of areas: peace and justice (the cause of the Aboriginals for example; next day I was to partake in a demonstration for Aboriginal land rights with some of their members), liturgy, forms of community that would be a countersign to a materialistic and harshly secular world, how best to relate to the traditional church, and youth of course.

Now and again a little one would stray in and sit on the lap of mummy or daddy, or lie down at their feet, be covered with a blanket, and fall asleep. The accommodation of the children, some of whom were in fact young teenagers, was beautiful to see. Can the reader think of a better way of introducing Christ and the gospel message to these children? I'm sure this small community, or family church, will serve as a beacon throughout their lives.

* * *

Summary
1) The essential components of the small Christian community meeting are: bonding (communion), spirituality, commitment, reality, and communication.
2) The session ought to be relevant, flexible, and adaptable.
3) As well as meetings proper, social encounters are effective means of building relationships.
4) There is the ordinary format for meetings based on the pattern:
- Life,
- Word of God,
- Life (action) and
- Prayer,
   which is very widely used and allows scope for variety (cf. pp. 102-3).

5) Some twenty-three examples of meetings are given, employing the following categories: exercise (group dynamic), worship, commitment, ecumenical, prophetic, planning, evaluation, communication, ordinary format, and miscellaneous.

6) The themes embraced are: community, sharing, unity, word of God, prayer, eucharist, reconciliation, commitment, kingdom of God, leadership, ecumenism, justice, environment, planning, evaluation, communication, self-confidence.

Question

How does what has been said in this chapter relate to what happens in your own small Christian community?

Suggested Bible passages: John 4:1-30 (Jesus' encounter with the Samaritan Woman). What do the participants in this meeting teach us, including the apostles who come in on the end of it?

Luke 24:13-35. Jesus meeting with the two disciples on the way to Emmaus. All the main elements of a small community meeting to be found in this episode.

CHAPTER 7

Pastoral Planning

I once heard a lay person plead for an end to drift and the making of a plan in this fashion: 'Fr A comes to our parish and does a lot of building. Then comes Fr B saying the people are the church, not bricks and mortar, and gets groups going. Comes Fr C and he believes that, if you get the liturgy right, everything else will automatically follow. The result is that we, the laity, are completely bewildered. Is there no way that the diocese could have a plan, so that all the priests are concentrating on the same things?'

The situation described is not uncommon, and it is a bad situation. Indeed it is not just bad but completely counter-productive, because through lack of follow-up each pastor is undoing what his predecessor did.

Difficult though it undoubtedly is in a world where all is sand shifting beneath our feet, we must nevertheless strive to plan. As already noted, a small Christian community ought to have a plan-of-action from the outset that will respond to some obvious needs round about. There might, for example, be a lot of elderly and housebound people in a district who would welcome a frequent visit. But as a community grows in maturity, it could feel the need of making a thoroughgoing pastoral plan for its area. This entails understanding the religious, political, social, and economic realities of a situation as seen by the ordinary people of the locality. To do this the group needs to make a careful study of the situation. I will outline a method that has been honed through practice and which, I believe, can be adapted to wider situations.

The planning method in question has eight steps that are fairly common to most planning procedures. All of them are of importance to the process, so there should be no shortcuts. *The process involved is just as important in terms of the resulting benefits as the plan itself, so it absolutely should not be rushed.* I have known people whose minds and hearts were changed during the course of planning; this too is an enormous gain. Depending on the size of the area, difficulty or ease of communication, we are talking of months, even a year or two. A far-flung province of my order spent three years making a plan. But, believe me, it really was far-flung. The steps involved are as follows:

1) The planning team positions itself.
2) The approach.
3) First meeting at grassroots.
4) Second meeting at grassroots.
5) Examination of problems / issues.
6) Analysis of systems.
7) An overall view.
8) Practical outcome or planning.

1) The team positions itself

The team, most of whom will be chosen from the small Christian community which will accompany them all the way in the task, must interest themselves in the total environment. If the group contains some persons qualified in relevant disciplines so much the better. Ordinarily, however, this is not possible, in which case the team chosen will equip themselves through the practical experience of doing the task. The appropriate disciplines would be theology, catechetics, psychology, sociology, anthropology, and economics. Of course there may be the option of calling occasionally on outside help.

To begin immersing themselves in the total environment, the team carries out a preliminary survey with instructions and questions that are crystal clear. Such clarity in queries and instructions must characterise the whole planning procedure. This survey should assist them in getting to know the place better as regards:

• climate;
• boundaries, mountains, hills, ravines (physical features);
• rivers, canals, lakes, and sea (waterways);

- roads, rail, electricity, gas, water supply, and sewage (infrastructure);
- buses, trains, and taxis (transport);
- post, telephone system, newspapers, radio, television, computers (social communications);
- living conditions, ethnic groups, customs, hospitals, schools, cinemas, and places of assembly (social, cultural, and educational factors).

The results of this preliminary survey are then written up and, if necessary, a map is drawn.

The team is engaged in pastoral planning and not in a merely social operation. The first step, therefore, and every phase of the planning, will be done in the light of the word of God, prayer, and church documents. And the same will be true of the subsequent implementation.

2) The approach

Despite the initial contact made in the foregoing phase, the planning team and small community may not be fully in touch with their people. They must do something to remedy this. In the first phase they will have come closer to some of the ordinary inhabitants of the area, so they can commence conversing with them on a variety of matters, including these:

- the family,
- position of women,
- situation of youth,
- treatment of children,
- working conditions,
- rate of unemployment,
- cultural events,
- main sicknesses,
- political involvement,
- religious practices.

From these conversations the team will draw up *a first version of a list of problems*. They must, however, understand that this initial approach will not produce a profound knowledge of the area.

There is a tendency of which the team must be aware from the start. It is a strong inclination on their part to colour all the findings with their own way of thinking. In short it becomes a matter of the problems *as they see them* and not as the people generally perceive the issues. There has to be a major effort to eliminate this weakness. So folk must be thoroughly consulted.

3) First meeting at grassroots

It is precisely to involve fellow-residents and delve deeper into the reality of the place that a first meeting at grassroots is held. The participants at this meeting will be the planning team, the members of the small community, and the persons whom the team have come closer to in the previous stages.

At the meeting those taking part should be presented with the first version of a list of problems, which was worked out in the second step, and asked to think carefully about it. They may add to or modify the list as they think fit.

The organisers of the meeting have to get beyond the point where the people may be telling them what they think they want to hear – another great pitfall in pastoral planning. This can only be done through establishing trust through patient, prolonged dialogue. It is therefore important to allow adequate time for this. I recall taking part in this first meeting at grassroots in a South American *barrio*. It seemed at the outset that the greatest worry of the people was to provide a steeple for the church – in an area where there was poverty, malnutrition, astronomical unemployment, lack of formal education, drugs, drunkenness, and prostitution. Lengthy dialogue showed that the steeple was among the least of their felt needs, and 30 years later the church is still without one.

This meeting ought to provide *a second more authentic list of problems.*

Incidentally, though this method is based on dialogue, the team may find it convenient here or at other points of the planning process to allow written submissions. These can be anonymous. This might prove helpful to certain shy individuals; personal attacks, however, and outlandish statements, unhelpful to the procedure, ought to be discarded.

4) Second meeting at grassroots
Up to this point the organising team, even without knowing it, may be unduly influencing proceedings. So they must try anew to eliminate any possible bias from the process.

Furthermore, people may be somewhat reticent of each other and of the team. Time is needed so that all concerned get to know each other better.

To solve such difficulties as these, a second meeting at grassroots is held. The number of participants is greatly increased from the previous meeting. After a brief introduction and, perhaps, a dynamic to relate people, they are presented with the second version of a list of problems. Then they are divided into convenient groups and urged to think carefully about the list and make relevant comments.

The planning team must be satisfied that there are a sufficient number of persons present to make the gathering authentic. Sixty, representing a good cross-section of the residents, would seem a desirable attendance. If there are not that many present, a repeat supplementary session could be held to ensure that a sufficient body of people are consulted

Following the group meetings a general session is held to pool ideas.

This encounter should root out most of the defects of the second list of problems and lead to a meeting of minds. Items may be dropped, added to, or altered. In short the team will likely discover a much more valid catalogue of issues. *This will represent the third and final list.*

And this is also the point in the planning process where we try to identify the generative problems on our list. *By generative problems we mean those that give birth to many others.* Abject poverty , for example, can lead to hunger, disease, crime, prostitution, and so on.

5) Examination of problems
Equipped with the third and finalised list of problems and perhaps even more importantly with a list of generative problems, the team must now move on to a more profound examination of the situ-

ation. Even if they have been proceeding in the planning process without professional help, they would do well to bring in some qualified person(s) at this particular stage. But again, only if it is possible.

So far the team has been dealing with the issues as they show themselves outwardly. Indeed, they have been striving to make sense of a most complicated reality. Now they must face an even greater challenge and endeavour to examine the root causes of the problems under consideration. This the team does with the help of the remaining members of the small community and some of their acquaintances from the district.

There are a number of questions that need answering, such as these:
- Is the problem new?
- If not, how far back does it go?
- Why wasn't something done about it long before?
- Has the make-up of the people (attitudes, how they see the world, their manner of thinking) anything to do with the problem?
- Can't the authorities, the law, or anybody remedy the situation?
- What can the participants in the meeting and people like them do about a solution?
- Do they need to organise?

These questions should help to winkle out relevant historical, religious, social, psychological, cultural, and economic factors that are at work in the situation.

6) Analysis of systems

The previous stage leads naturally to a consideration of how the society in which we live is organised. This can bring the participants face to face with oppressive structures which cry out for 'bold transformations and innovations that go deep.'[32] For four decades now the church has been insisting that we must look to the very structures of our society and do something about these. A dab of paint here or a nail there is not enough. Unjust structures divide people into haves and have nots, included and excluded, and condemn millions to real death or a living death through misery, hunger, and disease.

And oppressive structures give rise to values, attitudes, and actions that are widespread and utterly blighted by selfishness. To deal effectively with these we must get at the causes.

7) An overall view

As the team and its associates analyse systems, they inevitably find that the problems they encounter are widespread. They may have differing aspects from area to area, but basically they are the same. The evils found in the locality under consideration are to be found in neighbouring areas, in the province, nation, continent, and indeed in the whole world.

East and West, North and South, ordinary persons are the victims of powerful structures preserved by elites who inculcate false values, who gain profit at the expense of people, power at the expense of people. In this, unfortunately, they are often aided and abetted by the media and corrupt politicians. But the great mass of humanity founder in misery and powerlessness. One of the great causes of our time is that of the dispossessed of the earth, and not to involve ourselves is to remain on the margins of history.

8) Planning

When we come to planning, or what we are going to do in practice, we must look hard at root causes and generative problems and strike at these. It is best to be specific here. Let us return to the South American *barrio*, or poor urban district, that I mentioned above in stage 2. Remember its appalling list of problems? Grinding poverty, malnutrition, astronomical unemployment, illiteracy, lack of formal education, crime, drugs, drunkenness, prostitution, and so forth. When we came to getting to the root causes of these issues, we arrived at the following conclusions:

- *Oppression* and *marginalisation* at the hands of the wealthy and powerful elite who ran the country with military connivance were the main factors that blighted the lives of residents in the *barrio*. These internal forces of oppression were in league with multinationals and foreign banks that further exacerbated the situation. All of these agents engendered a poor self-image

among the people, deprived them of culture and a formal education, sank them in poverty, and caused disunity, because the
oppressor could easily sow division among them.
• There is a perversity that is to be found together with good in the
heart of every human being, even in that of the oppressed, and
this too has to be taken into account and combatted.
To deal with these we took the following course:

Solution
This would be provided by a liberating:
• evangelisation,
• conscientisation,
• education, and
• social action.
By the term *liberating* we meant that the solution would come
largely from the person himself in interaction with others.

Activities
Evangelisation or passing on the faith
(with a view to enriching folk spiritually and improving the moral
climate):
• youth ferment group,
• seven small Christian communities,
• courses,
• retreats,
• youth Mass,
• youth Easter,
• bringing gospel/human values to the home, neighbourhood,
spheres of work, study, business, and leisure,
• five catechetical centres, each with an attached children's club.

Conscientisation /Social Action
(the awareness which comes from continually reflecting upon the
issues of life and acting on that reflection so as to change the world):
• barrio magazine,
• notice boards,

- posters,
- meetings,
- conferences,
- discussions.

Education/Social Action
- literacy,
- accountancy,
- cooking and hygiene,
- dress-making,
- commercial crafts' centre,
- first aid,
- electrical installation,
- guitar,
- English,
- individual tutoring,
- a night school for people who had missed out on education and others who wanted it.

When it came to action, we could only work with the resources we had and, as we said, bring them to bear on the above evils. We did not have vast sums of money. What we did have was a good number of enthusiastic young people willing to help their *barrio* and this is reflected in the above plan-of-action. The area was in fact teeming with young folk and their well-being was a major concern. Thirty years later the area has lost its former notoriety and progressed greatly. I feel sure that the above effort played some part in this happy outcome. But there was always a solid core of some of the finest people I have ever met in that place. At the time of planning the district was bearing the brunt of migration as landless *campesinos* flocked into the city from the rural areas, signalling a dire need for land reform.

In chapter 5 on organisation we mentioned how small Christian communities have agreed principles, values, understandings and commitments. They would have had these long before setting out on the pastoral plan. Indeed sometimes the communities have four or five broad-based statements, or a Rule of Life, that express their aspirations for building the kingdom of God. Following the planning, they must now examine their Rule, whether it be implicit or explicit, to see how it squares up with the new scheme of things. The two together then provide a pathway into the future.

In going through the above exercise, we are following in the footsteps of the early Christians. During painful and confused times they looked at the reality of their lives in the light of Christ and forged paths into an uncertain future. I feel confident that the seeds of the church to come are already here in the present and that the Holy Spirit will help us to discern them. And we can move forward from there.

Implementation and evaluation

A pastoral plan must not just remain on paper; it has to be resolutely implemented. It also has to be evaluated periodically from all aspects: spiritual, intellectual, intuitive, human, and practical. Adjustments are made when required. The small community will do these things, yet everything should not be made to fall upon them. The eventual success of the endeavour will depend on the continued involvement of all whom it touches. All must own it. All must take responsibility for it. This list of questions may facilitate the work of evaluation:

- Are we making a persevering attempt as individuals and as a community to implement the plan?
- If not, why not?
- Do we need to make adjustments?
- Has there been progress?
- Have we sought to involve the people of our area, especially all those consulted in the making of the plan?
- Are we united and organised?
- Do we respect process, yet have a sense of urgency?
- Are our endeavours to implement the pastoral plan backed by a profound spirituality?

Implementation is of course the acid test. 'To make a ragout you must first catch your hare.' So said one Doctor Hill in a work entitled *Cook Book* (1747)[33] – at least the volume was attributed to him. One can imagine old Doctor Hill chuckling to himself as, tongue in cheek, he saw the double meaning in what he had written. Now making a pastoral plan is one thing; implementing it quite another. Implementing it is the pastoral equivalent of catching your hare. I hope the foregoing questions may help people to do so. But where hares are concerned, I prefer them running wild and free.

I might add here as a conclusion that, distinct from the *barrio* plan outlined above, I was later involved in pastoral planning with my own order. I now have the opportunity of looking back on that endeavour from a distance of twenty years and of talking to my confrères about it. What emerges is that, apart from any practical benefits that may have resulted, it was the process that was, above all, important. Over the three years work – ours was a far-flung province at the time – minds and hearts were changed, and minds and hearts met. Because we came together and talked so many times, potential gulfs, such as those between young and old, progressive and conservative never seriously emerged, as we absorbed the great insights of Vatican II. The priorities that were decided upon have entered the bloodstream of the province. In practical terms our work among homeless youth has been greatly extended, we have a considerable presence in the inner city – relative to our numbers – and, when confronted with the demands of the gospel, you really could not quarrel with any of our works. Even developments that have become much clearer since, such as the need to work with lay people and be sensitive to environmental issues, were anticipated at the time. Heaven knows we are far from complacent about ourselves and there is far more we would like to be able to do but, thankfully, the foregoing facts are true. For which we are grateful to God.

Undoing long-standing institutions to replace them with structures that are fresh, relevant, and foster community, rather than preserving the status quo, is no easy task. Oh it can be done on paper quite readily, and so new wineskins are set in place .But hearts don't change as easily; the problem is with the new wine. A colleague of mine once said, 'Things don't change; people die.' I don't think this is absolutely true, yet there is a point to it. It's surely high time now that we implemented the Trinitarian vision of Vatican II.

Summary
a) A small community would do well to have a plan that responds to obvious needs.
b) As a group grows in maturity it might feel a need to make a thoroughgoing pastoral plan for its area – the process is just as important as the eventual plan; it can change minds and hearts.
c) This is a demanding undertaking, involving an analysis of the religious, political, social, and psychological realities of the district as the residents see them.
d) The community selects a team to spearhead the endeavour, and then the following steps are employed:
   1) The planning team positions itself.
   2) The approach.
   3) First meeting at grassroots.
   4) Second meeting at grassroots.
   5) Examination of problems / issues.
   6) Analysis of systems.
   7) An overall view.
   8) Planning.
(These steps are dealt with succinctly in the text.)
e) The group resolutely implements, and periodically evaluates (questions provided) the plan.
f) Ideally all the people of the district will somehow be involved with the project.

Question
   Does your small Christian community or group have, or feel the need for, a plan?
   Suggested Bible passage: Luke 10:1-20.
   Does this passage provoke any thoughts on the matter of planning?

CHAPTER 8

Common Issues

Owing to the nature of this book, we are of course touching on practical issues all the way through. However, there are some items which I feel we ought to single out for special treatment, and I will do so now.

Diversity
Having completed a workshop in an Australian town, I returned with a sister who had organised the session to the bishop's house. As I went upstairs, I could not help but overhear the bishop say to the sister down below in a rather resigned voice, 'Well, what's the word this time?' To which the sister replied resoundingly, 'Flexibility.' Heaving a great sigh of relief, the bishop declared, 'Thanks be to God!'

There is no blueprint for the establishment of small communities, no one methodology, no one structure and no one way. So we must be open to diversity and allow for flexibility. If there is a method that helps me, well and good, but I cannot presume that it has to be the path for everyone. I always insist myself that I haven't got a neat package tied up in ribbons to deliver, only insights and guidelines drawn from experience to share. Insights and guidelines many of which I have learned from others in the field. I ask participants in workshops to look at these in the light of their own experience to see if there is anything that might be of help to them. The groups respond to, and are fashioned greatly by, the environment in which they find themselves. So it would be a considerable mistake to try and plant a Chilean model in Australia, or indeed a Rockhampton model in neighbouring Townsville. This whole phenomenon of small communities is only in its infancy in the modern era. It is not a time to be setting things in concrete. We have to be ready to sit humbly at the feet of experience and learn.

There is a desire in many human beings, particularly in the affluent world, to tie up loose ends. We find it extremely hard to live with the mess that being a member of our church often entails. We grasp at a particular structure or methodology as if it were a security blanket, stoutly refusing to entertain other possibilities. But what is the point of replacing one model of church that we regard as hidebound with another that is equally so?

As I said elsewhere, I do realise that people may need something solid to seize upon at the beginning; often they may be coming from a situation where the church is highly institutionalised. With time, however, flexibility should appear. Indeed the people, guided no doubt by the Spirit who is a great one for turning the world upside-down, frequently make their own communities more malleable.

Let me return once more to the constants of the groups, or those elements embraced by the terms:

- bonding (communion)
- spirituality
- commitment
- reality
- communication.

These ought to be factors in the life of every small Christian community in the world. They are the transcultural essentials. But once these vital ingredients are present, varying structure, method, and style should then grow most naturally from the native soil. There has to be the homespun Ballyjamesduff version.

Apart from diversity within the groups, there is diversity all around us. In the church we have progressives and conservatives, people who are advocates of a Vatican II model and those who go back to the pre-Vatican way; there are the active and the passive, those who are within and a growing number who are alienated. Many are trying to make some sense of their church and their lives. Oftentimes the debate between disparate elements has been high-pitched and acrimonious. Intolerance has presented its granite face. It is now time to turn down the volume, respect one another, listen carefully to each other, and strive to dialogue even with folk in the most extreme positions. There is no other way forward. We badly need the good Samaritans who will pour the balm of healing oil on our wounds and divisions.

For centuries we have had uniformity in the church. No more. In the third millennium we must learn to live with diversity, yet always speak our truth, and always be ready to challenge and be challenged. In short we have to learn to tolerate each other, never forgetting the words of St Paul: 'Let all be done in love' (1 Corinthians 16:14).

Liturgy is most important to us, and an example taken from that area could help. In a South American parish, where I worked, a youth Mass was put on at an appropriate time on Sunday evenings. There were guitars and lively hymns and the young people were as plentiful as potatoes, as they say in that part of the world. The whole thing was a heartening success.

But after one such celebration a lady came to me full of indignation. She didn't like guitars. The singing was raucous (it was!) and there was quite a lot of talking. In short she felt she hadn't been to Mass at all. This had to stop. I felt upset. However, a little voice in my head said, 'Now just a moment...' Her point of view had its validity. Anyway, I went on to point out quietly to her that this was a celebration for young people, and whatever about our own personal tastes we had to meet the needs of those teenagers. At least they were now coming to church which wasn't the case before. Getting them in at all wasn't easy. And as for the singing, sometimes we have to listen to the music of the young with the heart and not with the ears. Also in the parish there were other Masses of a subdued nature provided for persons like herself who preferred that style. She calmed down somewhat and I heard no more about it. The liturgy is a good example of a situation in which we have to be tolerant of, and cater for, diversity.

Finally, if we can cope with disparity in our own house, then we will have some hope of coping with the wide world out there characterised by an enormous variety of race, creed, and practice. And this we will do while remaining faithful to our own identity. Many people feel threatened by what is different in terms of ethnic origin, religion, or colour. Jesus on the contrary rejoiced in difference. The kingdom of God is like a great net, he tells us, that gathers all manner of fish (cf. Matthew 13:47). There is ample room for everyone.

I find that parable of the net intriguing. While in Australia I had occasion to visit the Great Barrier Reef Museum in Townsville, Queensland. My mind simply boggled at the numerous types of fish of every conceivable shape, size, and colour swimming about among the gloriously blooming coral. Some had beetling brows reminding one somehow of Socrates; others had a predatory look, still others an eager-beaver mien. As I gazed on their infinite variations, the thought came to me that our Creator just loves diversity.

Ecumenism

Closely related to the issue of diversity is that of ecumenism. It is urgent. One of the most heartfelt prayers of Christ coming towards the end of his life was:

... that they may all be one;

As you, Father, are in me,

and I am in you ... (John 17:21).

So the question is never whether we will or will not do something about ecumenism. The only question is what exactly are we going to do? What is the best course in our situation? A church is Christian insofar as it is ecumenical.

Where small Christian communities are concerned, we can identify two possibilities. There can be groups belonging to particular denominations and those composed of members from various denominations. Both are necessary. The interdenominational, or ecumenical, ones of course give a very powerful witness to unity and as such must be promoted and encouraged. In order that this should work, I believe it is important for the persons who compose an interdenominational community to be sure of their own identity. They have to respect one another's beliefs and not set out to proselytise each other. In short it requires a fair degree of Christian maturity. If we get confused Catholics coming together with confused Protestants, great could be the confusion thereof.

Even where small communities are denominational, they are still ecumenical. Our Dublin group, although situated in an area that is almost totally Roman Catholic, is nevertheless very ecumenically minded. We have tried to link up with the local Church of Ireland community, attended the meetings of interdenominational groups, invited people of other denominations, even other religions, to come and chat and pray with us. We have been in demonstrations of different kinds with members of various denominations and indeed of none. Olive, an ordained priest of the Church of Ireland, spent a year as a member of our community. Her cheerful presence enriched us enormously. The group, though mature, is youthful on the whole and seem to have no trouble in being marvellously open.

We have just noticed how people of disparate denominations get together to demonstrate for worthy causes. This is a level of commingling that should present no problem. To sink a well, build a bridge, or struggle to have prisoners-of-conscience released are matters on which we can all cooperate. After all, there is no such thing as a Catholic, Protestant, or Muslim bridge; bridges are ecumenical and allow everyone, whatever their race or creed, to cross a river in safety.

Regarding ecumenism, I have found Africa of great interest. Over most of that vast continent – there are some sad exceptions – it doesn't present the problems that it does elsewhere in the world, because even within extended families you have members of varying denominations. I heard a bishop tell of how in his extended family there were Roman Catholics, Anglicans, and Pentecostals. It really depended on the school they attended as children. Yet they all lived together in harmony; as the bishop so rightly said, 'We can't afford to do otherwise.'

An African Cardinal once told Pope John Paul, who marvelled at the story, that his father had been a chief, who professed the native religion and had eight wives. Indeed depending on where one lived in Africa, he could have family members belonging to, not simply other Christian denominations, but different religions as well. Relating to fellow Christians, therefore, is hardly an issue at all. I have a friend, Joachim, who is going on to be a Catholic priest, whereas his sister is studying to be a Pentecostal pastor. They both deeply love and respect each other, and the mother said, 'I am happy because you are both doing something good.' The Africans, fortunately, do not trail our historical baggage where ecumenism is concerned. Are they not perhaps saying to us that the eventual unity of all Christians will be a unity in diversity?

Members of different religions, Christian and Muslim for example, relate easily and work together. Again they can be from the same extended family so how could it sensibly be otherwise? Fr Tony in Sierra Leone was celebrating the eucharist on the occasion of the harvest festival in a small village. The church was packed largely with Muslims. Before the ceremony was finished, the muezzin in the tower of the nearby mosque started calling all his co-religionists for prayer, because it was a Friday. Nobody stirred in the church. All reverently remained until the Mass concluded. Then they trooped off faithfully to the mosque. I have been at Christian funerals where the great majority of those praying for the soul of the departed have been Muslims; the Christians would have the same openness. Here surely is a sign of great hope for the church and the world.

Residential Small Christian Communities

We find yet another manifestation of unity in diversity when disparate elements come together to make residential communities, such as, different families or laity and religious. There is a difficulty involved here but, before we deal with it, let us just note that when we enter a residential community, it is a much more intense experience than being part of a neighbourhood group. That is not to say that one form is better than the other; simply that they are different calls. However, there are persons who will want, and indeed even need, to go the road of residential community no matter what. If one is in doubt, it might be best to try a non-residential set-up first.

In South Africa – to return to our original point – I found three families who joined together in a big rambling house to make a residential community. I asked the teenage daughter of one of them how she felt about the project. She told me how at first she strongly opposed the whole idea, but was persuaded by her parents to give it a try. She did so and was totally won over to the experiment. Her fear at the beginning was that she would lose her family – that their identity would be lost in the melting pot. However, the group sensibly left space for family life; there were the times when the families were alone for sharing meals, prayer, and life, but also the times when they joined the others. It worked. The key to success being that space was made for the individual families. To do this, of course, there also has to be the physical room.

The same would, I believe, prove true for laity and religious coming together. They would have to be respectful of, and make space for, the different identities.

Small Christian communities and the traditional church
By and large small Christian communities have operated within their mainstream churches. At an international meeting of the groups held in Cochabamba, Bolivia, November 1999, it was noted that they had 'entered the bloodstream of the church'. They have existed in the margins at times and there may have been tensions between them and the official body, still they persevered. I think the position of my own community regarding the local parish would be fairly typical of many groups in countries where the church is long established. Our relationship with it is good. We worship there, have a member on the pastoral council, and others performing different ministries. The parish let's us be; no opposition on the one hand, but no great involvement with us on the other. I could say that we are in the margins. That is because ours is one model of church, the communitarian, while the parish would be in the traditional, institutional mode (there are straws in the wind that would suggest this might be changing). Many of the parishioners would in fact be of an advanced age; so it is the model that places us in the margins rather than any form of acrimony.

On the other hand numerous small communities are being fostered by the mainstream church. This is particularly so in economically deprived countries, but not only there, as we will learn from our historical profile (pp. 166-240). Throughout the world there are whole parishes and dioceses that have opted for the community model. Africa, for example, made a commitment to Family Church at its 1994 Synod. On that occasion a West African bishop declared, 'For us it's the only way.'

There is a debate in the church as to whether the seeds of its future are in the mainstream or the margins. What I have seen myself leads me to believe that both will play their part.

More than once we have referred to the need for networking – the value of linking groups together so that they get the experience of being a communion of communities. How might this come about? Where groups are plentiful, it makes the task easier. I have seen parishes, and dioceses, where communities come together for meetings and celebrations. Twinning between small communities in different countries, even on different continents, is now occurring. All this is good.

Regarding the situation of my own community in Dublin, there are only a few groups in our parish, so we are reaching out beyond its boundaries in an effort to network. It makes one wonder if we should not be too rigid about demarcation lines. Community not geography is the priority. Ideally, we should have the *oikos*, or house church, and beyond that the parish centre which would serve as a sort of staging-post for neighbourhood groups – be a place where they could be refreshed and motivated. It would not, of course, be all one-way traffic, because the parish centre would also be greatly enriched by the small communities.

There are those who question the parish and the diocese. Presumably they are speaking of the model in which they now operate and not the concepts, because, call them what you will, we are going to need those more enlarged entities where we can get the crucial experience of being a communion of communities.

Inculturation

We have already referred briefly to the inculturation issue in connection with the cultural sensitivity which is a feature of the spirituality of small Christian communities. However, we need to explore it some more.

Inculturation is important today both as a concept and a process. Its content is inherent in the words of John's gospel: 'And the Word was made flesh and dwelt among us...' (John 1:14). The good news has to be made flesh and blood in the lives and circumstances of those to whom it is proclaimed, and this is a gradual and complex procedure, as the Working Paper for the African Synod, no. 49 reminds us:

> The process of the church's insertion into people's cultures is a lengthy one. It is not a matter of purely external adaptation, for inculturation means the intimate transformation of authentic cultural values through their integration in Christianity and the insertion of Christianity into the various human cultures.[34]

When culture and Christianity interact, the result may not always be soothing. A religious provincial was once visiting a community of his province. A great wall topped with broken glass surrounded the building where they lived. The visitor wondered if the glass was there to keep the thieves out or the religious in, to which one wag replied, 'I suppose it cuts both ways, father.'

Well the gospel is a two-edged sword. What is good in our cultures it affirms; what is not good it challenges. Too easily we can appeal to culture to give the stamp of approval to something defective. Here in Ireland we have a delicate peace process. It has come after thirty years of violence during which Christians killed Christians. Muslims and Christians are still embroiled in the Balkan tragedy; all worship the one God. And there was the Rwandan catastrophe that shook Africa to its core, and the strife between Muslims and Christians in Northern Nigeria. Really, at the beginning of this new millennium, the churches must seriously question themselves as to whether or not they are reaching down and challenging cultures in depth. Paul was adamant with the sexually promiscuous Corinthians. They could not do those heinous deeds and still call themselves followers of Christ. No pussy-footing there. Nor does Jesus tread lightly when he declares:

You have heard
that it was said to those of ancient times,
'You shall not murder';

and 'whoever murders shall be liable to judgment.'

But I say to you

that if you are angry with a brother or sister,

you will be liable to judgment;

and if you insult a brother or sister,

you will bc liable to the council;

and if you say, 'You fool,'

you will be liable to the hell of fire.

(Matthew 5:21-22)

If the churches were as determined as Jesus and Paul in announcing the good news, it would offer enormous hope as we enter the third millennium.

When the problem of inculturation is discussed, usually it is connected with the missions in places like Africa and Asia. What we can forget is that the issue exists for all cultures. More so today than ever. In a world of headlong change cultures change too, and every generation has to receive the faith afresh. Culture is often associated with folklore and tradition; however, it is also the living and altering present and not simply the past. The word has to be made flesh in the here and now.

And there is the further complication nowadays that youth have their own culture and can only be reached in and through it. A parish I know put on a Mass for young people. The pastor insisted that they come properly dressed and with hair neatly combed. The celebration was poorly attended. The youth in fact went in good numbers to another parish where they could come with sunglasses, designer holes in the knees of their jeans, and hair untamed. Simon the Zealot probably looked something like that. We must try to understand and address the current culture of young people and, obviously, there will be aspects of it that go much deeper than dress or appearance. For example, their reluctance to commit themselves in a rapidly changing, wildly uncertain, and frequently dangerous world.

Music is the language of the youth culture; it speaks to the soul of teenagers more than any other medium. I once saw this ever so lengthy queue on a Dublin street; all waiting to buy U2's latest album. And I asked myself if we are really using music enough to communicate Christ and his message.

And there is the hunger for peace and justice which many young people have, and a tender concern for the environment … We could go on. There are also the darker aspects that need challenging of course – drink and drugs for instance. Not long ago fourteen Dublin youth and seventeen in Glasgow died through the use of flawed heroin.

While we strive to know and respect a different culture to the best of our ability, we can never fully enter into it. I can never be a Masai and, if I were to don their national costume, I'm quite sure it would cause them no little amusement.

And what of the basic Christian community in the context of inculturation? It is the privileged place in which inculturation can happen and a powerful unit for promoting it. The groups are indeed indispensable instruments of inculturation. This, I realise, is quite a claim, but the theological implications, already considered, justify it. Just to mention liturgy as an example. We cannot supply a recipe for the whole world; only the communities can bring it alive in their own situations.

Youth

What of youth and the small communities? Clearly, since the groups are truly cells of the church, they must be open to everyone; and the church accommodates and involves persons of all ages. Not surprisingly then we find youthful people in the communities throughout the world; oftentimes in the role of coordinator. This should be so. Having said this, however, there are considerable cultural difficulties in the way of their involvement in some places. In Africa, especially in the rural areas, youth tend to be somewhat muted in the presence of adults. As you can imagine, this puts a considerable block in the way of their meaningful participation. To solve this problem the youth in certain parts are forming their own Christian groups, run along the same lines as the small Christian communities, to parallel the adult gatherings. Nevertheless young and old look for occasions to come together for celebrations and sharing of experiences. In this way they hope with time to erode barriers. We might note here that people having groups of their own for strong cultural reasons is a possibility, provided they remain open to other communities and groupings. The need for young people to have their own groupings is now, I believe, being felt more widely.

And Africa is not standing still. Like the rest of the planet it too is changing. In the cities you can find the youth fitting easily into meetings with adults and speaking readily. I was at a gathering of groups in Nairobi a few years ago and a young man stood up and spoke out quite boldly and eloquently. Later one of the elders congratulated him for his courage and for having spoken so well. In years gone by the adult might have thought that this young upstart was overreaching himself.

Where young folk are concerned, there is another factor that has to be reckoned with nowadays. The reader will recall that, besides sharing the common culture of their ethnic groups, they have also developed their own youth culture whose spread owes much to the mass media. Naturally, in communicating Christ to them one has to take account of this factor. This is why I think it is good for youth to have their own Christian groups to discuss issues of concern to them and to pray together, even where they can also be part of the adult communities.

In Zimbabwe a few years ago I was giving a workshop in a distant mission that had no priest. There was a large and enthusiastic gathering, among them many teenagers who followed everything attentively. When there was group work, they all got together and had the most animated discussions. I felt boundless admiration for them, because they were keeping this group going themselves and were excited by some ideas they had picked up in the sessions. They were determined to try and do something about them. I really felt the presence of the Spirit among them and the words of the psalm came to me: 'I myself will shepherd them' (cf. Isaiah 40:9-11; Matthew 11:28).

Another heartening aspect of the episode was that right before my eyes, by the power of the Holy Spirit, I could see being realised the dream of Vatican II when it says:

The young should become the first apostles of the young, in direct contact with them, exercising the apostolate by themselves, taking account of their social environment (*Decree on the Apostolate of the Laity*, 12).

In parts of the West, also, this approach increases in importance as it becomes more difficult for adults to deal with young people. In Dublin, I have come across a youth community whose members came together spontaneously to support one another in living a Christian life in a consumer society ever more hostile to that ethos.

Women

Women form the backbone of small Christian communities around the globe. Yet in certain societies that are heavily dominated by males they are not allowed to realise their full potential and rarely would you find them in leadership roles. This too is changing. In Africa I am now beginning to come across some women coordinators, and for the sake of the communities one would hope that this trend continues and grows. The gifts of warmth, intuition, understanding, empathy, and spirituality that women bring everywhere in the world are the lifeblood of community.

Women's groups of various kinds flourish in Africa. In such gatherings they get to discuss their common problems and support each other, and they hone the group skills which they need in mixed communities. There is, then, a real point to these gatherings.

The question is often raised as to why women are much more of a presence in small Christian communities than men. When the question is put to myself, there is a little routine I go through. I ask these questions. Who travelled with Jesus ministering to him during his public life? Who came forth willingly and wiped his face on the road to Calvary? Who wept over him on that same road? Who stood by the cross when all the apostles save John had fled? And who were the first witnesses to the resurrection? The participants, especially the womenfolk, chime in with the appropriate responses. Then I put the final query: So what's new?

Regarding the original question, I might just point out that where small communities are vibrant and life-related, they seem to attract men and women equally.

Before leaving this subject, I should like to observe that giving women their rightful place in the church and world is one of the gravest problems facing us today. Though it may be more acute in certain developing countries, it is a universal issue – one that the churches and society generally will neglect at their peril. A specific issue that refuses to go away in the church is the possibility of ordaining women to the priesthood. Community would demand that the question be thoroughly considered.

The Eucharist
In various Christian denominations the eucharist is important to the groups, which does not necessarily mean that they manage to have celebrations frequently. In our small community in Dublin we have a meaningful eucharist together about once every three months. For the rest we go to our parish, if possible to the same Mass.

Sad to relate, though the eucharist is so central for many Christians, there is a veritable eucharistic famine in the world through a shortage of priests. Numerous communities – sixty per cent in fact[35] – can go without the eucharist for months, even years. A man from the Ecuadorean Andes once told me that his people were lucky if they had Mass once every two years. Which tends to make pointless Christ's injunction: 'Do this in memory of me' (Luke 22:19).

This issue exercises the mind of some communities a great deal and they hazard possible solutions: recall laicised priests who wish to serve, allow married and women priests, and so forth. It is a vexed and complex question. For one thing the traditional office of bishop, priest, and deacon go back to the beginning of the church's history. What is the significance of this? Another consideration would be that, if the number of priests were to increase dramatically in the church as it is now constituted, it might have the unwelcome complication of reinforcing clericalism. Hardly desirable as the laity struggle even now to play their full part in affairs.

I believe that this problem of priestly vocations can only be resolved in the context of a renewed communitarian church, as envisaged by Vatican II, and achieved through small Christian communities. From these groups the ministries needed can emerge. How many communities have we seen in remote villages and out-stations which are served by some exemplary persons, many of them married, who are really pillars of the church? Such people could be promoted and ordained. Communities in Latin America were beginning to produce their own vocations in the seventies and imaginative means were used to prepare them, but the approach was discouraged in favour of the traditional seminary. Maybe it is an idea whose time has now come. On a recent visit to Latin America (1999), I found that seminarists who took part in the life of the small communities while in the seminary, tended to become priests who were truly in touch with their people. According to the faithful, this became particularly evident in their preaching. In recent decades the Bible was put back in the hands of the laity with telling effect. Now our problem is how to give the eucharist back to the faithful.

Incidentally, a recent book by Bishop Fritz Lobinger in South Africa has opened up the whole debate of a renewal of the Roman Catholic priesthood in a constructive form.[36] Such initiatives are timely because, without doubt, the priesthood as we have known it is in crisis.

The RCIA and Small Christian Communities

Many parishes in recent years have been enthused by the RCIA Movement (Rite of Christian Initiation of Adults). Rightly so – it is an excellent programme. However, the enthusiasm wanes at times, because people who have been through the course somehow disappear off the scene and are no longer to be found in the parish. This is disappointing, yet, I feel, understandable. The participants usually have the experience of an intimate year together and then at the end of it they are often thrown back into the cold pond of the old-time parish. The shock to the system proves too much. So we are back to the futility of renewing the wine without renewing the wineskin. The RCIA will only fully succeed in a church that is utterly transformed by the vision of Vatican II.

Ideally, then, those who complete the RCIA programme should have vibrant small Christian communities into which they can merge, if they so wish. Better still, the initiation could take place in the context of such communities.

In a previous chapter I mentioned the case of the Dublin parish which had all those praiseworthy committees to run its activities on behalf of the disadvantaged of every kind. The extent of their work became clear in the course of a seminar on small Christian communities. The parish priest, or pastor, was away for the early sessions. On his return I was speaking with him and he informed me that there was still one group in the area who needed support, namely, young married couples, and he felt that the small Christian community would be the ideal 'committee' to take up this task. I said nothing at the time. But in group work at the end of the course, the parishioners made it quite clear that their understanding of small Christian community was not that it was just one more committee added on to the others, or a ready tool at the priest's disposal for any activity he might deem fit. For them it was a whole new communitarian way of being church. Action on behalf of young marrieds might well be part of their agenda, but then again, it might not. It was a matter for discernment within the community and this process had to be respected. The upshot of this for us priests is that we must be sensitive to the dynamics of these groups and never impose ourselves upon them.

Politics

Where does politics sit with the small Christian community? Politics is the dynamic way in which our whole secular life is organised; it concerns itself with health, labour, sport, finance, education, industry and commerce, communications, welfare, and so forth. That is why we have government ministries to look after all of these areas. Is the church and its communities at the grassroots to have nothing to say about such matters? Must Christians busy themselves with incense and votive candles or retire to the sacristy? This is precisely what our opponents understand by keeping out of politics. Of course this is absurd. We cannot opt out of politics, for to opt out of politics is to opt out of life.

Recently, in the Sunday homily, I raised the issue of our Irish neutrality, which seemed to me to be under threat from a creeping militarism. After the Mass various people thanked me for having made them aware of the problem, but one man quite vociferously told me, 'You are meddling in politics and are quite out of line!' If we cannot talk of a matter of life and death for people, particularly the young, what are we to talk about?

Having said that we can't opt out of politics, we must stress that the small community is not a party cell and it would be utterly wrong to use or manipulate it as such. It is a faith experience. In the course of this faith experience, however, the members are motivated to make what seems in conscience to them the appropriate political option. In the historical profile of the groups (cf. pp. 166-240), for example, we give examples of how they can effectively impact on the political situation

Communism is a failed system. But so too is free-market, or more accurately, dominant-market capitalism. It stands condemned by the forty million people who die of hunger or hunger-related diseases every year. A figure, as already pointed out, equal to the combined populations of Belgium, Australia, and Canada. Suppose we have a family of ten and there is a cake to be shared. If the two strongest were to run off with more than three-quarters of the cake, the remaining eight would be quite rightly enraged at the injustice of it. That, however, is an accurate picture of what is happening on this planet. We have 20% of the earth's inhabitants consuming 80% of its substance. It is a recipe for disaster. Liberal capitalism also stands condemned by the growing millions who are not simply marginalised from even its most minimal benefits, but totally excluded. How can any sane person expect to build happiness in such an unjust world?

Total collectivism is not the answer; neither is leaving everything to be somehow regulated by the free market. That seems to me to make as much sense as throwing all the pieces of a jigsaw puzzle into the air and expecting them all to fall, so as to form a perfect picture. The answer lies somewhere in the middle as it always does. What is required is an economic system that takes equal account of the social and human. If governments renege on their responsibility to govern for the benefit of all, then the law of the jungle prevails.

Speaking to me of the dominant-market system in Bolivia in 1999, a girl of little means in a small community said, 'It utterly disinherits us.' She is in a position to see clearly its dastardly effects. One of the things she observes, for example, is small local industries for the manufacture of garments being run out of business by affluent countries. Those wealthy nations flood the market with even cheaper products than locals can produce.

Good government – the type that a Christian could with a clear conscience support – would in the first place be deeply concerned with the weaker members of society: the old, the sick, the mentally and physically handicapped, the homeless, the unemployed, and so on. Having given priority to the weak, it would then preoccupy itself with the well-being of the whole national family. Yet, while being concerned for all, effective governance would not spoon-feed or be paternalistic to anyone; rather would it foster self-reliance and self-respect in every person. It would promote a society where there is harmony rooted in justice and obscene inequalities are eliminated. At the very least, it would work for a situation where no citizen would go without a wage that would allow her to live with dignity. Finally, it would not be so narrowly nationalistic as to be unconcerned about the well-being of other countries on the planet, especially those in the economically deprived South. Only attitudes and actions such as these will lead to the establishment of democracy in the world.

In a syndicated article, Professor Jeffrey Sachs of Harvard University makes the exciting claim that we are in a position to end indigence. He writes as follows: 'If the world – especially the US and other rich countries – would shift a small amount of its military spending to meeting the needs of the world's poorest people, our generation could free humanity from poverty's iron grip.'[37] A truly worthy project !

158 SMALL CHRISTIAN COMMUNITIES

Development

This issue of development is very close to the previous one and has importance for the small communities. I will begin by quoting a traditional African story from Tanzania:

> Long, long ago in our land there was a rainy season such as had never been seen before, or since for that matter. The water was everywhere and the animals were running up the hills to escape it. So fast did the floods come that many of them drowned, except for the monkeys, who smartly climbed to the tree-tops to avoid the rising water. From their vantage point they looked down on the raging waters and to their consternation saw the fish swimming and jumping about in the flood. The creatures seemed to be enjoying themselves, yet it had to be a false impression, the monkeys concluded. In reality those unfortunate souls were in a dangerous situation.

> One of the monkeys called out to a companion, 'Look down, my friend, at these poor creatures. They are going to drown. Do you see how they are fighting for their lives?'

> 'Yes, indeed,' replied the other monkey.

> 'What a shame! it was impossible for them to escape to the hills because they don't seem to have any legs. But what can we do to save them?'

> 'Let me see. If we wade in at the edge of the flood, where the waters aren't deep enough to cover us, maybe we can help them to get out.'

> So all the monkeys did just that. With much difficulty they caught the fish one by one and placed them on dry land. After a time, there was a great pile of them lying on the grass – all of them motionless.

> 'Do you see how tired these creatures are?' asked one of the monkeys. 'They are just sleeping and resting now. Had it not been for us, my friends, all these poor people without legs would have drowned.'

> 'Yes,' observed another, 'they were trying to escape us because they couldn't understand our good intentions but, when they wake up, they will be very grateful because we have brought them salvation.'

Too often in our development work, like those well-meaning monkeys, we completely misread the situation and save the fish from drowning. In other words we help in ways that do more harm than good. In Africa I have seen heavy machinery rotting in ditches for want of fuel or a spare part. I have seen a once proud hospital with trees growing out through the windows of what was formerly the operating theatre. These were projects that expatriates thought would be beneficial for the area, yet failed to involve the local people. They were never the projects of the local inhabitants. They never owned them. In the end people cannot be developed; they must develop themselves. The question is whether there is not something outsiders can do to assist this process. If so, well and good. The trouble is that too often they go with the answers and not the questions; they talk but they do not really listen. It is so important to listen carefully to what people are saying, whether it be in society or the church. It is there that true development starts, because folk have to be in charge of their own progress. It is so hard for even well-disposed development personnel to shake off the conviction that they know best.

Workers in developing nations are not lacking in ingenuity. They cannot afford to be; they have to survive. While walking through a township in Nairobi a few years ago, I saw cooking stoves which were manufactured locally and perfectly adapted to the needs of the residents. And in Zimbabwe I was shown a whole array of unsophisticated farm implements and machinery that was most suitable for the environment. Indeed one look at the arts and crafts of Africans would swiftly dispel any reservations one might harbour about their manual skills.

The relevant point about small Christian communities and any such groups, whether religious or secular, is that they are powerful instruments for development, because here we have people organised at the grassroots which seems to me to be the first and most important condition for development. In Sierra Leone, during its recent civil war, a network of small Christian communities provided the basis that made a whole series of development projects possible in the capital, Freetown. Its population had swollen with refugees from the war, and in the midst of all this the groups were engaged in a welter of activities: food distribution, provision of water, literacy work, technical courses, street cleaning, health and hygiene. And their Muslim brothers and sisters joined in heartily. Indeed at one point in the fighting they were the only ones who would give burial to the rebels left dead on the streets of the capital. In Zimbabwe – in better days – a man engaged in giving courses on self-reliance found that two thirds of the work was done where the communities existed, while in the same country a government development worker was loud in his praise of the groups as facilitators of progress.

Similarly in a variety of places on the African continent the communities are providing impressive support for those stricken with AIDS by getting them to the hospital, summoning the mobile clinic, sharing food, and helping with family chores. Their members also take part in Education for Life programmes which help to provide people who will instruct folk regarding all aspects of the AIDS pandemic. Above all they respect the dignity of the victims and encourage them to carry on living and doing something productive if they can. Going among those stricken with this dread disease you would expect to find utter desperation. Not so. In a room of terminally ill patients I found music, flowers, visiting friends and family, smiles and peace; all was transformed by the power of love. I realised that no matter how tragic things may be, where there is love, we find heaven. There was a playground full of children and every one of them had received the dire inheritance of AIDS. The person in charge said, 'We are doing our best to keep the children alive in the hope that in the future a cure may be found.' In that situation the laughter of the children became a hymn to life.

Still more recently I have been involved with an AIDS project in the diocese of Tzaneen, South Africa. I and my African team-mate, Matthew, were part of an endeavour in which others were also involved. We were specifically asked to explore how a Christian spirituality could help in preventing AIDS in the first instance and, then, in consoling those already stricken. The small Christian communities with which we worked were clear on what they considered the solution: fidelity in marriage, and self-control among young people. Other solutions might give some protection, but would not stop the spread of the disease. It was Easter. Africa, they said, must rise from the dead. The stark choice was to choose life over death. It may be providential that the small Christian communities and similarly concerned groups are multiplying in Africa. They may animate the counter-cultural movement that will give birth to the New Africa. Not indeed that traditional Africa encouraged sexual licence: the restraints within family and tribe were stringent.

The small Christian communities, then, can be powerful instruments for development. They empower people to speak their word and raise themselves up by their own endeavours. Because of this, groups such as these can provide a sure basis for the democratic process.

Maintaining momentum in small Christian community
A missionary friend of mine in Zambia once sent a badge to his sister in the United States. On the badge there was a cartoon of a hippopotamus standing upright and underneath there was the caption: *Things desperate: send chocolates*. He had a sweet tooth and said the chocolate kept him going. At least it had the virtue of being a benign stimulant.

We all need something to keep us going. Small Christian communities also require motivation. I have often put the question to groups at home and abroad as to what helped them to maintain momentum. Here are a list of the factors cited:
- the knowledge that of ourselves we cannot persevere and, if we do so, it is ultimately the work of God,
- persisting with conviction through good times and bad,
- knowing that we are called to be a loving open community like the Trinity,
- a strong spiritual life,
- a hunger for the word of God and the eucharist,
- alert, sympathetic, and challenging animation,
- full participation in decisions through dialogue and consensus,

- deep reflection on the life of the community,
- initial and ongoing formation,
- concern for others especially for the powerless ones of the world,
- a sense of process,
- regular encounters ,'formal' and social,
- a sense of humour,
- meetings that are varied, interesting, and down to earth, and
- most importantly, encounters that in time gain depth.

In the above mentioned diocese of Tzaneen, South Africa, there is a network of communities in place: some strong, some reasonably sound, and others struggling. The need of animation for the groups became apparent and a workshop was held with participants from all the parishes to work out practically how this could be done. Furthermore, a diocesan team of five was set-up, so as to back up those local activists. This brought home to me the great importance of animating our communities. We cannot initiate small Christian communities and then leave them to their own devices, hoping they will somehow survive. There ought to be support; where possible a support network. Such backing will go a long way towards assuring the perseverance of the communities.

Wounded members

Finally, there is an issue around members who are wounded, psychologically or emotionally. All the participants in a group must have the intention of striving to live in communion. Some do this better than others; the gospel of the talents is relevant here. If I only have one talent, that is all I can give. A Christian community must be ready to carry wounded members. However, you need a core of integral people to do this. If there are too many participants with a wing down, it does not work; the group implodes. Of course, the word 'integral' is relative; in a sense we are all vulnerable, all sinners in need of affirmation, and community is the solidarity of the weak.

With this chapter we end Part II on the practicalities (reality) of small Christian communities. Again we remind ourselves that these practicalities well up from the depths of the love of Father, Son, and Spirit, mediated to us by the incarnate Jesus. And the Almighty is in the functional details, revealing God through time.

Summary

1) Small Christian communities must be open to diversity and allow for flexibility.

2) Ecumenism, that we may all be one within the Christian family, is urgent. From this base we then reach out to all religions and to all our fellow human beings.

3) Our unity will never be uniformity but rather harmony in diversity.

4) Inculturation, or making the gospel flesh and blood in a particular cultural context, is an important issue for small communities. The groups are, above all, the places where it happens, and they are instruments for bringing it about.

5) Youth are an integral part of the communities; sometimes cultural reasons may oblige them to have their own groups, which nevertheless remain open to, and on occasions share with, adult gatherings.

6) Even where young people have no trouble in being part of the ordinary small communities, they may need their own groups so as to share about their specific problems and take account of their unique youth culture.

7) Action is required to solve the eucharistic famine by adopting the community model of church, and by opening up ministry to a greater variety of people and not just restrict it to male celibates.

8) Politics is the dynamic, or active, way in which our whole society is organised. The church and, consequently, the small Christian communities must therefore deal with political matters, though they are faith experiences and not political party cells.

9) Good government is a matter of looking after the weaker ele-

ments of society, fostering self-reliance and self-respect, and promoting a society where there is harmony rooted in justice.

10) People cannot be developed but must develop themselves; the question for outside parties is whether they can do anything to help realise this. They must not come with the answers, but be superb listeners. Again the groups are places where this can take place and are instruments for bringing it about.

11) Momentum in small communities is maintained in a variety of ways that are given above.

Question

Have you to contend with any of the issues mentioned in this chapter, or any other knotty problem in your small Christian community, and how do you cope?

Suggested Bible passage: Matthew 24:11-13; or Hebrews 12:1-4.

PART III

History

CHAPTER 9

A Historical Profile
of Small Christian Communities

Like a melody that is passed along through the various sections of
an orchestra, we have heard the music of the Trinity passed
through Jesus to the church, the kingdom, on into time, and away
towards eternity. It reverberates through history, as we will now
see.

Biblical and Pre-modern Times
James O'Halloran SDB

Until the 1960s a hierarchical model of church prevailed in the
world, but with Vatican II we entered a period of change. The council
called on the church to be community as the Trinity is community
(*Dogmatic Constitution of the Church,* no. 4; cf. also 10, 11, 12). In the
intervening years we have found that one effective way of realising
this vision is through small Christian communities, which then
combine into larger units to form a communion of communities.

The appearance of the groups was not a bolt from the blue. Their
history dates not merely from the 1940s and 50s; it reaches much
further back. And all of it is important. In the various countries
where I work, I find that those involved in the groups are most
curious to learn about similar experiences elsewhere, and about
the origins of the small communities in the first place. Which led to
my elaborating this profile. Not that the ordinary people need all
the details here recorded, yet having a general picture is most helpful.

This is so for a variety of reasons:
- When the folk in communities know that they are not alone in
  their experience, it can be a great support.
- They get a sense of the Holy Spirit at work everywhere.
- And a sense of the New Pentecost ushered in by John XXIII and
  the World Council of Churches.

- The power the groups have to communicate Christ and his good news also becomes obvious.
- And people are saved from having to reinvent the wheel or eternally repeat the mistakes of history.

Small Christian communities in the New Testament
'Who was the founder of the small Christian communities anyway? Was it you?' someone once asked me during a workshop on the subject.

'No,' I replied mightily relieved at not having to shoulder that Messianic burden.

'Who was it then?'

'Well, actually, it was Jesus Christ.'

In a sense the communities are as new as the shopping mall, yet as old as the gospel. They have their origins in the itinerant community that trod the dusty roads of Palestine with Jesus, in the gathering of the early Christians which formed in Jerusalem after the first Pentecost (cf. Acts 2:42-47; 4:32-37), and in all those groups that sprang up in the gentile world largely as a result of Paul's work.

If the reader would like to explore the life of those early Christian communities, there are a number of texts that would allow him to do so. Reflecting on them can tell us much about the joys and sorrows, sufferings and struggles of the early Christians. For the sake of convenience we list them here:

- *Jerusalem*: Luke 24:52-53; Acts 2:22 - 6:15; 7:54 - 8:4; 11:22; 11:27-30; 15:1-31; 21:7-20.
- *Antioch*: Acts 11:19-30; 13:1-3; 14:21-28; 15:1-35; Galatians 2:11.
- *Ephesus*: Acts 18:19-28; 19:1-41; 20:16-38; Ephesians 1:1-12; 6:21-24; 1 Corinthians 15:32; 16:8; 1 Timothy 1:3-4; Revelation 2:1-7.
- *Philippi*: Acts 16:11-24; Philippians 1:3-14; 2:25-30; 4:14-23; Thessalonians 2:2.
- *Corinth*: Acts 18:1-11; 19:1; 1 Corinthians 1:10-31; 3:3-9; 3:16-23; 4:17-21; 5:1-2; 6:5-11; 8:4-13; 9:1-7; 9:11-16; 10:14-22; 11:17-34; 12:4-31; 13:1-13; 14:1-33; 15:3-19; 16:10-12; 16:13-20; 2 Corinthians 1:12-24; 2:4.

There are those who believe that Christ left us a highly organised church, rather along the lines that we have experienced in modern times. Many scripture scholars would not agree. Raymond Brown, for example, has pointed out that even in New Testament times the church expressed itself in diverse forms.[38] They were as follows:

- The heritage that Paul leaves us in the pastoral epistles of Titus and 1 and 2 Timothy. This model emphasises *church organisation*. Authority is important. The apostles have disappeared off the scene and there is a delicate moment for leadership. As a result the role of presbyter-priest is stressed. The model proposes a *family* approach.
- Then there is the type that considers the church as Christ's *body to be loved* which can be found in Colossians and Ephesians, and is also traced to Paul.
- From the gospel of Luke and the Acts we get a third Pauline mode, namely, *the church and the Spirit*. This highlights the presence and action of the Spirit.
- In 1 Peter we find the Petrine heritage of the church seen as *people of God*, a form that makes a person feel a strong sense of belonging.
- There is the tradition of John in the fourth gospel which shows people as *a community of disciples personally attached to Jesus*.
- John provides a further model in his epistles: *a community of persons guided by the Paraclete-Spirit*.
- And, finally, there is the heritage of Jewish-Gentile Christians in the gospel of Matthew, which stresses *'an authority that does not stifle Jesus'*.

In the foregoing models the church as community, or people of God, is strongly represented. Where authority is emphasised it is never intended to be dominating, rather is it to be understood as service. As Hoornaert points out: 'Nothing could have been further from the spirit of primitive Christianity than the notion of a power or authority that would not be one of sisterly or brotherly service. The principle of a community of brothers and sisters forbade any arrogance of power and held up before the eyes of all the example of Christ:

> Though he was in the form of God,
> he did not deem equality with God
> something to be grasped at.
> Rather he emptied himself
> and took on the form of a slave … (Philippians 2:6-7).'[39]

It would be quite mistaken then to look back and read the history of the early Christians with spectacles tinted by our own times.

Paul's approach

For Paul the church is the body of Christ (cf. 1 Corinthians 12:27) and as such clearly a community. No doubt the words spoken by the Lord on the road to Damascus had branded themselves into his consciousness: 'Saul, Saul, why do you persecute me?' (Acts 9:4). Paul would understand community, or being together in Christ, as:

- living as a single, united body, where the Spirit of God brings forth the fruits of the Spirit (cf. Galatians 5:16-25).
- being able to discern matters for itself with the help of the Spirit (cf. 1 Corinthians 2:6-16; 4:6-7; 6:1-8; 7:10-12; 12:4-11).
- being responsible, or:
  - faithful to its call (cf. Galatians 3:1-5; 5:1; 5:13-15),
  - capable of drawing others to Christ (1 Thessalonians 4:9-12),
  - being ready to get involved with the groaning of all creation (Romans 8:18-25),
- struggling with various issues, such as:
  - the fact that the kingdom of God is already existing, yet will only be fully realised in the world to come (cf. 1 Corinthians 15:12-28);
  - the delay in Jesus' Second Coming, or the Parousia (cf. 1 Thessalonians 5:1-11; 2 Thessalonians 2:1-12),
  - anxiety over death (cf. 1 Thessalonians 4:13-18; 1 Corinthians 15:12-28);
  - morality and a false sense of security (cf. 1 Corinthians 3:18-23; 5:1-2; 5:8; 6:12-20; 8:1-13; 10:23 - 11:1; Romans 14:13-23; 15:1-6);
  - and the conflict between Jewish and Gentile Christians (cf. Galatians 2:1 - 3:14).[40]

In the Pauline communities, as indeed in all the early Christian groups, it is people who are important. Organisation and buildings are secondary. The faithful meet in homes; there are no churches. So in Acts 12:12 we read of their being gathered in the house of John Mark when Peter comes knocking at the door, and in Romans 16:5 Paul sends greetings to the church that meets in the house of Priscilla and Aquila (cf. also Romans 16:11 and 16:14-15). A significant fact emerges here: Christians met in homes and it was there that they got the experience of the intimate group.

But there was also the preoccupation of bringing the small communities together on occasions so as to get the equally important experience of being a communion of communities. The Temple in

Jerusalem was an early meeting point. And at Antioch later the Acts tell us of all the people being gathered together in one place by Paul and Barnabas, when they returned from what is known as Paul's first missionary journey (cf. 14:26-27).

Of course the communitarian thrust of the church was inspired by the example of Jesus. He formed a community of disciples, consisting of men and women, around himself, and as part of that community set about the task of preaching the good news. While growing up, he would have been aware of the many groups that were common in the Roman world: Scribes, Pharisees, Saducees, Essenes, Epicureans, Stoics, Cynics, and so forth. Each sabbath he frequented the synagogue.

Nazareth was situated on a great trading route. All manner of people would have passed that way, including Jews from every part of the Roman Empire on their way to worship in Jerusalem. Furthermore, Nazareth was only five kilometres from Sepphoris which was rebuilt during the youth of Jesus as a Hellenistic, or culturally Greek, city. Capernaum, where he later lived, was a northern border town to the Decapolis region of ten Hellenistic cities. So Christ grew up in a Galilee that we could almost describe as multicultural.[41] He must have come across wandering philosophers and gurus holding forth in the marketplace and undoubtedly learned from all his experiences (cf. Luke 2:52). One of the lessons that he must have absorbed was the effectiveness of the group. It is not surprising then that we find him adopting the strategy of the small community in his own ministry.

Sometimes there is the perception that all was smooth in the early Christian groups. By no means. And if we think our times are difficult, theirs were still more so. As we saw from the scriptural references given above, the fledgling church had to deal with a host of troubles. But the remarkable, and seemingly contradictory thing was that their unity was forged from the very struggle and suffering which they endured in common. This, surely, should be a source of encouragement for us in dealing with confrontation and conflict today.

Change with Constantine
With the coming of the Roman Emperor Constantine (288?-337 CE), the church changed from a communitarian model to a hierarchical

one. Though he was principally responsible for the change, it is only fair to say that small compromises can be detected even in The New Testament. Thus in 1 Peter 2:18 we read: 'Servants be submissive to your masters with all respect, not only to the kind and gentle but also to the overbearing.' Here we see the church adapting to survive; the old patriarchal, or dominating, order is reasserting itself. 'Be good servants and you will be considered as having worth' was the message – a modification of the gospel, where our worth comes from being human persons, children of God, and brothers and sisters in Christ. But at the particular time these words were written, patriarchy was being strongly affirmed right across the Roman Empire.

The seachange, however, came with the conversion of Constantine. The church ceased to be harassed and Christianity became the favoured religion of the Empire. It was fashionable to be a Christian and the church greatly increased in numbers, though it was not the case of a massive entry of pagans. Yet it lost the momentum of an entity that until then had been lean, persecuted, and more committed; the edge of witness became blunted. 'Not only did he recognise the bishops as counsellors of state, but gradually he extended to them juridical rights. He gave legal force to their solution of civil suits in 318 (CodTheod 1. 27. 1), permitted the emancipation of slaves in church (321), and recognised bequests to the church (ibid. 16. 2. 4).'[42] This gave birth to a church model that was both hierarchical and strongly institutional, a form that prevailed as the communitarian vision faded. The neighbourhood community, or house church (*oikos*), ceased to exist and the focus was placed on structures. With the departure of the house church a dimension that gave early Christianity much of its vitality was gone. And, truth to tell, the church has never been quite the same without it. Today the ordinary faithful are reclaiming their heritage as small communities increase in numbers around the world. That Christians enjoy this heritage is not simply an optional extra. It is a right; it is a necessity. I hope these things have become clear in the course of this volume.

Though the vision of church as community faded, it was never entirely lost. It was preserved in a rarefied fashion by the religious orders. We owe a debt of gratitude to figures like Basil, Benedict, Scholastica, Dominic, Francis, Clare, Ignatius, Teresa, John Bosco,

and Mary of Mornese. The founders of religious orders and congregations were often charismatic figures who valued relationships
above structures. Francis really lamented as Brother Elias boxed in
his creativity, and Don Bosco was deeply distressed the day he saw
his pupils being marshalled into lines to enter the classrooms. This
had not been the practice and was not the family spirit that prevailed in the early days of his Oratory. In short the religious orders
that appeared on the scene like a breath of fresh air often adapted to
the pyramidal church model, becoming little pyramids within the
great pyramid. Nevertheless the founders must be credited with
preserving a precious Christian memory.

In the sixteenth century the Anabaptists also were a grassroots
phenomenon that emphasised community. And with people of the
sea small Christian communities flourished among ordinary folk
on board ships and on land, owing to the Bethel Movement, in the
late eighteenth and early nineteenth centuries. So in some fashion
the small communities have always been present since the first ones
appeared following the Resurrection of Christ.

Modern times
As already mentioned, small Christian communities are once again
emerging among the baptised in our days. And it is happening
worldwide. The accounts that follow are contributed by people
from among the most informed in their regions.

North America (USA and Canada)

Rev Robert S. Pelton CSC

In the Post-Synodal Exhortation *Ecclesia in America*, Pope John Paul II twice recognises small Christian communities: once in the context of renewing parishes so that each might become a community of communities (41) and again when discussing the challenge of the sects, in which context the small communities are seen as especially capable of promoting interpersonal bonds of mutual support within the Catholic Church (73). Additionally, the institutional church recognises small communities as 'the primary cells of the church structure' and praises them as 'responsible for the richness of faith and its expansion as well as for the promotion of the person and development' (*Instrumentum Laboris* for the Synod of America, 64). These references strongly indicate that the Vatican is now relying upon small Christian communities to build solidarity within the church.

A prominent role

Many persons worldwide initially expressed surprise when they learned that the Holy Father envisions such a prominent role for North American and European small Christian communities as well as for their better-known counterparts in Africa, Asia, Latin America, and Oceania. Large numbers of Canadian and US Catholics seem not to have previously recognised that small Christian communities have been flourishing in their homelands during the past decade and a half – enjoying a strong and steady growth in their numbers, in their scope, and in the significance of their contributions to God and to humanity. Those of us who have a keen interest in the small communities, however, see compelling evidence that the small Christian communities will not only fulfil the challenges the Vatican has offered them, but will also continue making great contributions in numerous other spheres as well.

There are currently 37,000 such communities in the United States[43] and 7,200 to 7,500 in Canada.[44] The combined membership of Canadian and US small Christian communities totals approximately one million church-going Catholics who have strong loyalties to their faith, who actively participate in the missions of their small communities and of the universal church, and who build their groups upon a foundation of prayer, faith sharing, scripture, and concern for spirituality. Significantly, their rapid growth has occurred at a time when regular attendance at Sunday Mass was sharply declining from a previous high of 80% of parish members to a current level of 32% in the United States[45] and 12% in Canada.[46]

It seems clear, therefore, that the small Christian community phenomenon is achieving significant successes in helping large numbers of individuals to find the religious meaning of their Catholic faith, to relate their spirituality to daily life, to make living faith commitments, and to connect their 21st century lives with the very dawn of Christianity.

Well documented information
Until very recently, such conclusions could have been based only upon anecdotal observations and faith in the Holy Spirit. During the earliest years of the small Christian community movement in the US and Canada, there were few opportunities to conduct comprehensive empirical studies of the many thousands of grassroots communities that were spreading rapidly throughout two of the world's larger nations. Nor was it possible to form systematic theological reflections based upon verified data that accurately reflects the current state of the small Christian community phenomenon.

During the past five years, however, several initiatives have produced a wealth of documented information. Monsignor Timothy O'Brien, a senior priest of St Mary's Parish in Los Gatos, California, spent a sabbatical year studying small Christian communities. He shared his findings in the book, *Why Small Christian Communities Work*.[47] Another excellent overview is provided in James O'Halloran's *Small Christian Communities: A Pastoral Companion*.[48]

Latin American/North American Church Concerns (LANACC) of the Kellogg Institute actively promotes pastoral bonds between the churches of the Americas, a mission which includes sponsorship of conferences that study, assist, and promote small communities throughout the Americas. In 1990, LANACC convened a consultation that brought together representatives of the National Alliance of Parishes (which promotes the restructuring of parishes into small communities), The North American Forum for Small Christian Communities (which is composed of diocesan directors of small communities), and Buena Vista (which represents grass-roots communities which may or may not pertain to church structures). These organisations formed a joint task force at the University of Notre Dame, Indiana, to sponsor an ongoing series of national and international convocations. The 1991 International Consultation on Small Christian Communities at Notre Dame placed special emphasis upon comparing pastoral experiences. The 1996 Consultation, again at Notre Dame, provided the opportunity to delve more deeply into those theological dimensions that may influence our church in the new millennium. The 1999 Consultation in Cochabamba, Bolivia, took place in the context of the Synods of Bishops from all five continents. Small Christian communities have played a prominent role in the discussions and documentation of all these synods.

Fr Bernard Lee SM has written: 'There is no more central question than what kind of community the church needs to be today, faithful to its origins and interdependently interactive in the world in which it lives.'[49] It is our sincere hope that the fruit of the Notre Dame Consultations has contributed – and will continue to contribute – helpful responses to this crucial question.

Watershed study
Most recently, there has been a watershed study conducted by the Institute for Ministry of Loyola University, New Orleans, and made possible by a generous grant from Lilly Endowment Inc. Directed by Bernard J. Lee SM – with assistance from a team of prominent theologians, researchers, consultants, and representatives of many small Christian community networks – this study offered the first fully viable opportunity to conduct a complete census survey of small Christian communities, members, practices, attitudes, goals, and concerns.

The study team identified three primary types of small Christian communities:

1. The general (GSC) type includes about 24,000 individual communities, or about 65% of the small Christian communities identified in the study. Most of these communities are parish connected, and many of the members belong to national organisations.
2. Hispanic/Latino (H/L) communities number 7,500 at the mini-

mum, and represent 20% of small Christian communities. Nearly all are parish-connected, and the great majority stress family issues and family membership.

3. Charismatic communities (CHR) are minimally 4,500 in number, comprising 12% of small Christian communities identified. While most members of charismatic communities are parish members, the communities themselves do not tend to be parish connected.

Other Small Christian Community types, smaller in number, but often outstanding in commitment and achievement, include:

(a) Call to Action (CTA) communities and eucharistic central communities (ECC), which the study team grouped together because of their marked similarities. Numbering about 200 groups combined, CTA/ECC communities are the best educated and most affluent of all small Christian community types. They are both the most critical of the institutional church and the most responsive to the church's social teachings.

(b) College and university campus communities, about 1,100 in number, comprise about 3% of small Christian communities. These communities have not yet been fully studied due to lack of information in at least one crucial area, but they will soon be included.

(c) Communities associated with religious orders, many of which have most of the characteristics of small Christian communities. Although an independent survey conducted by two Franciscan Sisters indicates membership of at least 14,500, the study team learned of this network too late to complete full research.

(d) Women's groups who share feminist concerns undoubtedly exist, but the study team could not identify them or contact them in sufficient numbers to include them.

All-pervasive diversity

The diversity between the types is mirrored by the diversity within the types. Based upon her two decades of active involvement with the small community phenomenon, Nora Petersen reports: 'In Buena Vista we meet people who are members of various forms of small Christian community. The groups have varying life spans – from weeks to years. They are made up differently – meeting seasonally, weekly, biweekly and so forth. Some were begun by the official church as the action of a priest, pastor, or other staff member. Others were organised by members at the grassroots to fill needs not met by the organised church. While a few extra parochial communities operate in the margins, the vast majority have some links to local parishes or are made up of active parish members ... Most small Christian communities in my acquaintance are made up of members active in a parish, who meet around the word of God and/or study of church-related topics and who participate in the local parish celebration of the eucharist. Some communities are made up of members drawn from different parishes who come together as the groups described above and to share their lives of faith, to support one another and reflect on scripture together. They worship at eucharist in their own local parishes. A few communities, while seeing themselves as Catholic, operate extra parochially and regularly include celebrations of the eucharist which is presided over by a visiting or member priest.'[50]

In summary, Mrs Petersen has discovered that her twenty year involvement with small Christian communities has empowered her '... to ride out some difficult times, grow in the faith, and become ever closer to the church. To be Catholic, it seems to me, means to remain connected to that universal network of church that includes the Catholic family. Sometimes I can only do that with the help of fellow Catholics who love the church as one loves family, warts and all, and who seek to grow in participation in the mission of Jesus.'[51]

Exploring attitudes to church
The Institute for Ministry study team collaborated with the Research Center at the University of Maryland and with Dr William V. D'Antonio at Catholic University to explore the attitudes of small Christian community members regarding church, culture, loyalty, critical capacities, and ideologies, and to determine what factors motivate individuals both as Catholics and as small Christian community members.

In general, they found that small Christian community members tend to be active and highly committed Catholics. Except for Hispanic/Latino groups, many of whose members are recent immigrants who have not had adequate time to climb the socio-economic and educational ladders, members are better educated and more affluent than the general Catholic population. In the largest small Christian community group (GSC), which comprises two-thirds of small Christian communities, 33% are college graduates and another 23% have professional or advanced college degrees. CTA/ECCs are even more highly educated. They are an older group than the general population (53 to 76% of each type are over age 40), and women members outnumber men by a 2 to 1 ratio in the three largest community types. Most small communities are not ethnically diverse: Hispanic/Latino communities are 98% Hispanic, for example, while GSC communities are 92% Caucasian.[52]

In contrast to the small Christian communities of Latin America where members are predominantly the poorer members of the churches, Canadian and US small Christian community members are predominantly middle or upper middle class. A strong similarity, however, is that US/Canadian middle class has become the most important power base for justice and social change, just as the poorer people in Latin American communities have long been the power base for issues of justice and conscience.[53]

Participation in Sunday eucharist is extremely high, with group participation rates of 93%, 91%, 78%, 76%, 61% and 33%. Daily prayer is also the norm: the lowest group total was 46% and most groups reported percentages in the 70s and 80s. It is impossible to determine whether the most active Catholics are more likely to join small Christian communities or whether small Christian community membership promotes participation and frequent prayer. Unquestionably, however, there is a clear correlation.[54]

Small Christian community members of all groups want their voices heard in important decisions about church life and polity, most particularly in use of parish income, economic justice, welfare, and, to a somewhat lesser extent, in selection of parish priests and in ordination of married men or of women.[55]

In general Catholics join small Christian communities to search for meaning in their daily lives. Opportunities to 'Learn about Religion, God;' 'Prayer, Praise, Worship;' and 'Spirituality' were the most cited reasons for joining.[56]

Reasons for remaining members, and sources of greatest satis-faction from membership, seem to be of a more interpersonal nature. Here, 'Social Support, New Friends,' and 'Community' were the predominant considerations. This contrast is probably more apparent than real, however, since self-reported narratives of community members make it clear that much of the interpersonal satisfaction arises from the communal character of Christian discipleship, communal discernment of scriptures, and shared prayer. Thus, small Christian communities bring relief from cultural loneliness, social and familial fragmentation, and widespread hunger for community. Small Christian communities must, of course, be more than mere support groups, but this function should not be summarily dismissed.

As Dr Craig Dykstra, Vice President for Religion at Lilly Endowment Inc. recently observed: 'Just getting through life involves having to figure out what to do. The help most people really want is a community of people in whose company they can do their own "figuring" ... What a gift it is to be able to find a home place, a community of people who have really figured out how to go about figuring things out and thus lead genuine lives.'[57]

Over three quarters of all communities meet weekly or biweekly. Except for charismatic groups, who generally regard a parish meeting place as a ritual connection to the parish, most small Christian communities gather in members' homes – reminiscent of the house churches of Christianity's earliest times, when private homes were the normative church locations.[58]

Although Eucharistic Central Communities (ECCs) are larger, most communities include 8 to 12 adult members. Such groups are small enough so members get to know each other well, and so all members have opportunities to actively participate at every gathering. Despite marked differences between community types, over three-quarters of all communities met weekly or biweekly.[59]

Most small Christian communities display strong resistance to traditional leadership models. Many have little or no formal structure, while others rely primarily on volunteerism to choose leaders. While this avoids authoritarianism, power struggles, and other negatives, it may also deprive the communities of the many useful benefits of effective leadership.[60]

Prayer, faith sharing, and scripture reading are almost universal activities at all types of small Christian community gatherings. Spirituality, theological reflection, sharing visions, and evangelisation are also widely practised. Small Christian communities serve as welcoming places where individuals can bring their life experiences, both good and bad, and find help in reflecting on those experiences in the light of faith. Such dialogues between experience and faith frequently create and clarify meanings and reshape lives, and they provide a supportive community during the struggle for meaning and direction. If not for small Christian communities, many persons would have no place to talk about their faith and their relationships in the presence of others who care.

One of the study team's interpretive propositions is that Christian communities are both gathered and sent. As such, it was assumed that members would be concerned with both the welfare of the community's own members and also with the welfare of the world beyond the group's immediate membership (the reign of God) especially by providing resources and assistance. The team was 'a little dismayed' that only the CTA/ECC groups gave the highest priority to social justice issues, while all other types gave a clear preference to helping their fellow members. The study team concluded that 'support dynamics are clearly stronger than the dynamics of social concern' and that 'this area invites pastoral attention as the small Christian communities continue to develop.[61]

Clearly, the facts unearthed in the Lilly/Loyola Institute for Ministry Study paint a hopeful picture for the future of small Christian communities, yet it is one beleaguered by significant concerns. Although very real, the challenges the study has identified are far from insurmountable.

Foster need for communion
We must continue to foster the ever-present need for communion on every level of church life, and must foster changes of the very paradigm of the church by encouraging greater roles for the laity, better evangelisation, and greater emphasis upon the powerful role of small Christian communities in the development of ecumenism. It is essential that we maintain a spirit of reasoned dialogue, unity, and mutual trust with those bishops, priests, and lay persons who, for whatever reason, may hold apathetic or even negative views of small Christian communities. We must explore how official church teaching looks at small communities in the larger sense of communion, and determine whether communion is to be understood in a structural sense or whether we need to encourage a broader theological understanding of communion. There is, additionally, a never-ending need both for stronger lay formation and for a

182 SMALL CHRISTIAN COMMUNITIES

stronger missionary sense. Similarly, we need also to develop effective training programmes for small Christian community leaders to ensure that small communities have access to the full richness of Catholic tradition and teaching.

Autonomy/solidarity connection

It is essential to find the optimal nexus between the essential autonomy of individual communities and their equally essential solidarity with each other and with the universal church.

A top priority should be given to heightening awareness of social justice, both at home and abroad, and strengthening the small communities' commitment to social outreach. Perhaps the key is simple recognition that most small Christian community members are well-educated and relatively affluent. It is hardly surprising, therefore, that they view contemporary society, the Bible, and Catholic social teachings from a perspective of privilege, just as the marginalised tend to view the same society, Bible, and teachings from the viewpoint of poverty and discrimination. It seems highly probable that we can free middle class faith from its captivity by culture through exposing the communities to the social realities experienced daily by people who have far less power and far less resources. There is every reason to believe that middle class Christians will heed Matthew 25:31 and will become powerful forces for social justice.

Similarly, we must encourage twinning across diocesan, national, racial, and cultural barriers. Although each small community clearly derives its richness from its own cultural identity, they can become fully Catholic only by drawing from each other's strengths and sharing each other's weaknesses.

Organisations such as Buena Vista and RENEW are already actively promoting twinning. We should support their endeavours and should develop similar endeavours at every level.

Prayer of the essence

Finally, and most importantly, we must pray fervently for these small communities, this nascent church, which is such a splendid example of the Holy Spirit working in the People of God, which has so rapidly become one of the most powerful forms of Christian witness in the post-Vatican II era, and which has so much to offer our brothers and sisters, to our church, and to our Lord.

Our quest is vast, but the opportunities are limitless. Our mission will be aided enormously by a very generous implementation grant from The Lilly Endowment Inc, which is supplying the financial and motivational resources needed to carry out many of the steps necessary to increase the effectiveness of small Christian communities.

Speaking with the wisdom garnered from thirty years experience, Father José Marins told the delegates of the International Consultation on Small Christian Communities: 'The communities pose an alternative to a church closed to new expressions and ministries, but are committed to full communion. They are always in process and as such never finished products. They lie at the heart of the church and are not mere appendages. In the final analysis, they are not just one more activity but a priority.'

We enter the new millennium with further support for a theology of communion, and our steadfast dedication to small Christian communities will allow us to recapture the spirit of hope which we had as we finished the final session of the Second Vatican Council. At that time, speaking about a world to be built up, the council fathers looked to the moment when '... people all over the world will awaken to a lively hope (the gift of the Holy Spirit) that they will one day be admitted to the haven of surpassing peace and happiness radiant with the glory of the Lord' (*Gaudium et Spes*, 93).

Let us awaken to the present moment of lively hope.

Robert S. Pelton, during his fifty-one years as a Holy Cross Priest, has served as Professor of Theology and as Chair of the Department of Theology at the University of Notre Dame; as a peritus (expert consultant) to Cardinal Leo Suenens at Vatican Council II; as founder and director of the Notre Dame Institute for Clergy Education; as chair of the Theological Institute; as Episcopal Vicar of the Archdiocese of Santiago, Chile; as director of the Institute for Church Life at Notre Dame; as editor of the International Papers in Pastoral Ministry; as Departmental Fellow of both the Helen Kellogg Institute for International Studies and of the Joan B. Kroc Institute for International Peace Studies; and as a representative of LANACC (Latin American/North American Church Concerns) of the Kellogg Institute. LANACC promotes pastoral bonds between the churches of the Americas. Part of this is through the annual Romero lectures, and the promotion of small Christian communities. Eight years as a missionary in Chile convinced Pelton of the enormous potential of small Christian communities to give flesh to the biblical image of the church as people of God.

Latin America

José Marins

(Marins uses the expression basic ecclesial community, commonly used in Latin America, rather than small Christian community, often employed elsewhere. Basic ecclesial community would of course be more theologically accurate. — J. O'H.)

I should like to make the following observations regarding the basic ecclesial, or church, community in Latin America.

1. It is something *permanent*, not passing, in the church; not just one more charism, but an essential element. It can, of course, be embodied in varying church models about which issues can be raised.

2. It is by nature a *eucharistic* and missionary community, even when the expression of this identity is limited by pastoral and disciplinary concerns. This expression can vary depending on the historical context or church rite in which it is developing. Basic ecclesial community cannot be analysed from the outside, employing simply a historical, socio-political, or institutional viewpoint. Nor is it merely a democracy. It is much more than that. It is a community animated by the Holy Spirit. Because of this, it is, and always will be, a source of surprises that confound human logic.

In a document published in 1983, the Brazilian bishops applied *Lumen Gentium*, 26 to the basic ecclesial community; it declares that *it is church* and not just a sector or activity of the same. A document from 15 Mexican archbishops and bishops followed suit on the 7th of April 1989, as did a further document from the Bolivian bishops in preparation for Santo Domingo, 1992 (no. 259:1-13).

3. The basic ecclesial community does not have the same format as Catholic Action. We are not talking of a programme, movement, or apostolic activity. Nor is it a question of one pastoral approach among others. Similarities between basic ecclesial community and other Christian groups would be that they are all under the aegis of mother church – which provides a community dimension – refer to the Bible, and give importance to spirituality. Differences between the basic ecclesial community and other phenomena (movements, programmes, pastoral approaches) is a question of essence or being.

The various groups and movements are not opposed to basic ecclesial communities; they complement them. But the communities are
essentially different. Maybe a metaphor would help, though all
such comparisons limp somewhat. The difference would be similar
to that between a seed of maize and a leaf on the maize plant itself.

4. Basic ecclesial community did not appear in the twentieth
century in response to a socio-political situation – even though this
did have an influence – but rather *arose out of theological and pastoral
needs*. The basic ecclesial communities figured primarily as a
restructuring of the church itself and not as a social or lay movement. They are a comprehensive expression of the church's mission. In an article in *Concilium* (April 1974), I outlined the significant
Brazilian experiences that were influential for the beginning of
basic ecclesial communities. These experiences belonged to the
ordinary catechists in Barrada do Pirai and São Paulo do Potengi,
working along the lines of the Movimento de Natal. Bishop
Expedito Madeiros, who initiated this work and was pastor of those
barrios at the time, is still alive and active. And there were other vital
experiences. In Latin America one must not fail to mention the
Presidents of the Christian Assembly in Santiago de los Caballeros,
Dominican Republic; the Delegates of the word of God in
Choluteca, Honduras, who have now spread throughout Central
America; the communities on the outskirts of Panama City, in San
Miguelito com o Pe. Leo; and the groups of Corrientes, in Goya,
Argentina, characterised by a deeply rooted popular piety. Also
worthy of mention are the Chilean basic Christian communities –
the terminology used at Medellin 1968. Basic Christian communities in Chile were distinguished from basic ecclesial communities,
which for the Chileans would be more broadly based and institutional, incorporating a number of basic Christian communities.

5. The basic ecclesial communities arise to summon the baptised
around the basic tenets of the faith – the word of God, works of
charity, prayer and devotions. In Latin America, the Caribbean,
Africa, the Philippines, India, and so forth, they served from the
beginning as small local churches and, because of this, they implicitly represent the church in an 'official' capacity as community/
mission (sacrament). With the necessary permissions, the basic
ecclesial communities may appropriately baptise, preach, receive
new members into the church, and have ordained ministers in the

line of the apostolic succession. These would of course be in communion with the bishop. All this and more is possible because we
are speaking of *the church as such*, and not about a movement or
some branch of Christian spirituality.

In some parts of Latin America (Columbia, Nicaragua ...) the
basic ecclesial communities, denied official approval, called for the
formation of groups that were sometimes parallel groups or groups
in opposition to the hierarchy. This is something circumstantial, not
pertaining to the essence of basic ecclesial community. The situation is not normal and cannot be countenanced in a coherent theology
of church. In these circumstances we are not talking of real basic
ecclesial communities, but of movements with much goodwill that
find inspiration in the communities. On the other hand, we must
recognise that in some situations, particularly in cities, basic ecclesial communities are still merely Bible-study, prayer, or socio-political groups. They have not as yet been able to realise their full ecclesial vocation to be the rallying-point for baptised members of the
Catholic Church in their areas. Indeed from a theological perspective various expressions of church at the grassroots that were highly
controversial have always existed. Nowadays a 'refounding' of the
church means implementing the theological-pastoral model of
Vatican II. Its salient features would be the primacy of the kingdom
of God, the church as sacrament, ecumenical openness, inter-religious dialogue, lay involvement, liturgy as sacrament, a liberating
mission. Like Vatican II, the general assembly of the Latin
American bishops at Medellin, 1968, also produced a 'refounding'-
of-the-Church document. It was on the subject of *Team Ministry*
(Pastoral de Conjunto), and was approved by Paul VI. This was clearly
a founding text and not a mere pastoral suggestion. As such, it must
be read as defining the manner of being a communitarian church in
the reality of Latin America at the historical moment following
Vatican II.

6. The assembly at Puebla in 1979, following the line of Medellin,
always sees the basic ecclesial communities in the contexts of parish
and diocese. The basic ecclesial communities are the vantage point
for seeing reality, the place where a theological foundation can be
laid, and pastoral strategies decided. This is how Puebla wrote its
documents, using the see, judge, act dynamic. Significantly, the
document of Puebla does not have a separate chapter on basic eccle-

sial community, rather is the subject integrated with parish and diocese. These three levels of church present the reality, the clarification, and the proposals to be followed. Puebla obviously tries to make clear that we are dealing with an ensemble that must not be divided: basic ecclesial community, parish, and diocese. The basic ecclesial communities are not regarded as yet another movement; they are of the essence, they are church. Not part of something else, but complete in themselves.

7. The logic of the position taken by the bishops at Puebla regarding the basic ecclesial communities is that they get mentioned in all the principal documents. Being *the basic building blocks* of the new church model, they obviously have a bearing on catechesis, liturgy, justice, responsibilities of the laity, religious formation, seminaries, and so on.

8. The militant socio-political commitment of a people's party in Nicaragua, Haiti, and parts of El Salvador, was strong and, indeed, a source of conflict. Sooner or later, *a concern for social issues* surfaced in all the basic ecclesial communities. Commitment to the poor was in fact present in the communities from the beginning; a commitment that sought not just assistance or promotion, but liberation.

9. *Inter-Church meetings* first took place in Brazil; other countries only followed suit very slowly. Mexico was the first to imitate the Brazilian example, then Argentina, but now the practice has spread to all parts. At present a national team, with a bishop representing the episcopal conference, accompany the life of basic ecclesial communities in countries such as Argentina, Honduras, Chile, and Bolivia. Brazil has opted for inter-church meetings, bringing together a larger gathering of participants in basic ecclesial communities, to coordinate the life and work of the groups.

10. An important aspect of the basic ecclesial communities is that they are *part of church and pastoral structures.* This fact is a source of tension. On the one hand the communities cannot be taken over by the parish, and on the other they cannot be relegated to being a mere socio-political or spiritual movement.

No basic ecclesial community excludes clergy. On the contrary they want them to be present, not just as members or persons who accompany them, but more so because of their ministry. This is about presiding over the community of love, especially in the celebration of the eucharist. The majority of basic ecclesial communities were, after all, started by a priest or bishop.

11. Following the conference at Santo Domingo (1989), pressure was exercised to have the basic ecclesial communities classified as merely a type of movement. This favoured the position that they formed part of a general network of communities and movements, which, of course, created ambiguity. It seems that at Santo Domingo there was the intention to use generalised terms to facilitate the approval of the documents.

12. More recent papal documents approve the basic ecclesial communities and no longer warn them about good behaviour within the church – which they never did with movements, although some would have certainly deserved it! They even praise the basic communities. Nevertheless they do not favour the line that they be a fundamental church cell in which the baptised live their experience of community and mission. At the moment we can say that basic ecclesial communities are considered 'normal' provided they are spoken of as part of the parish network of communities and movements.This could well be providential insofar as it permits them to operate freely in church circles that were previously carefully guarded. Perhaps in this context the basic ecclesial communities will be enabled to show what they truly are. This is my hope, and I feel encouraged by the wise words of Gamaliel: '… let them alone … if this plan is of God, you will not be able to overthrow them …' (Acts 5:34-39).

13. More and more the basic ecclesial communities are to be found in *the world of the poor*, and less in the overall church.

14. It is necessary to assert the ecclesial identity of the basic ecclesial communities through a comprehensive juridical statement that would recognise their theological make-up. This would afford them space irrespective of the likes or dislikes of members of the hierarchy or those around them. They cannot just depend on the 'conversions' of members of the hierarchy, as was the case with Romero, Sandreli, Mendes Arceo, and Bartolome Carrasco. Such a statute could rescue them from being considered as mere optional extras in the church, like movements or associations. And it need not limit their scope as basic ecclesial communities to be a base for experiment that is lithe and diverse.

15. I notice a lack of constant self-criticism on the part of the assessors and members of basic ecclesial communities. This is particularly so with regards to what is linked to their historical identity.

I fear that in some circumstances we run the risk of becoming a hired vehicle that allows varied groups and tendencies which have something in common with the communities to come on board. This they do to take advantage of the strength of the communities, in order to communicate some message. The groups have a social clout that they themselves do not possess. It can also happen that we have preconceived, church-related ideas against groups, persons, movements, certain members of the hierarchy, and so forth. Let us be open to any criticism that comes our way.

Seven points that emerge regarding basic ecclesial communities:
1. The basic ecclesial communities are not a parallel church, but they are an alternative model of church.
2. They are not a point of arrival, but of departure, because the destination is the kingdom of God, not the church.
3. They are church, yet do not exhaust all the possibilities of church.
4. They are a process, not just a happening. Renewal comes from below, reform from above.
5. They are not simply an appendix in the church, but radical heart surgery that calls for a revision of roles, pastoral plans, and ways of operating.
6. They are priorities and not simply activities.
7. They are not only for the poor, but with, from, and like the poor, as was Jesus himself.

Fr José Marins was born in Brazil in 1931 and ordained as a Roman Catholic priest in 1956. He did his theological studies in the Gregorian University, Rome, and has been a member of the theological reflection team of CELAM (Latin American Bishops' Conference) since 1970. Fr Marins served as a theological expert at the Medellin Conference of 1968 and as a facilitator at the 1979 Puebla Conference. From 1973 to 1979, he was a consultant to the Pontifical Secretariat for Christian Unity. Author of many articles and books, he is the coordinator of an itinerant pastoral team serving the Churches of Latin America and the Caribbean for the last 29 years. As coordinator of the team, he has promoted basic ecclesial communities, or small Christian communities, in different parts of the world, including Belgium, Spain, Italy, England, Australia, Asia, and the USA.

Africa

James O'Halloran SDB

During the 1971 Synod of Bishops in Rome, the Africans present noted that small Christian communities already existed in Africa. And this quite independently of what had happened in Latin America. One cannot say for certain where the modern groups began. They sprang up spontaneously throughout the world at roughly the same historical period by spontaneous combustion of the Holy Spirit.[62]

When I first started to work with African communities in 1980, I noted two things that were often lacking. The first was that the members were not clear on a vision that accompanied the communities, and then there was no great urgency regarding justice. There was the mistaken notion that where you had a small number of people, there you had a small Christian community. Even among a reduced group you can of course find those who dominate, and this is definitely not community. Or some divided a parish up into zones as if the concept was about territory rather than people. Needless to say, the vision has been clarified during the intervening years.

In 1980 most African countries had been independent for a relatively short period and for the first time in recent history had their own governments. People were happy with this new-found freedom and not overly critical. However, with the passing years they have realised that not only colonisers oppress, but also your own politicians, when corrupt. Meanwhile the church has spoken out and acted in the cause of justice. Nelson Mandela in fact thanked the churches for the role they played in overcoming apartheid; South Africa had of course been politicised for decades on this issue. The Kenyan and Malawian bishops too have since been courageous in opposing oppression in their countries, and just recently the valiant Archbishop Pius Ncube of Bulawayo has condemned abuses of power in Zimbabwe.[63] We could give many more instances. Nor are prophetic documents wanting. The following are examples: *Seeking Gospel Justice in Africa*,[64] *Centenary of Evangelization in Kenya*,[65] *The African Synod*.[66]

The small Christian communities have also stood up on justice issues. According to animators in the field, the groups in Zambia played 'a considerable role' in that country's peaceful transition from one-party state to multi-party democracy. In Kenya too during the 1993 elections some ordinary community members surprised politicians by speaking out on what they felt was for the good of the country. In the past those politicians had been accustomed to dealing with the people through intermediaries such as pastors. One member of parliament even asked pointedly whether father were not present. The people answered no, but that they themselves would discuss the relevant issues.

Significant moments
The following proved encouraging landmarks for the promotion of small Christian communities in Africa, making it clear that they were a priority on the continent:
- the Fifth AMECEA (Association of Member Episcopal Conferences of Eastern Africa) Plenary Conference in Nairobi, 1973,
- Sixth AMECEA Plenary Conference at Nairobi, 1976,
- Seventh AMECEA Plenary Conference at Zomba, Malawi, 1979,
- the Apostolic Visit to Kenya by Pope John Paul II, 1980,
- The SECAM (Symposium of Episcopal Conferences in Africa and Madagascar) Assemblies at Yaounde, Cameroons, 1981, and Kinshasa, Zaire, 1984,
- the First Plenary session of IMBISA (Inter-Regional Meeting of Bishops of Southern Africa), Chishawasha, Zimbabwe, 1984,
- The pastoral letter of the Kenyan Catholic bishops entitled *Centenary of the Evangelization in Kenya*, 1989,
- the Eleventh Assembly of the AMECEA bishops, Lusaka, Zambia, 1992 ('Small Christian communities are no longer merely an option,' the meeting declared; an expression of conviction rather than a pulling of rank by the prelates),
- The African Synod of Bishops, Rome, 1994. Here the notion of family church emerged and, consequently, the communities received wide support. Bishop Jodo Siloto of Mozambique, for example, '… saw these communities as an expression of African communitarianism, and the only true way of inculturation for the African church. In fact, he said, any pastoral strategy that omitted small Christian communities would be creating a

church without a future.'[67] And Monsignor Patient Kanya-nachumbi of Zaire regarded the communities as 'schools' where we can learn what it means to be church, not just in theory, but in practice. (Synod Bulletin of the Holy See Press Office, no. 22).

• Then there was the visit of Pope John Paul II to the Cameroons, Kenya, and South Africa in September 1995 to launch the document *Ecclesia in Africa (The Church in Africa)* which resulted from the Synod of the previous year. In no. 63 of this Post-Synodal Exhortation the Holy Father reiterated the resolve of the gathering to implement family church. He then goes on to say:

> Right from the beginning, the Synod fathers recognised that the church as family cannot reach her full potential as church unless she is divided into communities small enough to foster close human relationships. The assembly described the characteristics of such communities as follows: primarily they should be places engaged in evangelising themselves, so that subsequently they can bring the good news to others; they should moreover be communities which pray and listen to God's word, encourage the members themselves to take on responsibility, learn to live an ecclesial life, and reflect on different human problems in the light of the gospel. Above all, these communities are to be committed to living Christ's love for everybody, a love which transcends the limits of the natural solidarity of clans, tribes or other interest groups.[68]

I have heard a number of African bishops express sentiments similar to those of Bishop Jodo Siloto above. We can understand what they are saying if we consider the realities of their situation: immense difficulties of transportation and communication, areas of open hostility, volatile political scenes, famine, refugees, the precarious position of missionaries and even of local priests and religious, an acute shortage of vocations to the priesthood and religious life. What can be done in the face of all this but strive to implement small communities that are autonomous, yet linked through the communion of communities? The words of Irenaeus are relevant here: 'Where there are three people, there is the church. Laity will suffice.' And he was not being patronising. After all, through baptism we all become part of a priestly people and even ministerial priests would not make much sense outside of this context. To whom would they minister? For convenience, we speak of 'laity' and 'clergy'; I have to say I'm not comfortable with this terminology. I prefer 'priestly people'; some may be ordained, others designated for specific ministries, but all share in the priesthood of Jesus.

Pastoral Centres

By training animators, pastoral centres have done much to promote the groups throughout Africa. Kenema in Sierra Leone, Gaba in Kenya, and Lumko in Southern Africa would be instances of this. Lumko's outreach programme *Call to Serve* would be a good example of this endeavour. But nowadays many dioceses have their own pastoral centres which also do admirable work in the field. Ave Maria Pastoral Centre, Tzaneen, South Africa would be a good example of this. They do sterling educational programmes there.

Also noteworthy is that the CUEA Institute in Nairobi now offers a Postgraduate Diploma in Forming Small Christian Communities. This is encouraging. Such courses need to be at the heart of third-level curriculums in church-related institutes.

At a conservative estimate there are reckoned to be 10,000 small Christian communities in East Africa.[69] It is true that some of them would be prayer groups at the moment rather than communities, yet they are moving in the direction of becoming family church. Before the troubles there were an estimated 300 cells in Sierra Leone, and in South Africa 70% of the parishes are working towards their establishment either directly or having been inspired by the RENEW programme. On a visit to Zimbabwe a few years ago I was told in one diocese that they had 600 groupings. Unfortunately there are no exact statistics for the continent; hence the sporadic nature of the foregoing. However, one can safely say that there are thousands and thousands of small communities and that their number continues to grow.

Integration in the mainstream

An interesting feature of the African small Christian communities is that they are well integrated into the mainstream church. It is true that the original inspiration came from the bishops rather than the grassroots, and some would consider this a weakness. However, we all belong to the family church and, such being the case, does it really matter where the inspiration comes from? The question is whether or not the people make it their own. My experience leads me to answer yes to this question. This is good, because though reform may come from 'above', renewal can only come from the grassroots. Indeed I feel that it was a pity our missionaries did not go to Africa with a communitarian model of church in the first instance, because traditionally there was a great sense of family and community there even before we arrived. Indeed their strong sense of family and community is the special gift of the African groups to the rest of the world. That communal instinct is under intense pressure nowadays both from within and without the continent; from without there comes an ethos of individualism and economic exploitation, from within the ills mentioned above together with the dire menace of AIDS. Nevertheless the family and the community are still holding fast. As already mentioned, this sense of solidarity often breaks down beyond the level of ethnic group, and here is where Christianity can make a significant contribution. Love extends even to enemies.

Generally speaking the communities throughout the world have remained within the mainstream churches. Some are situated at the heart of these churches, as in Africa, others in the margins. Many feel that the life is to be found in the margins and it is there we must look for renewal. There is the fear that, if the groups are mainstream, they can be absorbed into the institution and manipulated. I doubt it. I have seen many places where the communities are now thriving, yet initially they were warily received by the clergy. The decisive factor was the enthusiasm of the laity. We are entering upon the age of the laity and it is they who will largely shape the church of the future. As already noted, priests are in short supply. 'After all,' I once heard an African bishop say, 'Many of our people are lucky if they see a priest once a year.' Furthermore not only are the small communities manifestations of a fresh communitarian model of church, they can also be powerful instruments for creating it. Once the members take the Bible in their hands, reflect on the word of God, and take responsibility to act upon it, things can never be the same again.

So who is to say whether salvation is in the margins or the mainstream? I don't think we can confine the Holy Spirit to the one or the other. Very likely renewal will come in a variety of ways.

Problems

Finally, the African groups are not without their problems. We have seen something of this already. These are the main issues that preoccupy them:

- the difficulty of involving men,
- how to integrate youth,
- how women are to play their full part,
- problems in finding appropriate leaders,
- finding practical ways to animate the communities,
- wrangles over money,
- what to do about non-sacramental Christians,
- deciding a suitable agenda for meetings,
- and a whole plethora of issues surrounding culture (e.g. tribal divisions, superstition, and so forth),
- more and more the overwhelming problem not only for small Christian communities, but for everyone, is the fact of war and violence, leading to dislocation and death.
- and, then, of course, there is the AIDs pandemic that menaces Africa's very existence; it is the leprosy of modern times that afflicts, not only Africa, but the whole world.

The problem of AIDS in Africa we have already dealt with in our chapter on 'Common Issues' pp. 140-64. There we noted that the small Christian communities are providing a counter-cultural alternative that can lead to a regeneration of Africa. I found them adamant that despite efforts being made to deal with the issue, the only adequate answer lay in marriage fidelity, and self discipline among young people.

More than a strategy

Problems notwithstanding, small Christian communities are at the top of the agenda in Africa. In the African Synod document *Report at the Beginning*, no. 12, Cardinal Thiandoum refers to the small Christian communities as 'a well known African experience.' In *What Happened at the African Synod,* ed. McGarry, the writer notes, however, that there were many parts of the continent where they had not taken root. And where they did exist, they were often seen only as an important pastoral strategy. He goes on to say:

After the Synod they must be understood to be much more – not just a strategy but a way of becoming church that is communion,

the family of God in Africa. This is reflected in the growing cent-
rality of the small Christian communities in the minds of the
fathers and in the documents of the synod. As was seen they
only featured in passing in the *Outline*; by the end of the synod
they were understood to be essential if the synod is to take root
in the local churches and thus be effective and produce fruit.[70]

So at the African Synod we saw the bishops of a whole continent
opt for the communitarian vision of church proposed by Vatican II.
Hopefully we will soon see the episcopal conferences of all continents do likewise.

Asia

Bishop Thomas Dabre

I attended the International Consultation on Small Christian Communities in Bolivia, 1999. January 2000 found me at the Seventh Plenary Assembly of the Federation of Asian Bishops' Conferences (FABC), held in Bangkok, and at the General Assembly of the Asian Integrated Pastoral Approach (AsIPA) at the same venue in October 2000. From the deliberations of these assemblies it is clear that during the last thirty years systematic efforts have been made in different parts of the Asian continent to set up small Christian communities (variously called basic Christian communities, basic ecclesial communities, neighbourhood communities ...).

Already in 1990, the Asian Bishops had declared, 'The church in Asia will have to be a communion of communities, where laity, religious and clergy recognise and accept each other as sisters and brothers. They are called together by the word of God which, regarded as a quasi-sacramental presence of the risen Lord, leads them to form small Christian communities (e.g. neighbourhood groups, Basic Ecclesial Communities and 'Covenant' Communities). There, they pray and share together the gospel of Jesus, living it in their daily lives as they support one another and work together, united as they are "in one mind and heart".' (FABC – Bandung Conference, 1990).

In his post-synodal apostolic exhortation *Ecclesia in Asia*, Pope John Paul II says, '... drawing on their pastoral experience, the Synod Fathers underlined the value of basic ecclesial communities as an effective way of promoting communion and participation in parishes and dioceses, and as a genuine force for evangelisation. These small groups help the faithful to live as believing, praying and loving communities like the early Christians (cf. Acts 2:44-47; 4:32-35). They aim to help their members to live the gospel in a spirit of fraternal love and service, and are therefore a solid starting point for building a new society, the expression of a civilisation of love. With the Synod, I encourage the church in Asia, where possible, to consider these basic communities as a positive feature of the church's evangelising activity' (N.25). From the Holy Father's words it is quite clear that the small Christian communities are:

- an effective means for living the Christian life;
- a way of promoting communion and participation in the parishes and dioceses;
- a force for evangelisation.

The FABC (Federation of Asian Bishops' Conferences) has been promoting the renewal of the church in Asia for the last thirty years. Indeed the Final Statement of the Seventh FABC Plenary Assembly, Samphran, Thailand, 3 January 2000, summarises their intentions well: 'In the Asian church there is a movement toward an authentic community of faith. Fully rooted in the life of the Trinity, the church in Asia has to be a communion of communities of authentic participation and co-responsibility, one with its pastors, and linked to other communities of faith and to the one and universal communion of the holy church of the Lord. The movement in Asia toward Basic Ecclesial Communities (small Christian communities) expresses the deep desire to be such a community of faith, love and service and to be truly a communion of communities open to building up Basic Human Communities.' Noteworthy here is the expectation that the influence of the communities is expected to extend beyond the purely religious sphere. The bishops continue their statement: 'An effective means for our mission of love and service, will continue to be the Basic Ecclesial Communities, small gospel-based communities and ecclesial movements. The vision of a new way of being church , promoted by the FABC, is proving to be a great help in the growth and development of the Basic Ecclesial Communities and deserves our attention and support. Ecclesial movements, duly discerned by the local church with its hierarchy can also offer specific and creative contributions to the being and ministry of the church.'

The FABC has been promoting the small Christian communities through AsIPA (Asian Integral Pastoral Approach) which seeks to further a participatory church on the continent. The terms of the process we explain as follows:

- *Asian:* This involves implementing the Asian Bishops' vision and helping Christians of the continent to face Asian life in the light of the gospel. The universal church realises itself through local churches. These are characterised by their own circumstances and cultures. In order to provide the fullness of life that Jesus Christ imparts, the local situations and customs must be taken seriously and responded to appropriately. The small

Christian communities in Asia must tune into the concrete realities of that continent.

- *Integral:* This means that a balance be maintained between the spiritual and the social, the individual and the community, between hierarchical leadership and the co-responsibility of the laity. In the groups all the sections of the church, namely, bishops, clergy, religious and laity, fully participate. This ensures the involvement of all, which is expected in the common mission of the church. Because of lay involvement in the working of small communities, the social dimension of the mission is better taken care of, as the teaching of the church consistently demands.
- *Pastoral:* The laity receive training for their pastoral mission in church and world. The bishops along with the clergy are responsible for the pastoral life. They must exercise their authority with the collaboration of the faithful who are also required to be actively engaged in the mission of the church. The laity too are endowed with the charisms of the Holy Spirit and should, therefore, be given appropriate formation so as to develop the skills and gifts, which they use in furthering the kingdom of God.
- *Approach:* AsIPA texts are centred on Christ and community. The method inspires people to develop and experience the new way of being church in which all sections work for the mission in a participatory and co-responsible manner. Life in small communities is rooted in sacred scripture. The people discover the meaning of God's word in their lives, and the priests and lay animators inspire the communities to live up to their calling and potential. This approach is not selfish or dictatorial, but communitarian and participatory.

AsIPA Survey

As a result of systematic and sustained efforts over the last thirty years, small Christian communities have been formed in different parts of Asia. The AsIPA Desk of the FABC have conducted a survey of the situation and the following were the responses given from various nations:

- 'People have started to use the Bible ... The small Christian communities have common tasks in the neighbourhood, for example, repairing houses, cleaning roads, constructing buildings...' (*Sri Lanka*).

- 'They listen to the word of God more carefully. On account of cultural homogeneity the workings of the small Christian communities is smooth in Myanmar. In general our people have a close relationship with one another in accordance with their culture and tradition, and this makes it easier to introduce the groups. Neighbours already living in harmony with one another are a great help when gathering for gospel sharing and helping those who are in need. They feel united because socially, economically, and politically they are in the same situation.' *(Myanmar)*
- 'The word of God has become dear and meaningful to them; they have started to pray spontaneously.' *(India)*
- 'Participation of the people in liturgy and in other church matters has increased. Folk take more responsibility as members of the parish.' *(Bangladesh)*
- 'Through a short evaluation during a workshop and a longer one afterwards, we have been able to share our experience, make constructive improvements in both preparation and general presentation, and spot potential leaders and activities in each parish. We have been able to learn from, and feel that we need, each other, both for support and in carrying out this program. A sense of comradeship has grown among us, so that our lay members are open and critical with our clerical participants in a sense of common mission. All have found working as a team to be an enriching and challenging experience.' *(Indonesia -- words of Fathers Frans Kopong Kung and Eugene Schmitz SVD)*
- 'There is more concern for each other as members of the same community, especially in times of sorrow. Some small Christian communities are involved in inter-religious and inter-racial movements. Their members are more approachable and willing to share and open their houses.' *(Malaysia)*
- 'There is unity, cooperation and concern for others.' *(Philippines)*

The Philippines
Small Christian communities in the Philippines are of course helped by the fact that most people are Christian. Among others, they readily take up socio-political and economic issues. Indeed they have many success stories to tell about their social struggle (cf. FABC Papers, No. 921, p. 2). Not least of these would be the part

they played in bringing down the corrupt Marcos regime (1986). In recent history their problems have been like those of Latin America: oppression, cultural alienation, sexual exploitation – the work of Fr Shay Cullen to combat this is well known – environmental abuse, and a desperate need for land reform. They are elaborating an appropriate theology for their situation, not a theology of liberation, but a theology of struggle, accompanied by a Good Friday spirituality of the cross. One of the significant factors in the proliferation of the communities throughout the land has been the presence everywhere of valiant religious sisters some of whom did not hesitate to lie in the path of oncoming tanks in the overthrow of Marcos. Mindanao, Infanta, Quezon, and Nueva Segovia would be places strongly associated with the communities, and some prominent names in their development would be Bishop Labayan of Quezon, Bishop Escaler of Ipel, Bishop Francisco Claver SJ former bishop of Malaybalay, and Archbishop Quevedo of Nueva Segovia.

Korea

During the AsIPA Programme, Bangkok, October 2000, the South Korean participants spoke of the pain of separation felt by the people on both sides of the 38th Parallel. They also related the joyful stories about the reconciliation and reunification of the fortunate few. In such a situation they are promoting concern, interaction, and a spirit of harmony between the two Koreas, North and South, through small Christian communities.

The retired Archbishop of Seoul, Stephan Cardinal Kim, has said: 'A great number of newly-baptised members of the church will leave again unless they find a spiritual home in small communities.' Acceptance and fellowship are characteristic features of the communities. These afford new converts the support and sense of belonging they need in their changed situation.

India

In my own diocese of Vasai, I have set up a special office for the promotion of small Christian communities, and I have visited large numbers of them. These have brought the church closer to the people, resulting in greater harmony among the faithful. The liturgy has become more active, and all participate. It is such a joy to see our young people engaged in organising the celebrations.

Catechesis too evokes a better response in small communities. And the same holds true of dealing with local needs, such as cleanliness in neighbourhoods, protection of the environment and of civic facilities, and so forth.

The town of Vasai was once a peaceful, scenic locality. On account of growing industrialisation and domestic migration the population grew tenfold in a short span. Due to lack of a proper infrastructure, the ecology has been badly damaged and people are forced to live in unhygienic conditions. To protest against growing ecological degradation and demand suitable civic amenities, a community movement was launched. The organisers went to villages and small communities where they conscientised the people at the grassroots on the need to organise and struggle for the values at stake. A systematic plan was made in order to prepare the people. There was an amazing response. From a town of 700,000 people, over 100,000 assembled for a protest rally. For years now the agitation has continued, with some success.

In one community I found that people of other faiths were also mobilised and actively engaged in the community programme. The fellowship which I noticed there was a moving experience of inter-religious harmony.

There are about eight thousand tribal folk in the diocese, who eke out a meagre existence and are neglected and marginalised. I conducted a training session in which we interacted and celebrated with them. Overcoming their shyness and feelings of insecurity they warmly participated in the session with a certain degree of self-confidence. Some of these tribal people contributed out of their poverty to diocesan development projects; I wept as I received their humble, yet high-minded, offerings.

Not alone

Vasai of course is not alone in encouraging small Christian communities. Many dioceses have introduced them. Foremost among them would be those of Bombay, Kottar, Tuticorin, Trivandrum, Alleppey, Mangalore, Pune, Patna, Guntur, and Hyderbad.

Among many others, Bishop Bosco Penha of Bombay and Fr Edwin of Kottar have contributed much to the birth of the groups in our country.

As though to copper-fasten all the statements they have made regarding the communities, the bishops of India had this to say in their latest pronouncement: 'Since the small Christian communities ensure a participatory, active, vibrant and evangelising church, they should become a pastoral priority for the entire church of India, as mentioned time and again, especially by the recent National Assembly of Yesu Krist Jayanti, Bangalore, 2000. While recognising the important place that ecclesial movements and associations have in the church, they are called to a fuller understanding of their collaborative role in relation to small Christian communities ... In the Indian multi-cultural, multi-religious contexts, small Christian communities, while preserving their ecclesial identity, should network with all people to promote and nurture small human/neighbourhood communities that usher in a society based on love, justice, peace and harmony' (XIII Plenary Assembly of the Conference of Catholic Bishops of India, 2001).

China

The story of the communities in China , as related by Raymond Fung,[71] is amazing. We might have thought that everything Christian was destroyed by the persecution of Mao. Not so. When he disappeared off the scene and the situation eased somewhat, house churches, animated by lay people, surfaced in that great country – house churches whose faith was all the deeper for the untold hardships they had endured for long bitter years. There are, of course, small communities in Hong Kong.

Other nations

Besides the countries already mentioned, the communities are to be found in East Timor, Japan, Laos, and Pakistan. So the groups are widespread on the continent of Asia.

Further key meetings

In the course of this contribution on Asia, we have mentioned recent international gatherings. Here we add some earlier ones. Conscious that the church was essentially 'communion-koinonia, a people made one with the Father, the Son, and the Holy Spirit,'[72] Asian bishops encouraged small Christian communities in a number of assemblies:

- The Asian Colloquium on Ministries in the Church, Hong Kong, 1977,
- International Mission Congress, Manila, 1979,

- The Second Bishops' Institute for Missionary Apostolate of the Federation of Asian Bishops' Conferences, Ponmudi, Trivandrum, 1980 (limited to the countries of South East Asia: Pakistan, Bangladesh, Sri Lanka, and India),
- The Bangalore Seminar on Basic Christian Communities, 1981,
- The Third Plenary Assembly of the Federation of Asian Bishops' Conferences, Samphran, Thailand, 1982.

In general the cause of the small community has been furthered by pastoral centres. In this context it is worth mentioning the East Asian Pastoral Centre in Manila which has done much to propagate the idea.

It is clear, then, from the Asian experience that small Christian communities lead to a church where there is participation, a church that makes Jesus known, and a church which is vibrant. As John Paul II states, they help create a society based on love, justice, peace, and harmony (*Ecclesia in Asia*, 25).

Networking

In Asia the Christians are a mere blip on the radar screen. Hardly 3.5% of the 3.2 billion population. Many are the faiths and cultures in the vast continent, which is also beset with enormous social, economic, political, and cultural problems. Given this situation, for an effective Christian life, the small Christian communities must network with all people and organisations that strive for social reconstruction and renewal. This regardless of creed. As we know from the troubles in many parts of Asia – India, Sri Lanka, Pakistan, the Holy Land, Indonesia, and the Islamic nations of the Middle East – fanaticism, fundamentalism and tribalism are growing. It would be disastrous for Christians to live and work in isolation from others. To overcome these problems collaboration is vital.

Small human communities

In a globalised world, Asian countries too are becoming increasingly multi-religious and multi-cultural. Numerically, as we have said, Christians are insignificant. In such an overwhelmingly non-Christian context the faithful are called to be the light of the world and salt of the earth. This is why in Asia the small Christian communities must be seen to be small human communities as well. Anyway, being a good Christian is tantamount to being a good human. In fact there are small Christian communities who strive and hope to project themselves as worthy human communities in different parts of the continent. While being faithful to Christian revelation and the mission of the church, these people interrelate and interact with those of non-Christian faiths and disparate cultures round about them. With these they form small human communities. In these communities they live in solidarity with all people, sharing their joys and sorrows, concerns and aspirations. Together they work for justice and peace. They also engage in inter-religious dialogue with a view to promoting respect for different faiths and cultures while, at the same time, witnessing to their own creed. Though Christians participate in them, the small human communities are a distinct experience from small Christian communities. In a climate of growing religious violence and tribalism, such human communities do much to foster the religious tolerance and harmony so badly needed in the situation.

Inculturation

Ever since Vatican Council II, the church has been insisting on the need for inculturation. This would mean making the gospel flesh and blood in the area in which we find ourselves. John Paul II has clearly stated that, though Jesus was born on Asian soil, he is perceived as western in Asia. The spreading of the good news has had its limitations and failings, because we lacked respect for native Asian cultures and did not sufficiently inculturate Christianity. To make matters worse, globalisation has undermined and endangered local ways of life. The small Christian communities promote an ongoing dialogue with folk of other cultures, especially with the poor and marginalised. Such a dialogue is sure to facilitate the inculturation of the Christian faith in Asia and manifest other aspects of the one universal church, making her mission more meaningful as suggested by the Holy Father in his post-synodal exhortation.

The normal way

On account of their relevance and effectiveness, the small Christian communities are regarded more and more as the normal way of being church today. The large parish set-up will surely continue, but it has to be complemented by the communities if it is to succeed in its mission. Through such groups pastors and others engaged in ministry are in direct contact with persons and localities that would otherwise be in danger of neglect in the traditional organisation. In contemporary society, which seems to grow ever more individual-istic and materialistic, many suffer from isolation, stress, and loneli-ness, leading often to spiritual emptiness and psychological disor-ders. This happens not only where there is poverty, but also in the midst of affluence. Obviously the small Christian communities can offer the solace, support, and spiritual nourishment that this situa-tion calls for.

Formation in the faith
To remain firmly grounded in the faith in a highly secularised, indifferent and relativistic society, proper formation in one's reli-gion is necessary. Effective catechesis and the opportunity to expe-rience the Christian way of life can be adequately provided by the communities.

Scientific and technological progress have, unfortunately, led to much immorality. There is violation of human rights, degradation of human dignity, and a culture of death in the form of abortion, euthanasia, oppression, and terrorism. The church's social and ethi-cal teachings are vitally important in society at present. The rele-vant knowledge can best be provided and social consciences formed through small human communities.

Church personnel, therefore, should work through the small Christian communities as a normal way of performing their min-istry. And the faithful should also be ready to welcome the small communities together with the parish set-up.

Working together
The various organisations, associations, and movements in the parishes will obviously have to continue, as these are making a pre-cious contribution to the growth and vitality of the church. But they should not work in isolation from the small Christian communities and small human communities. Nor should they ignore them. It is becoming clear that all these must work in harmony and coordinate their efforts to build the kingdom of God.

Leadership

The small Christian communities require a new style of leadership. They are cells of the church which shift the perspective from the traditional parish to the lives of people at the grassroots in their concrete circumstances. The leadership of pastors and all their collaborators has to synchronise with the needs of the small communities. There must be active involvement with the lives and issues of the people. Leaders cannot maintain their distance from those they serve. They are animators who respect and trust persons as responsible partners in the mission of the church; they are ever mindful of the baptismal dignity and Christian vocation of the faithful. Domination is not their way, rather do they enable folk to live up to their Christian calling and potential. The leader is, then, a facilitator and not the one who knows everything and, consequently, dictates and commands, conscious in a self-centred manner of his juridical authority.

In virtue of baptism and confirmation, every Christian is a member of the mystical body of Christ. As members of this body, all are endowed with fundamental equality though their functions are different. Nevertheless everyone is called to build the one body of Christ, and each has an active role in promoting the kingdom. The small Christian communities are an effective means in achieving all of this.

For a sound pastoral ministry a narrowly spiritual approach or mere good intentions are not enough. The world is fast changing, so training and planning for ministry are crucial.

Since Vatican II, parish councils have been set up worldwide. The trend in various parts of Asia is to elect animators and pastoral agents from the small communities to parish councils. These folk are able to present a valid picture of the situation in the parish, which helps in the planning process and, especially, in deciding upon priorities. Implementation at the grassroots is also more likely in such a scenario.

Conclusion

There is a new dynamism in the Asian church because of small Christian communities. Pastors are more people-oriented, and the laity are becoming increasingly aware of their Christian calling. The results are that charisms are being released, problems addressed,

210 SMALL CHRISTIAN COMMUNITIES

and a spirit of joy and fellowship prevails in the church. The model of communion of communities is also taking shape, a communion that cherishes a vision of a better life for all people regardless of race or creed, a communion in which all are missionaries.

Dr Thomas Dabre is Bishop of Vasai (a diocese carved out of the Bombay Archdiocese) and Secretary General of the Conference of Catholic Bishops of India. He is a member of the conference's Doctrinal Commission and chairperson of its Committee for Inculturation (Western Region). Bishop Thomas was formerly professor at the Papal Athenaeum, Pune, and is a Marathai scholar. The Vasai diocese has a committee of thirty five animators (laity, religious, and priests), representing most of the parishes, which plans and reviews the work of small communities. A permanent office for the promotion of the groups with a full-time director and secretary has been organised at the diocesan centre. A bulletin on the groups is published regularly and has run into ten volumes, while a book on the functioning of small Christian communities in Vasai has also been produced. As bishop, Dabre undertakes visits to towns and rural and tribal areas to encourage the groups.

Oceania

Paul O'Bryan

The region of Oceania encompasses the territorial areas of Australia, Melanesia, Micronesia, and Polynesia and countries such as New Zealand, Papua New Guinea, Tonga, Samoa, Fiji, the Solomon Islands and Guam, to mention a few of the island nations.

Among the people who call Oceania home are the Australian aborigines, who are the direct descendants of the oldest surviving civilisation on earth. It is also home to the descendants of indigenous people who took to the seas and settled islands that were some of the last regions of the world to be populated. Today, Oceania is home to a diverse multicultural mix of peoples: indigenous peoples, descendants of the European colonisation of the Oceania region, and people who have emigrated to Oceania from all other parts of the world. Geographically, the region is as diverse as its peoples: small tropical islands and coral atolls surrounded by thousands of square miles of ocean; mountain ranges so rugged and dense with jungle that only narrow walking trails connect isolated tribal villages; modern industrial cities and coastal settlements; snow covered mountain ranges; large areas of rural and farming land; vast inland deserts and salt lakes; tropical rain forests; wetlands and native bush lands.

A new way of being church

It is in these diverse settings – across the whole of Oceania – that people gather together to experience a new way of being church, as members of small Christian communities (SCCs). For some, the opportunity to join a small Christian community is new, while for others, the small community experience has been one they have lived for nearly three decades. In some places, it is the mainstream churches that are facilitating the establishment of SCCs, while in others, people are beginning to seek a more meaningful and relevant experience of church by gathering in small communities and house churches.

The greatest challenge that I have experienced in writing this profile has been deciding what to include and what not to include. There is not just one Oceania story. There are many different stories and all I can hope to do is open a small window into a selection of those stories, knowing full well that the majority are being left untold. They are stories that come from many countries and different settings. Stories that have been shaped in the experiences and carried in the memories of people of different races, cultures, and denominations. They are the stories of individual communities, parishes, and in some cases, entire dioceses. Each one is unique. Each one is a treasure in itself, and to my mind, each little story is an essential part of the telling of the whole.

In 1999, a lengthy BEC poem was written in the Archdiocese of Adelaide (Australia). A small part of that poem captures, for me, the spirit of the small Christian community phenomenon in Oceania:

There is a growing recognition
That being church means being part of a eucharistic community
That calls us out to others,
Especially those who are struggling,
That community is the richest experience of life
And that we are missing out on this great treasure
Because we don't know our people.

Except we do.
They are our partners
Our children
Our sisters
Our brothers
Our friends
Our neighbours.

BEC Poem
Cathy Whewell and Susan Holoubek
Archdiocese of Adelaide

Different models and methods
Small Christian communities have had an enormous impact in the recent history of the Catholic Church in some parts of Oceania for up to 30 years, whereas in other parts, the SCC vision has yet to be promoted or discovered. Small Christian communities have emerged in different locations under a variety of titles such as: small church communities (SCCs), basic ecclesial communities

(BECs), neighbourhood communities, house churches, small faith communities, small island communities and so on, and their growth has been influenced by many different sources of information, different models and methods and a variety of people who have travelled through Australia and Oceania. In particular, the Marin's International Team, Rev Arthur Baranowski, the South African Lumko Institute, the Movement for a Better World, Rev Jim O'Halloran SDB, Bernard Lee SM and Michael Cowan, Dr Ian Fraser and Jeanne Hinton. In some parts of Oceania, SCCs are an essential part of mainstream churches, while in others, SCCs are viewed with wariness. Various forms of SCC have emerged in different Christian denominations and also in the margins of the mainstream churches. (This term was used and explained by Terry Veling in his recent book, *Living in the Margins*.) In addition, a broad network of house churches also exists across some parts of Oceania and is networked through the Oikos Network. However, without a detailed study or survey of SCCs across the Oceania region, it is impossible to accurately describe the scope of SCC development throughout the area, nor the exact nature of many existing groups.

The data that I am able to include in this section are available as a result of a broad consultation that I conducted prior to attending an International SCC Consultation in Bolivia in November 1999. The following paragraphs provide concrete information about some of the Oceania stories that can be told:

Tonga, Cook Islands, Samoa, New Zealand, Papua New Guinea
From Tonga, Bishop Soane Foliaki writes (28.7.99): 'In our diocese small Christian communities have been in existence for at least 20-25 years. They came into being soon after Vatican II in the efforts to build up a sense of community, to enable and empower each baptised person to live out their baptismal gifts and to give people a sense of ownership of the church. Each of the small communities has an evangelisation team who visit homes and have Bible sharing and prayer with some of the families who come together in one of the homes. They also have teams for education in Christian living and they provide adult education and catechesis for the children. In most parishes, the small Christian communities are flourishing. Much depends on the parish priest and the community leaders.'

From the diocese of Rarotonga in the Cook Islands, Bishop Stuart

O'Connell SM writes (3.8.99): 'The diocese is made up of fifteen island parishes. The majority of our parishes would come under the description of a small church community. We have six priests for these fifteen parishes, three of whom are over 70 years old. Travel to the isolated islands is infrequent, erratic and expensive. Some parishes see a priest only once every one or two years. Each island or atoll is organised by a catechist and his wife and these people organise the Christian community – the small island community.'

From Samoa-Apia, Cardinal Pio Taofinu'u writes (12.7.99): 'Ecclesial communities in a parish are divided into basic Christian communities. Each village, under the leadership of married catechists, becomes a basic Christian community.'

In New Zealand, there are various indications that people have endeavoured to build SCCs based on the Lumko and Movement for Better World models for many years; however, without detailed information, I am unable to offer specific examples of these. New Zealand is a country of about 3.5 million people with six Catholic dioceses. Patrick Dunn, Bishop of Auckland (11.3.99), describes a network of over 20 'Samoan' communities comprising 50-100 families and, in Auckland itself, St Benedict's Parish, under Fr Paul Rankin OP and Sr Mary Anna Baird OP, has successfully developed a network of small groups as a basis for their SCCs.

Don Brebner of Tauranga, in the diocese of Hamilton, writes (6.4.99): 'Our Pastoral Plan calls for a major effort in all parishes – in fact, in all dioceses – to launch a small groups program in 1999/2000 to be named Renew 2000 and to use this, hopefully, as a major launching pad for SCCs thereafter.' Perhaps we can look to a broader and more systematic approach to the establishment of SCCs across the dioceses of New Zealand sometime in the near future.

In an informative and practical book entitled *Community: Give It A Go!* Pauline O'Regan and Teresa O'Connor tell of what was done by a small group of community workers in a city suburb; this is a story set within the wider context of a network of small Christian communities within the parish of North East Christchurch, New Zealand. And casting their glance even further afield, the writers note correctly the connection between what their group is doing, and the work of such secular bodies as the Picot Committees, Maori Access, and area health boards. These initiatives they would undoubtedly support.

Gayle and Geoff Stevens have long been involved with the Kodesh Community in Auckland and, more recently, with the Orama Fellowship on Great Barrier Island which has set about an important rebuilding process.

In Papua New Guinea, the development of a SCC vision, at both parish and diocesan levels, has been an essential part of the growth of many dioceses over the last three decades. In November 1978, representatives of many of the 18 dioceses of Papua New Guinea gathered in Goroka for a broad ranging Consultation on Basic Christian Communities. In an eight page concluding document, the building of small Christian communities was spelt out as the pastoral priority for the church of Melanesia at that time. Part Three of this document describes the essential qualities of the small Christian community:

A Small Church Community has all the characteristics which belong to any human community. It is small enough to allow social interaction on a face to face basis. Its members realise that they depend on each other in a spirit of trust and sharing. It is a people-centred community in which everyone can be responsible. It analyses its needs, plans for activity, and finds its own ministers to meet these needs. Conscious of its Christian mission, it is a community which is opened out in service to all other communities. Its common prayer life is nourished on the word of God and expressed in the eucharistic liturgy.

As a result of the SCC Consultation, a broad range of SCC initiatives has been developed and tested throughout Papua New Guinea and the Solomon Islands. The major influences for these initiatives seem to have come from the missionary priests and religious, the Philippines, the Lumko Institute in South Africa and the Movement for a Better World. The Movement for a Better World, through its Community Animation Service (CAS) offers the Project for Renewal of the Parish (PRP) and the Project for Renewal of the Diocese (PRD). Both of these projects have been widely adopted by dioceses and parishes of Papua New Guinea – particularly in the dioceses of Daru/Kiunga, Mount Hagen, Wewak, Gizo, Madang, and Kundiwa. The diocese of Alotau has worked for many years using the Lumko Approach and in Port Moresby, the establishment of small Christian communities and the training of their leaders is supported through the Port Moresby Pastoral Centre.

Stephen Reichert OFM Cap, Bishop of Mendi, writes: 'There was a time when we tried to introduce basic Christian communities in a more traditional sense, small groups of fifteen or twenty individuals within the various outstations themselves. These groups were to pray together, hold discussions about the needs of the community and church and so forth. This approach never really caught on except in the sense of being small prayer groups. Here, real concerns of life are dealt with at the village community level by all the members of the community and to break that natural unit up is to try to impose something artificial. So now we think of the whole Christian community of an outstation as being a basic Christian community unit, even if the that community numbers in the hundreds. Many of these communities are in the 50 -150 range including children.

'Each community has various lay ministers providing leadership and pastoral care for the Christian community. They may also exert a certain amount of influence in the wider community. There is the catechist who acts as a teacher and pastor of the group. There are prayer leaders, ministers to the sick, church committees, youth leaders and worship leaders. All of these lay ministers make up the pastoral team, which is charged with the care of the whole Christian community. In this sense, the pastoral team is a basic Christian community, or small Christian community, within the larger basic Christian community of the outstation.'

Fr Salvator Dougherty OFM Conv, at St Martin's Pastoral Centre in Aitape, did trojan work to promote small Christian communities. Even as he was dying of a brain tumour, he did not stop working. Together with his religious and lay collaborators this courageous priest formed hundreds of animators of small Christian communities down the years. Sal, who has since died, received training himself at the Kenema Pastoral Centre in Sierra Leone, while trying to convince all his friends there regarding the invincibility of the All Blacks on the rugby field! Fr Eduardo and Sr Quentin, both missionaries, carried on the good work for some years. It is now in capable local hands. The area was deeply affected by a tidal-wave disaster a few years ago.

Australia
In Australia, there have been some very significant efforts to pro-

mote and establish small Christian communities, but these are generally more recent than in other parts of Oceania. The trend toward a small Christian community or 'small church' experience is not huge, but amongst a range of different trends that have been experienced by the traditional churches, the move is significant. The desire for small church has inspired the emergence of many individual communities both residential and non-residential across all Christian denominations. It has inspired people to gather in communities in the margins of the mainstream churches. It has inspired the formation of small Christian community networks and it has inspired the development organisations and projects that have been specifically created to foster and support the establishment of small Christian communities under a diverse range of titles such as, small church communities, basic ecclesial communities, small groups, cell churches and so on. Some of these include:

• *The Movement for a Better World:* The MBW has spread throughout Australia over the last 20 years or so. Currently, there are 24 parishes ranging over eight dioceses that are involved in the Project for the Renewal of the Parish, which envisions the establishment of basic Christian communities as an end goal to the endeavour.

• *Communities Australia:* 'Communities Australia' – A Christian Community Networking Newsletter was founded by Rev Jim Cranswick in 1987 following a two-day workshop on SCCs that was conducted by Jim in Melbourne. In October 1989, the first National Gathering on Small Christian Communities was held in Sydney and was sponsored by Communities Australia and the Paulian Association. Terry Veling was instrumental in the organisation of this gathering. This was the first assembly of its kind anywhere in Australia. It brought together about 250 people from all over the country in an ecumenical setting and was led by Doctor Michael Cowan – co-author of *Dangerous Memories -- House Churches and our American Story.* From that point on, a small editorial team led by Jim Cranswick of Melbourne promoted the Communities Australia vision until it became a national and international movement by:
-    telling stories about Australian communities and people's efforts to establish them:
-    helping to connect people across a diverse range of community-based movements and facilitating conversations;
-    sharing information about SCC initiatives and developments –

both in Australia and around the world;
- providing good theological articles and a forum for dialogue on community issues;
- giving publicity to SCC gatherings and community-based work-shops, consultations and conferences;
- sponsoring overseas visits from key SCC people.

The significance of Communities Australia – the magazine and the movement bearing the same name – for the development of SCCs can never be underestimated here in Australia. For while different movements and organisations began to develop and promote SCCs in a systematic way, Communities Australia always held the ground, where anyone could pitch a tent and tell their story, regardless of their denomination or connection to mainstream church.

In 1997, the Paulian Association of Sydney took over the publication of the Communities Australia newsletter and in 1998 sponsored a Second National Gathering in Sydney, which was based around a story-telling theme. The book, *A Story Book of Australian Small Christian Communities*, was published in conjunction with this gathering.

• *Oikos:* Oikos is an instrument for networking that seeks to provide a means of support, communication and information sharing for a diverse range of small communities and house churches which exist across Australia. This ministry is focused through the Oikos newsletter, which had its origins in Melbourne in 1991, under the inspiration of Bessie Pereira. Bessie continues to edit the newsletter with the help of a support team and continues to promote house churches by visiting them and supporting their establishment and ongoing growth. Since 1991, there have been three National Gatherings of House Churches in Australia.

• *The Australian Small Groups Network:* The ASGN grew out of the extraordinary vision and networking efforts of John Mallison, who is the author of the well known book, *The Small Group Leader*. The network is supported by a national committee and state committees, which co-ordinate its efforts to actively promote and support a small group approach to church: community groups, ministerial groups, recovery groups, cell church groups, youth groups and so on. The ASGN supports small group initiatives across all Christian denominations. State committees co-ordinate a networking facility among affiliated members, publish regular newsletters and conduct conferences for small group development and leadership training.

• *The Melbourne SCC Steering Committee:* The Melbourne SCC Steering Committee currently functions to promote, foster and support the establishment of small church communities throughout the Catholic Archdiocese of Melbourne and across Australia in general. The Steering Committee comprises priests, religious and lay people, who are committed to the development of SCCs and is representative of all four regions of the Archdiocese of Melbourne. It supports the development of a wide range of SCC models and methods and this approach evolved from the work that was developed by Sr Joan Power PBVM and Paul O'Bryan at the Catholic Pastoral Formation Centre (CPFC) of the Archdiocese of Melbourne. For nearly 10 years, beginning in 1990, CPFC sponsored a Project for the establishment of small church communities in the Catholic parishes of Melbourne and in this time, CPFC had a significant impact on the development of SCCs across Australia. Today, nearly 40 of the 235 parishes of Melbourne either have SCCs, or are moving toward their establishment. The work that began through CPFC is now being carried forward by the Melbourne SCC Steering Committee and Southern Cross Communities, a resource and training centre for SCC development, established by Paul O'Bryan in 1997.

• *The Basic Ecclesial Community Office of the Archdiocese of Adelaide:* (We recall here that basic ecclesial community, or BEC, is an alternative form of SCC.) In 1988, following the Adelaide Diocesan Pastoral Renewal program, Archbishop Leonard Faulkner issued a statement to the priests of the diocese in which he presented his vision of leadership for the people of the local church. In that statement, he named small Christian communities as a central part of the strategy of leadership formation in the diocese. This development emerged from a strong tradition of Cardijn-inspired movements like YCW and YCS and the Adelaide based Christian Life Movement, which supported over 100 groups across a wide range of parishes. The office for 'Community for the World' was opened round 1990 to develop and implement a diocesan pastoral plan based on the establishment of basic ecclesial communities. The implementation of this vision proceeded through various stages of development under the direction of Fr Bob Wilkinson and Sr Ruth Egar RSM. Critical to these developments was the challenge to find a way to engage the 100% of Catholics in the parish.

What has emerged is a unique model of BEC development, based on the regrouping of the parish into smaller geographical zones consisting of 100-150 Catholic households. This zone constitutes the BEC. The growth dynamic of the BEC resides in the hands of a neighbourhood pastoral team and home visitors who animate people toward social interaction, faith development and a sense of neighbourliness toward the growth of communal involvement. The Marins International Team has been instrumental in helping to develop this vision and the support of Archbishop Faulkner is reflected in his active involvement in the project and his pastoral teaching on BECs., for example, his pastoral letter of October 1994, titled, *Basic Ecclesial Communities*.

Today, the BEC Office of the Archdiocese of Adelaide is coordinated by Cathy Whewell and it continues to be an important influence for the development of BECs around Australia and into the Oceania region. Fr Bob Wilkinson continues as chaplain to the BECs. Of the 75 parishes in the Archdiocese of Adelaide, 34 are developing the BEC vision.

Various other Catholic dioceses, apart from those already mentioned, have pastoral teams that are actively encouraging the formation of SCCs. This is the case in Brisbane, Bunbury, Perth, Rockhampton, and Townsville. The Canberra team is in fact ecumenical. Bishop Benjamin of Townsville in Queensland has set forth a similar vision to that of Archbishop Faulkner for the people of his own diocese. It is called *The Townsville Experiment*.

• *Cells of Evangelisation:* In the last five years or so, the establishment of Cells of Evangelisation, based on the work of Don Pigi Perini of San Eustorgio of Milan, have begun to emerge in some parishes – particularly of the Diocese of Sale in Victoria. A number of other parishes in other dioceses are beginning to explore this methodology of forming cell churches.

• *The Paulian Association* is based in Sydney and has been promoting, developing and networking SCCs in Sydney and around Australia for over 10 years. Rather than pushing programmes for transforming parishes through SCCs, the Paulian Association has sought to work through the grassroots, listening and talking to people who are interested, slowly building awareness of the nature and value of SCCs. As previously stated, the Paulian Association has always had a close connection to Communities Australia and in 1997, took on sponsorship of Communities Australia.

Currently, there are a handful of 'Paulian Groups' which have been going for many years and some SCCs, which have grown out of Paulian initiatives. The Association has created a number of resources to facilitate the starting and running of SCCs and supports the growth of SCCs by sponsoring workshops and seminars for their development.

• *Southern Cross Communities* is an Australian Resource Centre for SCCs and opened in 1997. Paul O'Bryan has written a series of SCC resources and offers these resources together with consultancy and training to support the establishment and ongoing growth and development of SCCs across Australia. [sccobryn@ozemail.com.au]

A profound difference
These examples describe some of the SCC/BEC initiatives that have emerged in Australia over the last two decades, but really only 'scratch the surface' as far as telling the full story of the historical development of small Christian communities in Australia. There are many other individuals and communities that could have been mentioned in this profile and there are many other movements and organisations that work tirelessly for the promotion and establishment of small Christian communities. Each community has its own story to tell and all stories are important. There is no doubt in my mind that one community makes a profound difference in a local neighbourhood or parish. One SCC/BEC parish makes a profound difference in a diocese. And, one diocese, committed to the SCC/BEC vision, serves the whole region as a leaven for the gospel of Jesus Christ.

Note: Full details on books referred to in this section on Oceania together with Paul O'Bryan's own works, are provided in the bibliography.

Paul O'Bryan currently lives in Melbourne, Australia. He is married to Debbie and has three children: Damian 20, Emily 16 and Joshua 15. Paul and family are members of a small church community and Paul is currently the SCC Coordinator in his own parish of Belgrave. Beginning in 1990, he worked for the Catholic Archdiocese of Melbourne for nine years and during that time coordinated a project for the establishment of small church communities in the parishes of Melbourne. In 1995, he was awarded a Masters Degree in Theology for a thesis exploring the theological, ecclesial and pastoral implications of the establishment of SCCs in parishes. In 1997, Paul established Southern Cross Communities as a Resource Centre for SCCs and today utilises Southern Cross Communities as a resource, training and consultancy base for the support of SCCs around Australia. In November 1999, he led the team representing Oceania at the International SCC Consultation in Bolivia. (Note: Paul has now moved to join the Pastoral Planning Team of the diocese of Maitland-Newcastle, NSW.)

Europe

Ian M. Fraser: A Personal Report

A gathering on the island of Iona, Scotland, in August 1999 could provide an introduction to the development of these small communities on the European continent.

First, why Iona? An unlikely place to assemble 18 Central and Eastern Europeans with a slightly larger number of British and Irish representatives. Present in the assembly also from both East and West were members of the European Collective – of which more later – who were conversant with the situation of small Christian communities on mainland Western Europe. But, we repeat, why Iona? A tiny dot of an island on the the edge of Europe, not at all accessible! Sure, it was of special historical and religious significance. There St Columba, a missionary from Ireland, had established his monastic community in 563 AD, whose influence eventually spread the length of Russia. But in that century the sea was like a motorway. The centre of Scotland was difficult territory, with mountains and bogs to daunt any traveller. Iona was not, then, remote.

Modern Iona
That important heritage has been built on. In 1938 the Iona community was founded, with the island as its base. Its leader was Dr George F. MacLeod. I myself have been a member since 1941. For one thing the enterprise stressed from the start that the church needed to reshape its life as a community of communities. For another it put two things in place which anticipated the character of the later development of small Christian communities.

a) Members worked out a discipline of personal devotion and engagement in the world, to which they committed themselves.

b) They met in small family groups as well as plenaries, finding they could go deep into the faith and get deep with one another if two or three (actually eight or ten) were gathered, with Christ in their midst. From the earliest days they thought of themselves as a 'John the Baptist sign', the precursor of a significant advent, no more, no less.

Hungary

The Hungarians who took part in the Iona August '99 gathering came not only from Hungary itself but from regions around Hungary. Before my wife Margaret died we had twice been in Hungary, trying unsuccessfully to make contacts. The communists were in occupation at the time, the early 1980s. We knew that there were small Christian groups in the underground – as an astronomer knows there is a planet on which he cannot get a telescope focused. The disturbance in the sky around, caused by pulls of gravity, is a sure sign. But we had to be very sensitive in our approaches – otherwise we might have unwittingly led the Secret Police to the small communities. A third visit in 1987, three months after Margaret's death, again seemed to be getting nowhere – when a secretary at a church headquarters intervened quietly. She said she knew the link-person for the communities and could see if he were free. He met me, and I was hooked into 6000 small communities which had persisted as a church of the underground, about 5000 of them were Roman Catholic and 1000 Protestant.

After the fall of communism in 1989, I was able to be present at a conference in Budapest where, now established in five networks (one of which, Bokor, went back to 1948), the small Christian communities met. They did so to discern the political and social responsibilities which pertained to the faith which could not have been fulfilled under communism. The groups now number around 10,000. Jim O'Halloran, from the Salesian House in Dublin (we have worked closely together for over two decades) is one of those who have kept open vital links through visits.

Czechs and Slovaks

In 1991, at a conference in Brno, I made contact with Czechs and Slovaks. They had endured severe persecution, but had met in small Christian communities as 'The Church of Silence.' The Vatican gave them a certain freedom to manage their life as far as that was possible under communism, once the contact with Rome was definitively severed. Jesus said of fruit-bearing Christians that the Father prunes them that they might bear more fruit. The Czech/Slovak church (at that time the countries were not divided) pruned back its life to essentials and survived all through that traumatic time. Jesus Christ remained at the centre of their fellowship.

The scriptures sustained them. Prayer and eucharist kept them firm about gospel priorities. Bishop Fridolin, who had been jailed for six years, said, 'You must never invite persecution. But if God gives gifts at a time of persecution, you don't jettison them once the persecution is lifted.' So, when the communists' grip was removed, he and others once again invested in the parish churches; but, with others, he refused to jettison the small Christian communities, as traditionalists had wanted him to do. There were of course other communities apart from those represented by the Bishop Fridolin, which also had to operate in secrecy. Representatives from both the Czech Republic and Slovakia took part in the Iona gathering. The Church of Silence spoke perceptively.

Poland

The European communities had wanted contact with small communities whom they heard were found throughout Poland in Warsaw, Lodz, Katowice, Ustron and a few other cities. Two Dutch representatives were appointed to accompany Margaret and me to visit in 1986. One of the two Polish delegates on Iona provided testimony to the continuing development of the small Polish communities; her companion was one specially well informed on the relationship of Polish communities to the broader European context in the life of the churches.

Yugoslavia, the Ukraine, Transylvania, Lithuania

Yugoslavia, the Ukraine, and Transylvania participated and contributed. Lithuanian representation was secured through the Craighead Institute. When this pioneering enterprise first made contact, they found that communist influence had dumbed down people, so that they followed routines without establishing relationships.

Teachers in the same school would not know one another's names, would be afraid to step out of line. It was the Craighead approach of working with them in small groups which gave them confidence to break out. Iona was a place to discover other communities on the European continent and set up relationships with them. It proved to be a freeing experience.

Ireland,England, Scotland, The European Collective

Fr Jim O'Halloran was present from Ireland where constructive groups of all kinds, both religious and civil, have according to a recent survey been proliferating. A report is pending which bears this out, but O'Halloran has been reliably informed of the foregoing by Aileen Walsh,[73] a member of the survey team. Some of these are already small Christian communities, while many of the religious groups ('prayer', 'faith-sharing' and so on) are moving in that direction. These groupings at the grassroots are, at the moment, low-key and mostly unconnected – maybe it is a case of relishing space in a country where the institutional church has been traditionally dominant. The survey team felt they were seeing the seeds of a new church.

Representatives from the small Welsh communities were unable to accept our invitation, yet some participants were knowledgeable about them. England had established a coordinating body 'New Way of Being Church' -- this entity, Family Groups and several independent communities were drawn into the Iona consultation. Scotland was represented by the Iona Community itself, family groups, and some others. As already noted, there were a few representatives of the European Collective – well acquainted with the communities in mainland Western Europe.

Western Europe

While Christians in small communities in Eastern and Central Europe had particular problems to face under communist occupation, those in Western Europe went from strength to strength. In my own judgment there was a significant expansion in 1968. The riots and near-revolutions of that year gave traditionalists in the Vatican opportunity to argue that Vatican Council II had loosened up the structures of authority dangerously. It was time to retrench. The response of those who found the work of the council liberating was expressed through a proliferation of small Christian communities, bent on church renewal. Since the very beginning, fresh forms of worship, prayer and a great variety of struggles for justice went hand in hand.

Over the second half of the last century, the development of West European small Christian communities has been impressive. Principal Grainger, then of St Andrew's College, Selly Oak,

Birmingham, England, found it so when he spent some days examining the interviews of 300 communities available in the Baker Library, Scottish Churches House, Dunblane. They derived from every continent. He had been principal of a Baptist College in Brazil and was in a position to compare the Latin American development with the West European. His personal conclusion was that the latter provided more pointers to what the church catholic could become in the future. The West European experience was not too closely bound to hierarchy; it won more space for new venturing.

Italy drew on the insights of Vatican II. In 1984 a team of eleven representatives from British churches spent sixteen days visiting small Christian communities from Turin in the north to Naples in the south. They were particularly struck by the attempt made to forge an understanding of church which differentiated the church 'born from below' from 'the church of power'. The following words stuck in the mind: 'The people of God must be self-convened before the Living-Word-In-Christ, without human masters.'

It was the fear of a restoration of domination by 'human masters' that held up the French development in the early years. Members had suffered greatly from dominating structures in the institutional church. Because of this, attempts to provide regional coordination for small Christian communities, for example in Lyon, were resisted. The fear was that new centres of power might be produced and play a dominating role once more. Over time it became clear that light structures provided means for sharing insights and experiences without the return of church paternalism. Members eventually accepted regional meetings and then even moved forward to benefit from national gatherings.

Great integrity was shown in the search for truthful ways of living. Dutch groups asked themselves what was the essence of Christian discipleship. This in view of the fact that even the word of God and the Mass could be used by clerics as means of control. So where did the essence of Christian discipleship lie? In establishing justice on earth, they concluded. But before too long, they came back to where they had started. 'We don't know what justice is without the Bible. And we are not nourished for struggles without the sacrament,' they said. The courage to question traditions that seemed to founder and yet not lose sight of them, in case there was more to them than they had at first realised, led to a joyful discovery. This was the relation between the quest for justice and Bible and sacrament.

In Austria a somewhat similar discovery concerned who were to be companions-of-the-road. When it became clear that Christians needed to meet in small communities, those concerned invited people who seemed to be compatible. It did not work; maybe it was too cosy. Only when members were sought because they were on a search to live authentically – however diverse, even awkward they might be in their different outlooks – were creative small Christian communities established.

The groups in the Oporto area of Portugal were marked by a gift for sharing. Spare keys were cut so that no one who needed a bed should be short of one. If a member became unemployed, the others reduced their own incomes to the point where these could make up the income lost. In Spain Fr Juan Nieto spoke of the great gift given to the small group who dared to assemble in the underground during Franco's dictatorship, namely, his own imprisonment. It meant that the group had to develop its life as a priestless church. In Louvain-la-Neuve, Belgium, fourth-world small communities developed strongly among those who were at the very bottom of the social heap. Swiss communities came from a well-off backgrounds, yet were equally imaginative.

European coordination

The first coordinating action on a European scale was taken by the Dutch who, in 1983, set up the first Congress of Small Christian Communities in Amsterdam and surrounding areas. At the end of the Congress the need for continuing contact on the European scene resulted in the formation of the 'European Collective', a body with representation from various parts of the continent. Margaret and I were asked to represent Britain on it. Its job was to assess European congresses or seminars and plan forward in the light of experience. Congresses were large gatherings that could exceed a thousand; seminars more cohesive meetings of a couple of hundred. Besides representation from Scotland, England, Ireland and Wales, the following are also participants in the Collective: Austria, Belgium (French and Flemish speaking), Spain – Basque territory – France, Italy, Netherlands, Portugal, Switzerland (German and Romande-speaking). At first, following the watershed year of 1989,

Hungarians and Czechs were a bit dubious about joining the Collective – their experience under communism had been so different from that of West Europeans. But now they are very much part of this coordinating body. An all-European gathering is again in the offing; it will hopefully take place in 2003. These occur at around three year intervals.

Vatican II and the World Council of Churches
I think it should be said that the coming into being of the World Council of Churches and the work of Vatican II had provided space in which the small Christian communities could take root and grow. The whole development is ecumenical in character. My own roots are in the Reformed tradition, yet I have been accepted by and worked with Roman Catholics all over the world. In November 1999, an International Consultation on Small Christian Communities was held in Cochabamba, Bolivia. It was sponsored by the Institute for International Studies, Notre Dame University, Indiana and The Maryknoll Missionary Institute, New York. Fr Jim O'Halloran was asked to bring a delegation from Europe. He found it natural to make a team, to accompany him, of one Roman Catholic, one Anglican, and one Reformed. The small Christian communities are instinctively ecumenical. They appreciate the tradition from which they have sprung. Yet they have a wider vision of church.

Interestingly, at the Cochabamba Consultation it emerged that in the *Instrumentis Laboris* (Working Document) for the European Synod of Bishops 1999, which overlapped somewhat with the Consultation, the communitarian model of church put forward by Vatican II was again proposed as the way forward (cf. nos. 33, 34, 45, 46, 48, 73 for this and closely-related issues).

Noteworthy too, from a European perspective, was a most encouraging statement made by Cardinal Cormac Murphy O'Connor of Westminster in his keynote address to the National Conference of Priests in Leeds, England, on 5 September, 2001:

> Then there are the communities of our parishes and in particular our need for small communities. It seems to me, and I do not think I exaggerate, that most Catholics in the future, apart from their Sunday Mass, will need to belong to some form of small community ... I often think that these small communities are the secret for the future of the church.[74]

Spontaneous combustion

In 1980 I was able to visit communities in Mexico, Guatemala, El Salvador, Nicaragua, Panama and Venezuela. In two of these countries I was asked, 'We hear that there are thousands of small Christian communities also in Europe. How can there be in affluent Europe?' By the time the question was asked, I had got to know the development in the country concerned. Instead of answering in the abstract, I gave stories of small Christian communities that resonated with their own. 'That is astonishing,' came the reply. 'They have a different context of life from ours. They don't have death squads trying to eliminate their young folk. They don't have Molotov cocktails thrown against their back doors or through their windows. But, allowing for the different situation, they are our kin. We are on the same search to live the Christian life, to establish justice. How can this be? We didn't spark them off, they didn't spark us off. The broad Atlantic lies between us!'

In no time we came to this conclusion. We put down the whole proliferation of small Christian communities to spontaneous combustion by the Holy Spirit.

Ian M. Fraser is an ordained minister of the Church of Scotland and a BD, MA, Ph D of Edinburgh University. He became a member of the Iona Community in 1941, and in 1942 went into industry as a labourer/pastor. Later work included 12 years as a parish minister in Rosyth: the establishing of Scottish Churches House in Dunblane as a house of the churches together; working for the World Council of Churches on Laity and Studies and the Participation in Change programme (while here he collaborated with some of the work of Vatican II); and service as Dean and Head of the Department of Mission in Selly Oak Colleges, Birmingham. His pride and joy is his family – wife Margaret (died 1987), three children, and nine grandchildren.

Maritime Mission

Roald Kverndal

A philosopher in ancient times was once asked: 'How many living people are there compared with those who are dead?' The old sage is said to have answered: 'First you will have to tell me where I am to place seafarers – among the living or the dead?' Traces of that thinking have continued through the centuries. Seafarers have all too often been seen as separate beings from the rest of the human race. But seafarers are people just like the rest of us, so they must have our deep concern. They have physical, emotional and spiritual needs like other human beings. The only difference is seafarers follow an incredibly hard, hazardous yet vital vocation.

Who are seafarers?

Precisely who are seafarers in today's world? In Pope John Paul II's 1997 *Apostolic Letter on the Maritime Apostolate*, the subject is identified as 'People of the Sea'. These consist of three categories:

1. Seafarers as such, or those actually on board merchant ships or fishing vessels. The inclusive term is used rather than 'seamen'.

2. Maritime Personnel who, in addition to seafarers, also include seafarers in training or retirement, as well as port and oil rig workers.

3. People of the Sea who comprise not only seafarers and other maritime personnel but also their dependents ashore as well as all regular maritime mission workers

The word *sea* is in this case taken in the very broadest sense, including not only seas and oceans but also inland waters, like lakes, rivers and canals. Of some 15,000,000 seafarers worldwide, currently up to 1,500,000 are merchant seafarers, some 13,500,000 fishers. Of these, 5,000,000 are industrial fishers, the rest traditional fishers serving in coastal or inland waters. With other seafarers' and port workers' dependents, the total number of 'People of the Sea' worldwide is close to 300,000,000.

Why should Christians bother about people of the sea? The answer is simple: Because the Christ whom Christians claim to follow did! He did so implicitly, through two major directives to his followers everywhere. In Christ's Great Commandment (Matthew

22:37-39) his call to love one's neighbour as oneself clearly applied to all fellow-humans, however unlovable (Matthew 25:31-46; Luke 10:25-37). There was not the slightest hint of any exception for sea-farers. Neither was the universal scope of Christ's Great Commission (Matthew 28:18-20) ever at issue. His call to go make disciples of all people made no exception for people of the sea. In his global plan of salvation all were included (Mark 16:15; Acts 1:8).

Christ Gave Them a Unique Role

Nor could Christ have been more explicit in his choice to head his global mission enterprise. By the shores of the Sea of Galilee it was a small band of seafarers he called to be his first followers, and even-tually go with his gospel to the waiting world. In a book about 'Small Christian Communities,' it seems noteworthy that Christ not only based his missionary methodology on the cell group model, but by making that model a maritime small community, he specific-ally singled out seafarers. Why? Two sociological factors seem rele-vant – seafarers' traditional marginality and inherent mobility.

Selecting precisely such a marginalised group was in perfect harmony with Christ's own stated policy. In Luke 4:16-21 we hear how he publicly proclaimed his primary concern for the poor and disadvantaged (cf. Matthew 25:35). Christ's intentional choice of society's so-called 'losers' lies at the very core of his gospel of grace (1 Corinthians 1:26-31; cf. Luke 1:46-55). This is reinforced by Matthew's emphasis on the ethnic origin of those first followers. They were not only seafarers. They were Galilean seafarers, hand-picked from the region the religious elite despised as that low-grade 'Galilee of the Gentiles'. By such a shocking choice of messen-gers Christ reveals the heart of his mission: cross every boundary and accept the unacceptable – bar none! (Cf. 1 Corinthians 1:28; Galatians 3:28).

Again, the basic mobility of seafarers may well have been another important consideration. In an age when modern media were unthinkable, the role of seafarers was indispensable to any form of international communication. Without such 'nautical nomads' there was no way the good news could be conveyed to where it was meant to go – literally to the ends of the earth (Acts 1:8; Romans 10:15). Not only the marginality but also the mobility of seafarers would be crucial to any plan of salvation socially and geographically inclusive enough to be truly universal.

SMALL CHRISTIAN COMMUNITIES

Highlights from History
Biblical Beginnings (Initiation: c. 30-c. 60)

The conclusion is clear. Seafarers did not later on become the bene-
ficiaries of a segment of Christian mission known as 'maritime mission'. It was seafarers Christ called to launch *all* Christian mission,
including maritime mission! The New Testament is replete with
maritime references. Not only from Jesus' ministry, but also from
that of his apostles, not least Peter, 'the Big Fisherman'. Among the
apostles, the role of Paul, 'the Great Missionary,' was remarkable,
given the opportunities his many sea travels offered to share the
gospel with seafarers. This is graphically illustrated in chapter 27 of
the Acts of the Apostles, where Paul's ministry on a storm-tossed
grain-ship bound for Rome around the year 60 AD makes him the
first on biblical record to fill the role of a ship's chaplain.

A Puzzling Pause (Improvisation: c. 60-1779)

Why did nearly 17 centuries roll by before the church of Christ
began developing any specialised organisational structure to reach
seafarers of the world with the gospel? Despite that puzzling pause,
significant sporadic efforts, however improvised and inadequate,
were nevertheless made by the Mediaeval Roman Catholic Church
during this period. There were seagoing priests and monks and
special Masses for those deceased or in peril at sea. Later, the
Protestant Reformation resulted in a flurry of devotional literature
for seafarers, as well as other measures. Still, it was not till the turn
of the 19th century that seafarers of the world would come into
their own, in terms of an organised mission of the Christian church.

The Bethel Movement (Formation: 1779-1864)

When it finally happened, it did not begin by bureaucratic action of
the institutional church but by seafarers themselves. Nurtured by
the burgeoning Bible Society Movement that emerged in both
Britain and America in the late 1700s, seafarers spontaneously
formed a widening network of worshipping and witnessing cell
groups at sea. As the Spirit again 'moved upon the waters' (Gen.
1:2), the 'Seafarers' Mission Movement' first took the shape of maritime small Christian communities, a typical case of self-empower-
ing, grassroots 'mission from below'.

Let us emphasise the significance of this. What we are really saying is that the small Christian communities, which are beginning to prove so significant in the modern church, were already to be found among seafarers in the 1700s!

It was the British wartime navy that saw the first signs of this movement. Scriptures came from the non-denominational Naval and Military Bible Society, founded in London in 1779. This date is now seen as the start of organised maritime mission. It was seasoned 'veterans' of this 'Naval Awakening' who helped ignite a similar cell group movement in Britain's post-Napoleonic wars merchant fleet.

In 1817, while anchored in London's Thames River, some of these latter hoisted their own emblem as a signal for lay-led worship on board. They called it the Bethel Flag (Hebrew for 'House of God'). The effect was electric. In just five years, committed captains and crews carried both the Bethel Flag and the Bethel Movement across the seven seas, leading eventually to maritime mission initiatives on every continent. As one committed sailor put it, simply yet forcefully, 'I cannot go to heaven alone!'

From Sail to Steam (Transition: 1864-1920)
The year 1864 marks the beginning of a distinct geographic expansion from a solely British-American enterprise. That year the Norwegian Seamen's Mission was founded in Bergen, Norway, and was soon succeeded by similar Lutheran-linked organisations in the other Nordic nations. The Germans and Dutch followed with Lutheran-Reformed and Dutch-Reformed organisations in 1886 and 1893, respectively.

Perhaps the most vivid evidence of the advent of a new era was in the means of marine transportation. By the mid-1860s the transition from sail to steam had begun in earnest. Meanwhile, this technological transition, combined with the mid-Victorian theological shift toward stronger social concern, generated a new model of maritime mission. Improvised worship facilities called 'Bethels' were replaced by purpose-built 'Seamen's Institutes', offering a wide range of welfare services.

Dealing with Disunity (Cooperation: 1920-1974)
The year 1920 marks the beginning of another era in maritime mission history. That year in Glasgow, Scotland, three Catholic laymen

initiated what would become the worldwide Apostleship of the Sea (AOS), destined to see remarkable global growth during the decades that followed. With few exceptions, 19th century organised maritime mission had been virtually a Protestant enterprise. From now on, how could Catholics and non-Catholics avoid 'fracturing the face of Christ on the waterfront?'

First Protestants would need to get their own house in order. In Philadelphia in 1932 there finally emerged a North American Maritime Ministry Association (NAMMA). With the cooperative climate resulting from the Second Vatican Council, NAMMA in 1969 invited the AOS to join non-Catholic agencies to form an International Christian Maritime Association (ICMA). Since then, ICMA has made church history, linking maritime ministry in no less than one thousand seaports worldwide.

Responding to Revolution (Globalisation: From 1974)
The institute-based welfare model of maritime mission that emerged during the transition from sail to steam managed to survive the ordeals of two world wars and continue up to the 1970s. Nevertheless, the 'Maritime Christian Fellowship Movement', with its seafarer-centred model of 'mission from below', remained virtually marginalised during the whole of this period – quite a change from the heyday of the Bethel Movement. Its basic concept was simply at odds with the prevailing 'top down' agency-centred institute model. The result was a patronising view of seafarers as passive objects of mission, rather than active subjects of mission, thereby robbing Christian maritime mission of its most powerful potential partner – the Christian seafarer!

But as so often happens, it was darkest before dawn. A new day for the seagoing small Christian community phenomenon. – and for maritime mission as a whole – arrived in the last quarter of the twentieth century. It resulted from the combined effect of the post-World War II global economy and the so-called 'Maritime Industrial Revolution'. But that story belongs to the awesome challenge confronting current-day maritime mission.

The Shape of Today's Challenge
In 1974 the exclusively Western-world monopoly in maritime mission ended with the founding of the first indigenous non-Western

maritime mission agency: Korea Harbor Evangelism in Seoul. Moreover, in the mid-1970s it became clear that maritime mission must now deal with global change in the shipping industry which was more radical than ever before.

The Dual Challenge

Since World War II the tremendous technological breakthroughs in the design and operation of ships have led shipping companies to cut soaring costs by now hiring their crews from the low-cost labour markets of the world's developing countries. This has confronted modern-day maritime mission with two compelling theological issues:

1) Since these seafarers typically have little or no union representation, they have all too often become the vulnerable victims of blatant human rights abuse.

2) Because so many of these seafarers now come from Asia, they are (with the exception of Filipinos) mostly from a non-Christian religious background, deprived of any truly authentic offer of the gospel.

A Dual Response:

1) In 1982 an Anglican-affiliated Center for Seafarers' Rights was founded in New York to work for justice in the name of Christ in the maritime world, with Anglican and Catholic associates later in London and Barcelona, respectively.

2) Beginning in the late 1970s, American Catholics, Baptists and Lutherans, also (from 1982) the indigenous Pusan-based Korea International Maritime Mission, launched programmes for Maritime Follow-up Ministry. In so doing, they have already seen the growth of many hundreds of Asian small Christian communities at sea, reminiscent of the original Bethel Movement – surely a sign of great hope!

How can Small Christian Communities at Sea Make a Difference?

As virtual 'Maritime-Base Communities', seagoing small Christian communities can now offer hope for self-empowerment wherever they encounter dehumanising conditions at sea. Also, through their daily walk of faith and Christian community on board ship, they offer a non-coercive gospel alternative to non-Christian fellow-seafarers. Otherwise these might well be denied their most basic human right – the freedom to choose their own ultimate destiny. Instead, some might even return with a new-found faith to home communities in countries closed to conventional mission.

However, if today's Christian seafarers are to fulfil the mission potential pictured by Christ himself, it will require a fundamental reorientation. While shore-based centres still need to play an important supportive role, recent research in the International Association for the Study of Maritime Mission affirms that the wave of the future belongs to ship-based seafarer-centred maritime mission. 'Without commitment to seafaring disciples as the primary agents of mission in the seafaring world, maritime mission will remain only at the level of welfare services to seafarers' (Paul G. Mooney).

Is a New Bethel Movement, articulated through small Christian communities, underway? Given the fact that most of the earth's surface is covered by the sea, without the people of the sea as active co-workers, how else can the earth one day be 'filled with the knowledge of the Lord, as the waters cover the sea?' (Habakkuk 2:14)? In short, how can the church universal ever become the church triumphant, without the church maritime – and therefore its key component, the seafaring disciple?

Roald Kverndal comes from a Norwegian background and was educated in England. He holds a doctorate from the University of Oslo. Before entering ministry he worked as a merchant seafarer and marine lawyer. Since entering, he has served as seafarers' chaplain in seafarers' centres in many parts of the world. He is President and Co-founder of the International Association for the Study of Maritime Mission (IASMM), former Executive Secretary of the North American Maritime Ministry Association (NAMMA), former Maritime Ministry Consultant for the Lutheran World Federation and the Evangelical Lutheran Church in America (ELCA), Co-founder and Board Member of the Lutheran Association for Maritime Ministry, Associate Member of the National Catholic Association for Seafarers, and Consultant for the Tacoma Seafarers' Center, coordinating agency of the international, nondenominational Ministering Seafarers' Program. He has had a particular concern for justice in the seafaring world and in the younger indigenous churches of Asia and Africa. Roald lives in Seattle with his wife Ruth. They have four children and eight grandchildren.

Universal Declarations

James O'Halloran

Where small communities are concerned, there have of course been statements of a universal nature. We take note of the following:

• The Second Vatican Council 1962-65 launched the vision of a fresh communitarian model of church (cf. *Dogmatic Constitution on the Church*, nos. 4, 10, 11, 12, 26).

• Interest of the World Council of Churches' Uppsala Assembly (1968) in creative church initiatives led eventually to a worldwide contact with small Christian communities. As a result, community experiences were recorded by Dr Ian Fraser and his late wife Margaret and are to be found in a Resource Centre at the Scottish Churches' House in Dunblane. A compendium of these experiences now exists in book form, entitled *Reinventing Church*. Enquiries regarding it could be made at Scottish Churches House.

• The International Catechetical Congress held in Rome, 1971, cited the small community as a particularly suitable environment for passing on the faith and confirmed this in a follow-up document, *General Catechetical Directory*, no. 93, 1971.

• *The Evangelisation of Peoples* of Paul VI, 1975, has an entire section (no. 58) on the communities. Paul sees them as offering hope to the whole church provided they are faithful to its teaching, united to the local and universal churches, and avoid thinking themselves superior to other groups and movements. He also urges the members to grow as missionaries in their awareness, fervour, and zeal. And he makes the important point that the small Christian community is an authentic cell of the church – in other words it is of the essence.

• In his Address to the Brazilian Basic Ecclesial Communities, 1980, John Paul II repeats that the small communities are church and insists on the need for their lay animators to be in communion with their pastors, prepared in the faith, and of exemplary life.[75]

• John Paul's *Redemptoris Missio* , 51, describes small Christian communities as 'a sign of vitality within the church, and instrument for formation and evangelisation, and a solid starting point for a new society based on a "civilisation of love".'

• Finally, in his Exhortation: *Vocation and Mission of the Lay Faithful*, no. 28, 1989, John Paul again affirms small groups.

And so ends our historical profile. In the course of it we noted some of the key meetings held and official statements made on the subject of small Christian communities. Such events are, I believe, a sign that something important is happening among the people of God. Real history takes place at the grassroots. As mentioned earlier, reform comes from above, renewal from below.

Question

Do you think the history of small Christian communities is important? Why?

Suggested Bible passage: Acts 1:15-26

Conclusion

With the foregoing historical profile ends our treatment of the vision and practice of small Christian communities. It is a story of a torrent of love emanating from the Blessed Trinity and channelled to creation through Jesus, the Word made flesh; a torrent that seeps into the mind of the theologian and the arm of the missionary.

An anecdote that I tell has somehow endeared itself to many people, and, because of its relevance, I repeat it here:

In the early 1960s Pearl, a frail little lady in her 70s, was demonstrating outside the White House against racism. She was arrested and tried.

'My goodness,' said the judge, 'you are such a frail little lady, I don't know what to do with you, even though you have been breaking the law.'

'You must do what your conscience tells you,' retorted Pearl feistily, 'just as I do what my conscience tells me.'

Well, the judge did what his conscience told him, and sent her for a stint in prison.

While in prison she had a heart attack and was been driven in an ambulance with flashing blue lights and wailing siren to the nearest hospital. She came to and asked what had happened. The attendants told her.

'What hospital are you taking me to?' she enquired.

They named the hospital.

'Does it admit Americans of African origin?'

No, it was for whites only.

Despite her condition she stubbornly refused to go, and the ambulance driver, swearing profusely, had to turn his vehicle round and speed to a hospital at a much greater distance that accepted folk of all races. And having survived the prison and the heart attack, back she went – to demonstrate in front of the White House.

Twenty years later, I met Pearl at a meeting protesting the nuclear threat. To me she seemed a most experienced, wise, and holy person, so I thought I would put an important question, perhaps the most important question, to her. 'Pearl,' I asked, 'what is happiness?'

Without hesitation, out of her long experience and great wisdom, she replied, 'Happiness is belonging.'

That simple statement neatly sums up the meaning of life. It is about the heart; it is about relationships. By befriending each other in God, we lead one another to God who is love. Whenever we care for others, we make the music of the Trinity, just like Patrick, the Apostle of Ireland, did all those centuries ago, when he gave us that eloquent hymn:

I bind on to myself the name,
The strong name of the Trinity;
By invocation of the same,
The Three in One and One in Three;
Of whom all nature hath creation,
Eternal Father, Spirit, Word;
Praise the Lord of my salvation –
Salvation is of Christ the Lord! Amen

APPENDIX

Passages for Bible Sharing

Community/Church
- Genesis 1:26-27. "Let us make human beings in our own image...male and female God created them."
- Psalm 133 (132). "Behold how good...when brothers and sisters dwell in unity!"
- Matthew 5:13-14. "You are the salt of the earth..."
- Matthew 6:25-34. God cares for us, motive for self-confidence in ourselves as persons.
- Matthew 7:15-28. Matthew's idea of Church...false prophets within...a community that does the will of God.
- Matthew 8:18-27. Church – a community that follows Jesus come what may.
- Matthew 10:5-42. Church missionary – God sends Jesus – Jesus sends community to the rest of the world – world must respond.
- Matthew 11:28-30. Church – a community that takes on the yoke of Christ – appears heavy – not so really.
- Matthew 12:22-28. "Every kingdom divided against itself is laid waste..."
- Matthew 13:24-58. Good and bad found in the church – weeding expeditions dangerous – a sorting out to take place at the appropriate time.
- Matthew 18:7-35. Seriousness of following Jesus.
- Matthew 18:20. "...where two or three are gathered in my name..." (cf. also Matthew 10:5-15; Luke 10:1-20 – apostles go out in twos).
- Matthew 19:16-30. Give up anything in order to follow Jesus.
- Matthew 21:28-32. Doing is crucial in the church community.
- Matthew 22:37-39. The Great Commandment.
- John 15:5-10. "I am the vine..."
- John 15:11-17. "...love one another as I have loved you."
- John 17:20-26. "I pray that they may all be one." The mutual indwelling.
- Acts 2:42-47. The early Christian community.
- Acts 4:32-37. The early Christian community.
- Acts 9:1-8. "Saul, Saul, why do you persecute me?"

243

1 Corinthians 11:17-34. Division in community.

1 Corinthians 12:14-27. "...you are the body of Christ."

- Galatians 3:28-29. There is neither Jew nor Greek, there is neither slave nor free..."
- Ephesians 5:29-31. "The two shall become one."
- 1 Thessalonians 4:13-18. Anxiety over death.

Note: For the life of the early Christian communities, exhaustive list of references given on p. 167.

Community/Eucharist.

- Luke 22:14-23. "Do this in remembrance of me."
- John 6:35-58. "I am the bread of life..."
- 1 Corinthians 10:16-17. "...we who are many are one body..."
- 1 Corinthians 11:17-22. "...it is not the Lord's supper that you eat."
- 1 Corinthians 11:23-26. "Do this in remembrance of me."

Commitment/Conversion/Perseverance

- Matthew 24:11-13. "But the one who endures to the end will be saved."
- Luke 9:57-62. "Leave the dead to bury their own dead..."
- Luke 13:22-30. Enter by the narrow gate.
- John 12:20-26. "...unless a grain of wheat falls into the earth and dies..."
- Mark 10:17-31. The Rich Young Man.
- Luke 9:57-62. "No one who puts a hand to the plough..."
- Luke 13:24. "Strive to enter by the narrow door..."
- Luke 19:1-10. Zaccheus.
- Acts 9:1-13. The conversion of Saul.
- Galatians 2:20-21. "...it is no longer I who live, but Christ who lives in me..."
- Galatians 3:1-5. "Having begun with the Spirit, are you now ending with the flesh."
- Galatians 3:28-29. "There is neither Jew nor Greek..."
- Galatians 5:1. Stand fast.
- Galatians 5:13-15. "For you were called to freedom..."
- Ephesians 4:1-16. Attaining "to the measure of the stature of the fullness of Christ."
- Philippians 2:5-11. The great graph of descent and ascent.
- Hebrews 12:1-4. "...let us run with perseverance..."
- 1 Peter 3:13-18. "...make a defence to anyone who calls you to account for the hope that is in you...."

Dialogue/Discernment

- Ecclesiasticus (Sirach) 5:9-13. Firm in resolution, careful in speaking.

- Ecclesiasticus (Sirach) 23:7-14. Wisdom in silence.
- Ecclesiasticus 27:4-7. The test of a person is in conversation.
- Ecclesiasticus (Sirach) 37:16-18. Communication through silence.
- Matthew 12:33-37. "For out of the abundance of the heart the mouth speaks."
- Luke 1:26-38. Listening and speaking well.
- Luke 2:41-52. "listening to them and asking them questions...and his mother kept all these things in her heart" (cf. also 2:19).
- Luke 24:13-35. Jesus listens.
- John 4:1-30. Jesus listens.
- Acts 15:1-41. The apostles enter into dialogue.
- 1 Corinthians 2:6-16; 4:6-7; 6:1-8; 7:10-12; 12:4-11. Discernment with the help of the Spirit.
- 1 Corinthians 16:13-14. "Let all that you do be done in love."
- Ephesians 4:10-16. "...speaking the truth in love..."
- James 3:1-12. Listening and speaking well.

Diversity/Ecumenism
- Genesis 1. Diversity in creation.
- Matthew 13:47-50. Fish of every kind gathered in the net.
- 1 Corinthians 12:4-31. The body of Christ has many parts.
- Mark 9:38-41. Openness (cf. also Luke:9:49-50).
- John 17:30-26 "...that they may all be one."

Environment/Creation
- Genesis 1 and 2. God found everything that had been created good.
- Psalms 8, 19 (18), 24 (23), 29 (28), 50 (49), 136 (135), 139 (138),147 (146), 148
- Daniel 3:35-68. "Bless the Lord, all works of the Lord..."
- Matthew: 6:25-34. "Consider the lilies of the field..."
- Romans 8:18-25. "We know that the whole creation has been groaning in travail together until now."

Freedom
- Isaiah 58 "...let the oppressed go free..."
- John 8:31-38 "...the truth will make you free."
- John 14: 1-7. "I am the way, the truth, and the life."
- Galatians 5:13-15. "For you were called to freedom."

Friendship
- Ecclesiasticus (Sirach) 6:5-17. "...the person that has found one [a friend] has found a treasure...."

- Matthew 11:1-15. "...among those born of woman...no greater than John the Baptist..."
- John 11:1-44. Lazarus raised from death; "...he whom you love is ill... Jesus wept...deeply moved."
- John 20:1-18. Mary Magdalene consoled by the appearance of Jesus.
- Luke 10:38-42. Jesus' deep friendship with Martha and Mary (cf. John 11).

Formation
- Matthew 12:34-35. Formation relational.
- Luke 2:22-40. "And the child grew and became strong..."
- Luke 2:41-52. "And Jesus increased in wisdom and in stature..."
- Ephesians 4:7-16. Attaining "to the measure of the stature of the fullness of Christ."
- Ephesians: 4:22-24. "You were taught to put away...your old self."
- Colossians 3:9-10. "Do not lie to one another, seeing that you have stripped off the old self with its practices, and clothed yourselves with the new self, which is being renewed in knowledge according to the image of its creator."

God
- Psalm 139. God is with us.
- Psalm 92:1-5."It is good to give thanks to the Lord; 12-15. "The righteous flourish like the palm tree."
- Isaiah 40:28-31. "The Lord is everlasting God."
- Isaiah 43:1-3. God unfailingly present.
- Jeremiah 29:11-14. "For I know the plans I have for you..."
- Habakkuk 3:17-18. "I will rejoice in the Lord."
- 1 Kings 3:16-28. The wisdom of God in Solomon.
- Matthew 1:23. Through Christ and the Church (Christian community), God is present in the world.
- Matthew 3:1-17. "It wasn't that a dove descended, because it doesn't say that a dove descended but "like a dove.' It was the love of God that descended on him." (Sally and Philip Scharper, eds., *The Gospel in Art by the Peasants of Solentiname,* New York: Orbis Books, 1984, p.22).
- Matthew 6:7-15. "It is a loving name [i.e. Abba] that's given to God...we don't have to be formal when we chat with God and give the name 'papa.' " (Sally and Philip Scharper, eds., *The Gospel in Art*, p.32).
- Matthew 6:28-34. Abandonment - put ourselves in God's hands.
- Matthew 7:1-5. God would not have us judge.
- Matthew 18:21-35. The parable of the Unforgiving Servant – our God is forgiving (cf. also Luke 17:3-4).
- Matthew 20:1-16. The Workers in the Vineyard – God's justice much more ample than our notions of justice.

- Luke 1:46-55. The Magnificat - "My soul glorifies the Lord..."
- Luke 1:68-79. The Benedictus - "Blessed be the Lord, the God of Israel..."
- Luke 10:25-37. The Good Samaritan; Luke 15:1-7, The Lost Sheep; Luke 15:8-10, The Lost Coin. These passages testify to God's unconditional love, compassion, patience – loves to the point of foolishness (old man running) – patiently gives the barren fig tree another chance when all others would have given up on it – God a loving parent, not a scorekeeper.
- John 3:16. "For God so loved the world that he gave his only Son..."
- Romans 14:7-9."If we live, we live to the Lord..."
- 1 John 4:7-21. "...for God is love." God is good.
- Revelations 4:1-11. "Holy, holy, holy is the Lord God Almighty."
- Revelations 22:1-5. The water of life flowing from the throne of God.

(God) Holy Spirit.
- Joel 2:28-29. I will pour out my spirit on all people.
- Matthew 1:23. Emmanuel - God with us.
- John 14:8-14. The person who sees Jesus sees God.
- John 14:15-16, 23-26. The Holy Spirit will teach you everything.
- John 15:26-27; 16:12-15. The Spirit of truth will lead you to the complete truth.
- John 20:19-23. "...receive the Holy Spirit."
- Acts 2:1-11. They were all filled with the Holy Spirit and began to speak.
- Acts 15:22-29. "For it has seemed good to the Holy Spirit and to us..."
- Romans 8:8-17. Everyone moved by the Spirit a child of God.
- Romans 8:22-27. The Spirit pleading for us.
- Romans 12:1-8. Gifts of the Spirit.
- 1 Corinthians 12:3-7, 12-13. In the one Spirit we were all baptised.
- Galatians 4:4-7. God has sent the Spirit of the Son.
- Galatians 5:16-25. The fruit of the Spirit. With the Spirit we achieve more.

God, love of

- Genesis 22:1-33. "For the sake of ten I will not destroy it."
- Isaiah 49:14-18. I have inscribed you on the palms of my hands.
- Luke 10:25-37. The Good Samaritan; Luke 15:1-7, The Lost Sheep; Luke 15:8-10, The Lost Coin. These passages testify to God's unconditional love, compassion, patience – loves to the point of foolishness (old man running) – patiently gives the barren fig tree another chance when all others would have given up on it – God a loving parent, not a score keeper.

- John 3:16. "For God so loved the world that he gave his only Son..."
- John 15:12-17. "...love one another as I have loved you."
- John 17. God's love for us.
- Romans 14:7-9."If we live, we live to the Lord..."
- 1 John 4:7-21; "...for God is love"...God first loves us...

God, will of
- Matthew 26:36-46. "...not as I will, but as thou wilt."
- John 4:31-37. "My food is to do the will of the one who sent me..."

Inculturation/Word
- Jeremiah 1:9-10. The power of God's word impacting upon creation.
- The text that throws open for me the challenge of our times is Mark 1:1. "This is the gospel of Jesus Christ the Son of God." Gospel being a term used to describe Roman propaganda of victories in battle on the borders of the empire: Mark 'steals' the term and turns it to a new advantage. In describing Jesus as "Son of God," Mark is also jousting at the titles offered to the Roman emperor on the coins – "Caesar – Divine son of God," and points to the authentic "Anointed One" – Christ Jesus, "who saves his people". This text presents Jesus as the one who offers a gospel – good news of victories over the powers and principalities which have governed and controlled human affairs; offering a kingdom of justice, love and peace (Bishop Peter B. Price). It also treats of a Jesus deeply immersed in our reality.
- Luke 11:27. Word of God has to be implemented...made flesh.
- John 1:1-18. "And the Word became flesh and lived among us..." Basis for all inculturation.
- Acts 2:1-11. All hear in their own native language.

Jesus
- Matthew 3:13-17. Baptism of Jesus – "...we shall do all that God requires."
- Matthew 4:1-11. Temptations - Jesus does the will of God.
- Matthew 5:21-48. Jesus calls for more - the kingdom demands it.
- Matthew 7:15-20. Jesus a doer - a person for others.
- Matthew 8:5-13. For Jesus faith (trust) indispensable.
- Matthew 9:18-38. Jesus a healer – a person for others.
- Matthew 11:1-6. Jesus makes an option with the poor – kingdom breaks in.
- Matthew 11:25-30. Jesus knows the Father – yoke of Jesus may appear heavy, but in reality light.
- Matthew 12:15-21. The mercy of Jesus - he "does not break off the broken reed."

- Matthew 16:21-35 (cf. also Mark 8:31- 9:1; Luke 9:22-27). Prophecies of the Passion – suffering is part of the deal for those who follow Jesus.
- Matthew 18:21-35. Parable of the Unforgiving Servant – Jesus is forgiving.
- Matthew 24:29-31. Christ will come again.
- Matthew 25:1-13. The Parable of the Ten Virgins – we must be ready for the coming of Jesus.
- Matthew 25:31-46. "...for I was hungry and you gave me food, I was thirsty and you gave me drink..." This is one of the most eloquent pleas for justice in the Bible.
- Matthew 26:14 - 27:66 (shorter form, 27:11-54). The Passion.
- Mark 14:1-15:47 (shorter form, 15:1-39), and 3-9, the perceptive act of anointing. The Passion.
- Luke 22:14-23:56. (shorter form 23:1-49). The Passion.
- Luke 24:13-35. Road to Emmaus.
- John 1. "In the beginning was the Word..."
- John 14:6."I am the way, and the truth, and the life."
- John 14:8-9. "Whoever has seen me has seen the Father."
- John 18:1-19:42. The Passion.
- Galatians 2:20-21. To live Christ.
- Colossians 1:11-22. Christ in the universe; 3:1-4. New priorities.

Justice
- Exodus 3:1-20. God the liberator.
- Exodus 6:2-13. God the liberator.
- Exodus 12, 13, 14. God liberating the children of Israel from oppression.
- Exodus 22:20-24. "You shall not wrong or oppress the stranger....You shall not afflict any widow or orphan."
- Deuteronomy 10:16-20. "He expects justice for the fatherless and widow, and loves the sojourner..."
- 1 Kings 21:1-16. A grave injustice. (What are the injustices in your own area?)
- Isaiah 3:13-15. Injustice condemned.
- Isaiah 58. True fasting is a matter of establishing true and loving relationships.
- Isaiah 61. Justice / Freedom / Promise.
- Amos 2:6-8. "...they that trample the head of the poor..."
- Amos 5:15-24. Justice is asked for not ritual acknowledgment.
- Amos 6:1-7. "Woe to those who are at ease in Zion..."
- Amos 8:4-7. "Hear you who trample the needy..."
- Micah 6:8. "Do justice, love kindness, walk humbly with our God."
- Matthew 5:27-30. Good must triumph over evil.

- Matthew 5:38-42. Good must triumph over evil.
- Matthew 6:33. The kingdom (and its justice) a priority.
- Matthew 25:31-40. "I was hungry and you gave me food..."
- Luke 4:16-21. Jesus' mission - option with the poor.
- Luke 1:46-55. The Magnificat, Mary's Manifesto. "He has brought down the powerful from their thrones, and lifted up the lowly; he has filled the hungry with good things, and sent the rich away empty."
- Acts 20:35. "...more blessed to give than receive..."
- Galatians 3:26-29. Away with all barriers.

Kingdom
- Genesis 9:8-17 (taken with Hosea 2:16-22 and Romans 8:18-25). The covenant and the hope of redemption is for all creation.
- Matthew 5:3-12. The values of the kingdom – turn worldly values on their heads.
- Matthew 5-7 Requirements of the kingdom.
- Matthew 6:33. The kingdom (and its justice) is the priority.
- Matthew 10. The messengers of the kingdom.
- Matthew 13. Parables of the kingdom; mysteries of the kingdom.
- Matthew 18:21-35. The position of little children in the kingdom.
- Matthew 18:21-35. Forgiveness, reconciliation.
- Matthew 18:24-25. Those who work for the kingdom must be watchful and faithful.
- 1 Corinthians 15:12-28. There is tension - the kingdom is here, and yet to come.
- Galatians 6:15. The kingdom is "a new creation."

Note: For succinct treatment of the kingdom in Old and New Testaments see chapter 4.

Leadership/Coordination/Animation/Facilitation
- Matthew 20:20-28. Authority is for service (cf. Mark 10:35-45; Luke 22:24-27).
- Mark 1:14-28. Starting. Jesus commences his mission.
- Luke 10:1-2. Teamwork.
- Luke 22:24-27. Be a servant.
- John 4:1-30. Meeting. Jesus' meeting with the Samaritan Woman (cf. also Luke 24:13-35. Meeting with disciples on the road to Emmaus).
- John 13:1-20. Jesus washes his disciples feet.
- Acts 12:12; Romans 16:3-5. Small Christian communities meeting in home (cf. also Romans 16:11; 16:14-15).
- Luke 24:52-53; Acts 5:12. Meeting places for the communion of communities.

- Galatians 2:11-21. "But when Cephas came to Antioch I opposed him to his face."

Love (cf. Community)
- Mark 4:35-41. Jesus calming the storm, "lack of love in the world, that's the stormy lake." (Sally and Philip Scharper, eds. *The Gospel in Art by the Peasants of Solentiname*. Maryknoll, New York: Orbis Books, 1984, p. 28).
- Luke 9:10-17.The Multiplication of the Loaves; "...The gospel doesn't mention multiplication or miracle. It just says they shared..." (Sally and Philip Scharper, eds., *The Gospel in Art*, p.42).
- John 13:35. "...all will know that you are my disciples if you have love for one another."
- 1 Corinthians 13. " If you speak in the tongues of men and angels, but have not love..."
- 1 John 4:7-21. God is love – love of neighbour – love drives out fear.

Option with the poor/ Mission (cf. Jesus)
- Matthew 10:5-15 (cf. Mark 6:7-13; Luke 9:1-6). The mission of the twelve.
- Matthew 21:12-17 (cf. Mark 11:15-19; Luke 19:45-48; John 2:13-22). The clearing of the Temple – we must not dare use religion or a holy place as a hideaway – "den of robbers."
- Matthew 28:18-20. The Great Commissioning.
- Mark 10:17-31; "...sell what you have, and give to the poor..."
- Luke 4:16-21. Jesus is rejected at Nazareth – Jesus' mission: an option with the poor.
- Luke 10:1-20. The mission of the seventy-two.
- Luke 16:19-31. The rich man and Lazarus – scraps from the rich man's table totally inadequate.
- Luke 18:18-30. Jesus against possessiveness.
- Acts 11:19-30. Mission to Antioch where the term Christian originated.
- 1 Thessalonians 4:9-12. Christians to be witnesses.

Peace
- Leviticus 26:3-13. The elements of peace.
- Judges 6:19-24. Peace the gift of God.
- Psalm 35:27. God desires peace for us.
- Isaiah 2:1-5. Turn swords into ploughshares.
- Isaiah 9:5-7. Messiah the Prince of Peace - peace without and within the kingdom.
- Isaiah 32:16-17. Justice the basis of peace.
- Isaiah 48:17-19. Peace the fruit of obedience to God.

- Isaiah 48:20-22. No peace for the wicked.
- Isaiah 54:13-17. If Israel is just, there will be peace and prosperity.
- Isaiah 60:17-22. There will be peace and righteousness.
- Jeremiah 6:13-15. Peace the fruit of justice, not of a lie.
- Ezekiel 13:10-12. Saying there is peace when there is none is to white wash a crumbling wall.
- Matthew 10:11-13. A greeting of peace, once uttered, has a power of its own (cf. Luke 10:5-6).
- Matthew 26:51-53. Non-violence (cf. Luke 22:49-53).
- John 14:25-27. Peace of Jesus the only true peace (cf. John 16:33).
- Romans 8:6-8. To enjoy peace one needs to be spiritually minded.
- Romans 14:13-19. Peace is right relationships (harmony).
- 1 Corinthians 7:12-16. God has called us to peace.
- 1 Corinthians 14:26-33. Peace is right relationships (harmony).
- Ephesians 2:14-17. Peace is union with God – Jesus our peace – unites us with God.
- Ephesians 6:10-20. Preaching the gospel brings peace.
- Philippians 4:4-7. Peace of God communicated through Jesus passes all understanding.
- Colossians 3:14-15. We are called to peace because we are one – the body of Christ.

Planning and Evaluation
- Luke 10:1-20. Christ prepares the apostles for their mission.
- Acts 6:1- 7. The apostles evaluate a situation and plan.
- Acts 15:1-35. The apostles evaluate a situation and plan.

Prayer
- Matthew 6:5-15. The Lord's Prayer.
- Romans 8:26-27; "...the Spirit pleads with God for us..."
- Luke 6:12-16. "...all night he continued in prayer to God."
- Luke 18:1-8. Pray without losing heart.

Prayer/Action (cf. Jesus – Doing – Doer)
- Matthew 7:21. "Not everyone who says to me, 'Lord, Lord,' shall enter the kingdom...the person who does the will of my Father..."
- John 1:1-14. The Word became flesh.
- Isaiah 29:13-14. Lip service not enough.
- James 1:22-25. "but be doers of the word, and not hearers only..."
- James 2:1-17. Practical signs of a new life style.
- James 2:14-26. "So faith by itself, if it has no works is dead."

Process
- Ecclesiastes 3:1-19. A time for everything.
- Mark 4:1-8. "The plants sprouted, grew, and produced corn..."
- Mark 4:26-34. Seeds slowly growing – The Parable of the Mustard Seed (cf. Matthew 13:31-32; Luke 13:18-19).
- Luke 2:52. "And Jesus increased in wisdom and stature..."
- Ephesians 4:1-16. Attaining "to the measure of the stature of the fullness of Christ."

Readiness
- Genesis 12:1-5 (taken with Hebrews 11:8-16). In obedience be prepared to leave safe territory.
- Luke 10:13; 10:23-24; 11:29; 12:16-21; 12:35; 12:43-46; 12:54-56; 12:57; 13:1-5; 13:6-9; 14:16; 14:28; 16:1-8; 17:26-30; 19:5; 19:11-27 (cf. Matthew 35:14-30).

Reconciliation
- Psalm 129 (130). "Out of the depths I cry to you, O Lord."
- Proverbs 24:15-16. "...a righteous person falls seven times, and rises again..."
- Isaiah 53:1-12. "...it was our sorrow that he bore..."
- Luke 1:67-79. Salvation through the forgiveness of sins.
- Luke 3:1-6. "Prepare the way of the Lord..."
- Luke 7:36-50. The woman who was a sinner anoints Jesus; "her sins are forgiven...for she loved much."
- Luke 15:11-32. The Prodigal Son.
- Luke 17:1-4; "And if the same person sins against you seven times a day...you must forgive."
- Luke 18:9-14. The Pharisee and the tax collector.
- Luke 19:1-10. Zacchaeus building bridges of reconciliation.
- Luke 23:33-43. "Father, forgive them, for they know not what they do..."today you will be with me in paradise."
- John 8:1-11. The woman taken in adultery.
- 1 Corinthians 13:1-7. Sin a failure to love.
- 2 Corinthians 12:5-10. Strength in weakness.
- Ephesians 4:7-16. Attaining "to the measure of the stature of the fullness of Christ."
- Ephesians 4:22-24."You were taught to put away...your old self."
- Colossians 3:9-10. "Do not lie to one another, seeing that you have stripped off the old self with its practices, and clothed yourselves with the new self, which is being renewed in knowledge according to the image of its creator."

Vocation

- Jeremiah 1:4-10. God's strange, imperious call. God knows us intimately and calls us before we are born.
- Matthew 4:18-22.
- Mark 1:16-20; 2:13-14; 10:17-31 (The Rich Young Man).
- Luke 5:1-11.
- John 1:35-51.

Women

- Genesis 1. God created human beings in the image and likeness of God – male and female God created them.
- Joshua 2:1-24. Rahab astutely saves her family.
- Judges 4:4-23. Deborah saviour and leader of her people.
- Ruth 1-4. Valiant women.
- 1 Samuel 9:11. Michal, Saul's daughter and David's wife, saves David.
- 1 Samuel 25:14-42. The discreet Abigail prevents David from wrongfully shedding blood and saves lives.
- 2 Samuel 21:7-14. The devotion of Rizpah.
- 2 Kings 4:8-37. The woman of Shunem – wisdom and devotion.
- Judith 13:1-20. Judith saves her people.
- Esther 7:1-10. Esther saves her people.
- Matthew 15:21-28. Jesus heals the woman of Syria (cf. Mark 7:24-30).
- Matthew 25:1-13. Jesus appreciates the concerns of women.
- Matthew 26:6-13. Jesus anointed by a woman at Bethany – defends her against her critics.
- Mark 1:29-31. Jesus cures Peter's mother-in-law (cf. Matthew 8:14-17; Luke 4:38-41).
- Mark 5:21-43. Jesus raises the daughter of Jairus and heals the woman with the haemorrhage (cf. Matthew 9:18-26; Luke 8:40-56).
- Luke 7:11-17. Jesus takes pity on the widow of Naim.
- Luke 8:1-13. Women listed with the men as helpers of Jesus – various women later witnessed his death and resurrection.
- Luke 10:38-42. Jesus' deep friendship with Martha and Mary (cf. John 11).
- Luke 13:10-17. Jesus heals woman with the deformed back.
- Luke 15:8-10. The Lost Coin. Jesus appreciates the concerns of women.
- Luke 18:1-8. The Parable of the Widow and the Judge.
- John 4:1-42. Jesus' respect for, and frankness with, the Samaritan woman – Jesus sends the apostles on mission two by two, but the Samaritan woman alone converts a whole village – Jesus' conduct towards women revolutionary.
- Acts 1:12-14. Women important in the church from the outset.
- Acts 12:12. Key role of women in the early church.
- Acts 16:11-15. Lydia readily hears the word of God.

- Acts 18:24-28. Priscilla and Aquila equal partners in mission.
- Galatians 3:26-29. Clearest statement of equality of the sexes in the New Testament.

Worship
- 1 Corinthians 14:26-33. Worship built up "from below."

Youth
- Exodus 2:11-15. The young Moses.
- 1 Samuel, chapters 16, 17, 18. The young David.
- Tobit (Tobias) chapters 1-14. Much to say to modern youth.
- Proverbs 1:8-9; 6:23; 10:1; 15:32; 17:25; 23:25; 27:17. Youth and the family.
- Canticle of Canticles (Song of Solomon), chapters 1-8. A song of human love.
- Jeremiah 1. The young Jeremiah.
- Daniel 13: The story of Susanna (or book of Susanna).
- Ecclesiasticus (Sirach), Youth and the School: 1:22-24 (patience); 3:17-20 (humility); 3:21-23 (study of the law enough for the wise person); 3:25-29 (invitation to meditate); 4:20-31 (critical awareness); 5:9-13 (firm in resolution, careful in speaking); 6:2-4 (dominating one's passion); 7:4-7 (no need to be ambitious); 7:11, 32 (being compassionate); 18:30 - 19:3 (controlling one's desires); 20:27 (don't be easily influenced); 22:16-18 (reflecting well before a decision); 23:7, 12-14 (wisdom in silence); 33:4-6 (be wise and consistent); 37:7-15 (value of God's counsel); 37:16-18 (communication through silence); 38:24-39:11 (eulogy of the teacher); 41:14-42:8 (a middle way between false modesty and brashness).
- Matthew 9:20. Jesus appreciates youthful frankness.
- Mark 5:35-43. Jesus helps the young girl.
- Mark 10:13-16. "...whoever does not receive the kingdom of God like a child."
- Mark 14:51-52. Curiosity of the young man in Gethesemane.
- Luke 2:41-52. The young Jesus provokes wonder.
- Luke 15:11-32. Prodigal Son – harrowing experience, conversion.

Christian Family and Community, caring for:
- Ephesians 5:22 - 6:9; 6:1-4.
- Colossians 3:18- 4:1.
- 1 Timothy 2:15; 3:4; 4:12; 5:4, 10.
- 2 Timothy 3:15.
- Titus 1:5-6; 2:6-8.
- Hebrews 12:7, 10.
- 1 Peter 2:13 - 3:7.
- 1 John 2:13-14.

256

Annotated Bibliography

Andrews, Dave and Engwicht David. *Can You Hear the Heartbeat?* Sydney: Hodder and Stoughton, 1989. Describes the radical alternative to a me-first lifestyle in which the strong get power and the weak go to the wall.

Andrews, Dave. *Building a Better World*. Sutherland, NSW: Albatross Books,1996. A set of realistic, tested strategies for changing the world – and us – for the better.

Azevado, Marcelo, de C., SJ. *Basic Ecclesial Communities in Brazil*. Washington, D.C: Georgetown University Press, 1987. A thorough investigation of the "fascinating reality of Brazilian Basic Ecclesial Communities." The book is geared to the academic.

Banks, Robert and Julia. *The Church Comes Home*. Peabody, MA: Hendrickson Publishers, 1998. A visionary and practical handbook for those interested in home churches by two deeply experienced people. An excellent read.

Banks, Robert. *Going to Church in the First Century*. Blacktown, NSW: Hexagon Press, 1985. An historically accurate fictionalization of one pagan's encounter with a first-century house church. Helps peel away our cultural misconceptions of church by seeing what things were like in the early church. Interesting and provocative.

— *Paul's Idea of Community: the Early House Churches in their Historical Setting*. Grand Rapids, MI: Eerdman's Publishing, 1980. A fantastic rereading of the New Testament which will change your view of church! Scholarly in tone yet easy to read, this book lays a solid biblical and theological foundation for church as community.

Baranowski, Arthur R. *Creating Small Faith Communities*. Cincinnati, Ohio: St. Anthony's Messenger Press, 1988. A methodology for establishing small Christian communities in parishes, written by one who has had considerable experience in the field.

Barret, Lois. *Building the House Church*. Scottdale, PA: Herald Press, 1986. A valuable guide to starting home churches by an experienced leader of a network of home churches in Wichita, Kansas. Deals with questions such as written covenants, worship, relationships, decision-making, growth strategies, and so on. The book's only flaw is an over-emphasis on structure and order.

Barriero, Alvaro, SJ. *Basic Ecclesial Communities – The Evangelization of the Poor*. Maryknoll, New York: Orbis Books, 1982. This simply written book shows the power of the poor for evangelisation, particularly when this power is harnessed in basic ecclesial communities.

Biagi, Bob. *A Manual for Helping Groups to Work More Effectively*. University of Massachusetts, Amherst, MA. A book that reads easily and may be adapted for use by small Christian communities; it has useful suggestions for group dynamics or exercises.

Boadt, Lawrence. *Reading the Old Testament: An Introduction*. New York: Paulist Press, 1984.

Boff, Leonardo. *Ecclesiogenesis: The Base Communities Reinvent the Church*. Maryknoll, New York: Orbis Books, 1986. The author explains how the Brazilian basic Christian communities are a new way of being church.

— *Jesus Christ, Liberator*. Maryknoll, New York: Orbis Books, 1978. Refreshing insights on Jesus.

Bonhoeffer, Dietrich, *Life Together: A Discussion of Christian Fellowship*. New York: Harper and Row, 1954. A perceptive analysis of the biblical reasons for residential community and for the style of community. A classic.

Brown, Raymond E. *The Churches the Apostles Left Behind*. Mahwah: New Jersey, Paulist Press, 1984. In New Testament times the church was not a monolith – there were various models operating.

— *An Introduction to the New Testament*. New York: Doubleday, 1997. A monumental piece of scholarship that speaks to experts and novices alike. "If a person could only have one book on the New Testament, this is the one to have."

Burke, Harriet, et al. *People, Promise, and Community: A Practical Guide to Creating and Sustaining Small Christian Communities*. New York, Paulist Press. Deals with the nuts and bolts of being a small Christian community, step by patient step. Useful for beginners.

Byrne, Tony, CSSp. *Working for Justice and Peace: A Practical Guide*. Ndola, Zambia: Mission Press, 1988. A practical and easy to read guidebook for people who wish to encourage and motivate themselves and others to take action for justice and peace. Byrne is very experienced in the field.

— *How to Evaluate*. Ndola, Zambia: Mission Press, 1988. A practical guide to evaluate the work of the Church and its organizations.

Carroll, Denis. *What is Liberation Theology?* Cork: The Mercier Press. Many people ask this question. This book provides an excellent answer.

Center for Conflict Resolution. *Building United Judgments: a Handbook for Consensus Decision Making*. Madison, WI., 1981. Although not a "Christian" book in itself, this is an invaluable how-to guide to the form of decision-making most appropriate for Christian community: consensus. Extremely practical and thorough. Highly recommended.

Clark, Stephen, B. *Patterns of Christian Community: A Statement of Community Order*. Michigan, Ann Arbor, Servant Books, 1984. Useful overview of what constitutes Christian community from the perspective of a Roman Catholic live-in community, but with an attempt to be ecumenical.

Concilium. London: SCM; New York: Orbis Books, vol. 2, 1993. A most enlightening number regarding the Church in Asia.

Cook, Guillermo. *The Expectation of the Poor – Latin American Basic Ecclesial Communities in Protestant Perspective*. Maryknoll, New York: Orbis Books, 1985. The most complete treatment of this theme, adapted from a doctoral thesis.

Cowan, Michael A and Lee, Bernard J., SM. *Conversation, Risk, and Conversion: The Inner & Public Life of Small Christian Communities*. New York: Orbis Books, 1997. Gathers reflections on the likely future of small Christian community phenomenon. A must read especially for those interested in small Christian communities.

Crosby, Michael H. *House of Disciples – Church, Economics and Justice*. Maryknoll, New York: Orbis Books, 1988. Through an in-depth exploration of Matthew's gospel and its socioeconomic milieu, this book shows how the world of the early church continues to challenge Christians today. It makes a unique contribution to both New Testament scholarship and the practice of contemporary spirituality.

Cruden, Alexander, M.A. *Concordance of the Holy Scriptures*. London: The Epworth Press, 1969. Most useful in helping resource persons to locate scripture passages.

Culling, Elizabeth. *What is Celtic Spirituality?* Nottingham:Grove Books Limited, 1993. In this book we find brief, clear, quality thinking that addresses its subject capably.

Cunningham, Loren with Rogers, Janice. *Is That Really You God?* Seattle: YWAM Publishing. The Youth With A Mission (YWAM) story. A spellbinding book that describes how YWAM was formed. Community is an essential component of the organisation.

Dearling, Alan, and Armstrong, Howard. *The Youth Games Book*. I.T. Resource Centre, Quarries Homes, Bridge of Weird, Renfrewshire, Scotland, 1980. Useful exercises for youth.

de la Torre, Ed. *Touching Ground Taking Root*. Quezon City (Philippines): Socio-Pastoral Institute, 1986. This book gives an account of small Christian communities in the Philippines.

de Sales, Francis and Jane de Chantal. *Letters of Spiritual Direction*. New York: Paulist Press, 1988. A rich correspondence which reveals the joint spirituality of two great experts in the spiritual life. The Introduction too is really valuable.

Donders, Joseph G. *Empowering Hope: Thoughts to Brighten Your Day*. Mystic, Connecticut: Twenty-Third Publications, 1985. This simple down-to-earth book is a collection of inspirational radio and television presentations broadcast in many parts of the world; could provide excellent material for meetings.

Donovan, Vincent, CSSp. *Christianity Rediscovered*. Maryknoll, New York: Orbis Books, 1982. An account of a missionary endeavour among the Masai people in Tanzania which makes one think about the church in a wonderfully creative way.

Dorr, Donal. *Option for the Poor: A Hundred Years of Vatican Social Teaching*. Maryknoll, New York: Orbis Books, 1983; Dublin: Gill and Macmillan, 1983. An excellent scholarly survey of the period under consideration.

— *Mission in today's world*. Dublin: Columba Press, 2000; New York: Orbis Books, 2000. Dorr explores the meaning of 'mission' for today and comes up with some absorbing insights. Dialogue and an openness to different religions and spiritualities would be important. He so insists on serious religious dialogue with the value system of the modern world.

Drane, John, *Introducing the Bible*. Oxford: Lion Publishing, 1990. A simple introduction. Exists only in hardback.

Dublin Diocesan Committee for Parish Development and Renewal. *Parish Development and Renewal*. Dublin: Veritas Publications, 1993. An account by the committee of the attempts being made to animate parishes.

Dulles, Avery, SJ. *Models of the Church*. Dublin: Gill and Macmillan, 1976; New York: Image Books, Doubleday and Company, 1978. This book shows us that the church is not just one simple reality, but can express itself in various forms or models.

Eagleson, John, and Scharper, Philip (eds.). *Puebla and Beyond*. Maryknoll, New York: Orbis Books, 1979. Included is the opening address of John Paul II to the Bishops' Conference in Puebla.

Earley, Ciaran, OMI (ed.). *Parish Alive Alive O!* Dublin: The Columba Press, 1985. This is an account of efforts to establish small Christian communities in a variety (urban and rural) of Dublin parishes.

Edwards, Denis, and Wilkinson, Bob. *The Christian Community Connection: A Program for Small Christian Communities*. Adelaide, Australia: Community for the World Movement, 1992. This book introduces small communities to the changing world, changing church.

Ela, Jean Marc. *African Cry*. Maryknoll, New York: Orbis Books, 1986. A profoundly prophetic voice from the African church. Strong on issues of justice and inculturation.

Ellsberg, Robert. *All Saints*. New York, Crossroad, 1997. A wonderfully ecumenical collection of saints – not all are officially canonised, not all are Christian. Each fascinating vignette carries some intriguing reflection on its subject. Excellent material for small Christian communities.

Figueroa Deck, Allan; Tarango, Yolanda; and Matovina, Timothy M (eds). *Perspectives: New Insights into Hispanic Ministry*. Kansas City: Sheed and Ward, 1995. A work that probes the tensions, issues, and options facing the church as Hispanic ministry continues to develop and deepen in the United States.

Flannery, Austin (ed.). *Vatican II: Conciliar and Post-Conciliar Documents*. Dublin: Dominican Publications, 1975; New York: Costello Publishing Co., 1975.

—— *More Post-Conciliar Documents*. Dublin: Dominican Publications, 1982; New York: Costello Publishing Company, 1982.

Fraser, Margaret and Ian M. *Wind and Fire: The Spirit Reshapes the Church in Basic Christian Communities*. Basic Communities Resource Centre, S.C.C., Dunblane FK15 OAJ, Scotland, 1986. This book gives us the opportunity to feel the life of the small Christian communities. In it the communities speak for themselves.

Fraser, Ian M. *Reinventing Theology as the People's Work*. Glasgow: Wild Goose Publications, 1988. Shows how theology is not just the project of the academic but of the entire Christian community.

— *Living a Countersign*. Glasgow: Wild Goose Publications, 1990. The enormously experienced author seeks to explain basic Christian communities in terms of their historical roots, their distinctive features, and their experiences of struggle.

— *Strange Fire: Life Stories and Prayers*. Glasgow: Wild Goose Publications, 1994. This work brings together 90 stories from Ian Fraser's many years among Christian communities around the world. Inspiring, well drawn, and always thought-provoking, they bring to life the profound faith of ordinary people, often in extremes of hardship and danger. Each finishes with a prayer or reflection which lets us link the stories with those of our own daily lives. The volume could prove an invaluable resource for meetings of the small Christian communities.

Fraser, Margaret and Ian M. *Salted with Fire, Life-stories, Meditations, Prayers*. Edinburgh: St Andrew's Press, 1999. An ideal resource book for church and pastoral work, and for use within the field of religious education.

Fung, Raymond. *Household of God on China's Soil*. Maryknoll, New York: Orbis Books, 1983. A refreshing collection of first-hand experiences of fourteen Chinese Christian communities during the turbulent Cultural Revolution years.

Gaba Publications. *African Cities and Christian Communities*. Spearhead No. 72, Eldoret, Kenya, 1982. A good study by people with local knowledge.

Galdamez, Pablo. *Faith of a People – The Life of a Basic Christian Community in El Salvador*. New York: Orbis Books; Melbourne: Dove; London: CIIR, 1986. An account of a basic community in an area that has suffered much.

Galilea, Segundo. *The Future of Our Past*. Notre Dame, Indiana: Ave Maria Press, 1985. One is struck by how relevant the spirituality of the great Spanish mystics is to modern times, and it is particularly suited to the small Christian communities.

Gilkey, Langdon. *Message and Existence*. Minnesota: Seabury Press, 1972.

Gill, Athol. *Life on the Road – The Gospel Basis for a Messianic Lifestyle*. Scottdale: Herald Press, PA 15683, 1992. An in-depth study of the gospels, emphasising their differences from each other and the necessity of breaking with cultural chains if one is to truly follow Jesus.

Gish, Art. *Living in Christian Community*. Scottdale, PA: Herald Press, 1978. An excellent book on Christian community. Written from an Anabaptist perspective, it comprehensively addresses the important theological and organisational issues. Both solidly theoretical and extremely practical.

Gutierrez, Gustavo. *A Theology of Liberation*. Maryknoll, New York: Orbis Books, 1973. A most important book that created a watershed in theology.

Haight, Roger. *Jesus Symbol of God*. New York: Orbis Books, 2000. A scholarly book, already hailed as a landmark in contemporary Catholic theology.

Harper, Michael. *A new Way of Living – How the Church of the Redeemer, Houston, found a new lifestyle*. London: Hodder and Stoughton, 1973. A description of household communities with Harper's perspective of the biblical basis for such.

Healey, Joseph G., M.M. *A Fifth Gospel: The Experience of Black Christian Values*. Maryknoll, New York: Orbis Books, 1981. Gives valuable insights into the workings of small Christian communities in Africa.

Healey, Joseph and Sybertz Donald. *Towards an African Narrative Theology*. Nairobi: Paulines Publications, Africa (Revised Edition, 2000); New York: Orbis Books 1999. For those interested in the church in Africa and beyond. Well received in Africa.

Healy, Sean, SM and Brigid Reynolds. *Social Analysis in the Light of the Gospel*. Dublin: Folens and Co., 1983. A useful volume that emerged from a series of workshops. From the Justice Desk of CORI (Conference of Religious of Ireland) these authors have produced a series of publications relevant to their brief; they deal with Irish and European issues mainly.

Hebblethwaite, Margaret. *Base Communities – An Introduction*. London: Geoffrey Chapman, 1993. A recommended resource.

— *Basic is Beautiful*. London: Fount (Harper Collins Publishers), 1993. This volume deals with the issue of how to translate basic ecclesial communities from the Third World to the First. Includes valuable accounts of, and reflection on, practical experiences.

Hennelly, Alfred T., SJ., ed. *Santo Domingo and Beyond*. Maryknoll, New York: Orbis Books, 1993. Documents and commentaries from the historic meeting of the Latin American Bishops' Conference.

Hinton, Jeanne. *Communities*. Guildford (Surrey), Eagle: Inter Publishing Service; 1993. Gives the instructive stories and spiritualities of twelve European communities. The volume is enhanced with photographs by Christopher Phillips.

— *Walking in the Same Direction*. Geneva: WCC Publications, 1995. The author, who has considerable experience, examines the new church that is emerging in the world largely through the vision and action of the small communities.

Hirmer, Oswald. *How to Start Neighbourhood Gospel Groups*. Lumko Missiological Institute, P. O. Box 5058, Delmenville 1483, South Africa. A kit with posters and textbook for learning a method of gospel sharing by a man very experienced in the field.

Hodgson, Ralph. *Poems*. London: Macmillan, c. 1917.

Holland, Joe and Henriot, Peter, SJ. *Social Analysis: Linking Faith and Justice*. Maryknoll, New York: Orbis Books, 1983. A valuable book by two experienced practitioners. Suited for animators of groups.

Hoornaert, Eduardo. *The Memory of the Christian People*. Maryknoll, New York: Orbis Books, 1988. This excellent work reveals striking similarities between the church's first communities and the grassroots communities transforming the church today. It puts us in touch with useful documentation from the early church, thereby providing a sound historic base.

Hope, Anne, and Timmel, Sally. *Training for Transformation: A Handbook for Community Workers*. 3 vols. Gweru, Zimbabwe: Mambo Press, 1984.

These volumes are excellent for justice formation and provide useful group exercises or dynamics.

Huelsmann, Rev. Peter, SJ. *Pray – An Introduction to the Spiritual Life for Busy People*. Mahwah, New Jersey: Paulist Press, 1976 (comes with a Moderator's Manual). A "course" in prayer to be used alone or in groups. Some communities in the United States have found this book most helpful.

Hurley, Michael. *Transforming Your Parish: Building a Faith Community*. Dublin: Columba Press, 1998. This book is an excellent introduction to a creative way of living the gospel as a community, employing the cell system.

Icenogle, Gareth Weldon. *Biblical Foundations for Small Group Ministry*. Inter Varsity Press, Dowers Grove, Il. 60515, 1994. We must begin with the word of God. This book gives the biblical foundations for small group ministry.

Imboden, Roberta. *From the Cross to the Kingdom*. San Francisco: Harper and Row, 1987. Basing herself on the philosophy of Sartre, the author says much that is of interest to small Christian communities; brilliant and original.

Jackson, Dave and Neta. *Living Together in a World Falling Apart*. Altamonte Springs, Florida: Creation House Publishers, 1974. This book sparked much interest in small Christian communities when first published. Years later it is still relevant. Deals with the most basic questions – from theology of community to issues of who does the housework – in a very readable way.

Janzen, David et al. *Fire, Salt, and Peace: Intentional Communities Alive in North America*. Evanston, Ill: Shalom Mission Communities. Explores the narrative method by profiling 29 communities. There is an ecumenical mix, "chosen from thousands of such communities worldwide."

John Paul II. *Redemptor Hominis*. London: Catholic Truth Society, 1979.

— *Laborem Exercens (On Human Work)*. London: Catholic Truth Society, 1981.

— *This is the Laity* (Simplification of *Christifideles Laici*). England: The Grail, 1989.

Justice and Peace Commission of the Kenyan Bishops' Conference. *We are the Church*, Lenten Campaign '94. Nairobi: St. Joseph's Press, Kangemi, 1994.

Kalilombe, Patrick A. *From Outstation to small Christian Community*. Eldoret, Kenya: Gaba Publications, 1981. A study, adapted from a doctoral thesis, by a person who was himself one of the pioneers in fostering small Christian communities in Africa. Shows how having a small number of people doesn't necessarily constitute a small Christian community.

Knox, Ronald. *Autobiography of a Saint, Thérèse of Lisieux: Journey of a Soul*. London: Fontana Books, 1960. A spiritual masterpiece.

Latin American Bishops. *The Church in the Present-Day Transformation of Latin America in the Light of the Council* (Medellin documents).

Washington D.C. (Secretariat for Latin America, National Conference of Bishops), 3rd ed., 1979.

Lee, Bernard J. and Cowan, Michael A. *Dangerous Memories*. Kansas City: Sheed and Ward, 1986. Explores home churches in the United States. Includes valuable discussion of mutuality, political action, and servant leadership. Contains an especially useful treatment of the role and potential of communities in the context of American individualism.

Lee, Bernard J. SM. with D'Antonio, William V. *The Catholic Experience of Small Christian Communities*. Mahwah, NJ: Paulist Press, 2000. Results and reflection upon a valuable, widescale sociological study of small Christian communities in North America.

Lernoux, Penny. *Cry of the People*. Middlesex: Penguin, 1981; New York: Doubleday, 1980. An excellent resource book regarding the justice issue in Latin America. Particularly good on the National Security State and the role of the multinationals.

Le Shan, Lawrence. *How to Meditate*. Boston: Bantam Books, Little Brown and Company, 1974. A book that many people have found helpful.

Lobinger, Fritz. *Building Small Christian Communities*. Lumko Missiological Institute, P.O. Box 5058, Delmenville 1483, South Africa, 1981. A kit with large posters and textbook for starting small Christian communities; widely used, especially in Africa (Lumko has a selection of excellent pastoral materials).

— *Like his Brothers and Sisters*. Quezon City, the Philippines: Claretian Publications, 1998. This book takes a constructive look at a possible means of renewing the priesthood.

Lohfink, Jerhard. *Jesus and Community, The Social Dimension of Christian Faith*. Philadelphia: Fortress Press, 1984; New York: Paulist Press, 1982. Implementing the Christian ethic must be done by groups of people who consciously place themselves under the gospel of the reign of God and who wish to be real communities of brothers and sisters. A challenging book.

Marins José. *Church from the Roots*. London: CAFOD, 1989. Proceeding from modern-day parables, the author and his team, who have shared worldwide on small Christian communities, draw valuable conclusions for the groups.

McCarthy, Flor, SDB. *Windows on the Gospel: Stories and Reflections*. Dublin: Dominican Publications; Mystic, Connecticut: Twenty-Third Publications, 1992. This simple collection of stories and reflections is offered to all who are searching for a spirituality based on the gospel; excellent material for meetings.

McConnell, Frank. *Find Quickly in the Gospels*. Sevenoaks (Kent): Petrus Books, 1990. An extremely user-friendly guide for locating gospel texts – an ordinary person's concordance.

McDonagh, Sean. *The Greening of the Church*. Maryknoll, New York: Orbis Books, 1990. Effectively highlights the crucial environmental issue.

McGarry, Cecil SJ, Editor. *What Happened at the African Synod?* Nairobi: Paulines Publications Africa, 1995. A must for anyone interested in the church generally and the African church in particular. The subject of the small Christian communities is at the core of African pastoral concerns.

McGowan, Phelim SJ. *Welcome Home.* Dublin: Dominican Publications, 1998. A prayerful reflection on the sacrament of reconciliation. Also has a section containing excellent "Services of Reconciliation", by Flor McCarthy SDB.

Mellis, Charles J. *Committed Communities.* William Carey Library, 533 Hermosa Street, South Pasadena, CA, 19030, 1976. A very insightful evaluation of the importance of community in missions, historically; gives the implications for today.

Merton, Thomas. *Elected Silence,* or, *Seven Storey Mountain.* London: Burns and Oates, 1961. A spiritual classic.

— *The Non-violent Alternative.* New York: Farrar, Strauss, and Giroux, 1980. Excellent.

Mesters, Carlos. *Defenceless Flower.* Maryknoll, New York: Orbis Books, 1989. Shows a marvellous use of the Bible in Brazilian small Christian communities. A significant contribution to methodology in scripture reflection.

Miller, Hal. *Christian Community: Biblical or Optional?* Ann Arbor: Servant Books, 1979. A solid theology of Christian community, demonstrating from the scriptures that community was part of God's plan from the beginning and that Jesus restored community through the kingdom.

Myers, Ched. *Who Will Roll Away the Stone? Discipleship Queries for First World Christians.* New York: Orbis, 1994. A thought-provoking book.

NACCAN (National Association of Christian Communities and Networks, Britain). *Directory of Christian Communities and Networks.* JAS Print, 1993.

National Secretariat and Hispanic Teams. *Basic Ecclesial Communities.* Missouri 63057: Ligouri, 1980. Simple, theologically rich, and practical.

— *Guidelines for Establishing Basic Christian Communities in the United States.* Missouri 63057: Ligouri, 1981.

"New Way" has produced a very useful set of booklets related to the life of small Christian communities e.g. *Living Faith through Word and Action, Reflections on St Matthew's Gospel for Small Christian Communities,* by Peter Price; *Small and in Place – Practical Steps in Small Christian Community Formation,* by Jeanne Hinton and Kathy Galloway; *Celebration, Games and activities for fiesta,* by Magdalen Smith. For information contact: Pauline Lamming, Lodge Farmhouse, Groton, Sudbury, Suffolk CO10 5EJ, UK.

O'Brien, David J. and Shannon, Thomas A. *Renewing the Earth.* New York: Image Books, 1977. The single most comprehensive available collection of primary documents on Catholic social thought from Pope Leo XIII's *Rerum Novarum* (1891) to John Paul II's *Centesimus Annus* (1991). Documents are accompanied by introductory essays and helpful notes.

O'Brien, John, CSSp. *Seeds of a New Church*. Dublin: Columba Press, 1994. This deals with twenty-two group experiences in the Irish context and their implications for the church of the future. Important and challenging reading for anyone connected with the church, particularly in Ireland.

O'Brien, Monsignor Timothy. *Why Small Christian Communities Work*. San Jose: Resource Publications, 1996. Useful documented information.

O'Bryan, Paul. *Regathering the Parish: A Beginning Program for the Parish SCC Core Team*. Melbourne: Southern Cross Communities Australia (Revised Edition), 1997. Useful material from an experienced team. Also recommended:

— *Growing the SCC Vision*. do., 1998.
— *The SCC Gathering Format*. do., 1997.
— *Leadership in the SCC Parish*. do., 1999.

O'Connell Bisgrove, Margaret. *Where Two Are Gathered*. Winona, Minnesota: St Mary's Press, 1997. This book is important because it offers an assortment of stories about real people who candidly share their successes and failures as they build the Reign of God.

Ó Donnchadha, Proinsias. *A Stack of Stories*. Dublin: Night Owl Early Bird Bureau, 1995. Beautiful short reflections that could provide valuable materials for meetings.

O'Donnell, Hugh. *Mrs Moody's Blues See Red*. Limerick: Salesian Press, 1980.

O'Gorman, Frances Elsie. *Base Communities in Brazil: Dynamics of a Journey*. Rio de Janeiro: FASE-NUCLAR, 1983. An account of Brazilian small Christian communities by one who has been deeply involved with them in the favelas of Rio de Janeiro.

O'Halloran, James, *Signs of Hope: Developing Small Christian Communities*, Maryknoll, New York: Orbis Books, 1991; Dublin: Columba Press, 1991. This book developed from Living Cells "which has been for some years one of the best introductions to the small Christian communities" (*Tablet*, 22 February 1992).

— *Small Christian Communities: A Pastoral Companion*. Dublin: Columba Press, 1996; Orbis Books, Maryknoll: New York, 1996; builds on the two foregoing volumes.

— *The Least of These*. Dublin: Columba Press, 1991. A book of short stories, some of which have been used in catechetical programmes and courses on peace and justice.

— *When the Acacia Bird Sings*. Dublin: The Columba Press, 1999; available at: Victoria, Australia: John Garratt Publishing. "This novel is a must for anyone who wishes to understand the pain of separation suffered by migrants and refugees. If ever a book should be on the national curriculum, this is it." 'Books of the Year'. *The Irish Times*.

O'Hanlon, Joseph. *Beginning the Bible*. Slough (England): St Paul's, 1994. A user-friendly, integrated introduction to the Bible. The general reader will find this amenable.

O'Regan, Pauline, and O'Connor, Teresa. *Community, Give it a Go!* Christchurch, New Zealand: Allen and Unwin, 1989. The authors describe their work in building community: how to establish networks, how to start a coffee group, ways of arranging childcare, kinds of celebrations, relationships between local community workers and professional groups.

Parker, J. Palmer. *The Promise of Paradox – A celebration of contradictions in the Christian life.* Indiana: Ave Maria Press, Notre Dame, 1980. The section on community is worthwhile reading.

Paul VI. *Populorum Progressio (On the Development of Peoples).* London: CTS, 1967; Mahwah, New Jersey: Paulist Press, 1967.

— *Evangelii Nuntiandi (Evangelization Today).* Dublin: Dominican Publications, 1977. Commentary by Bede McGregor OP.

— *Evangelica Testificatio: Witness to the Gospel* (cf. above, Flannery. Vatican Council II, p. 680ff.).

— *Octogesima Adveniens (On Social Justice).* London: CTS, 1971.

Pelton, Robert S.,CSC. *Small Christian Community: Imagining Future Church.* Indiana: University of Notre Dame Press, 1997. A thought-provoking book, edited by a man of vast experience in small Christian communities.

Perkins, Pheme. *Reading the New Testament, An Introduction.* New York: Paulist Press, 1977.

Prased Pinto, Joseph, OFM Cap. *Inculturation through Basic Communities: An Indian Perspective.* Bangalore: Asia Trading Company, 1985. The author explores the potential of basic communities to create a church that will be "deeply rooted in the Indian values of religiosity, poverty, joy, and festivity."

Price, Peter, B. *Seeds of the Word: Biblical Reflections on Small Christian Communities.* London: Darton, Longman and Todd, 1996. This book brings an originality and realism to Bible reflection in small groups that will inspire practical action and enable the footprints of God to be seen in the life of the local community. An excellent resource.

Rahner, Karl, SJ. *I Remember.* London: SCM, 1984. An autobiographical account, taken from an interview, of one who has been described as the "quiet mover" and "ghostwriter" of Vatican II, and even as "the Father of the church in the 20th Century." The volume gives his thinking on the council.

Raines, John C. and Day-Lower, Donna C. *Modern Work and Human Meaning.* Philadelphia, Pennsylvania: Westminster Press, 1986. This work deals with social problems in the United States. It has the considerable merit of allowing the poor to speak for themselves; listening to their voice is even more critical in the present political climate..

Reichert, Richard. *Simulation Games for Religious Education.* Winona, Minnesota: St Mary's Press, Christian Brothers Publications, 1975. Useful resource material.

Research and Development Division, National Council of Young Mens'
Christian Associations, 291 Broadway, New York, 10007. *Training
Volunteer Leaders – A Handbook to Train Volunteers and Other Leaders of
Program Groups.* Contains helpful resource material and group exercises.

Saxby, Trevor J. *Pilgrims of a Common Life – Christian Community of Goods
Through the Centuries.* Scottdale: Herald Press, 1987. A review of intentional residential Christian communities from New Testament times to
the 20th century and of the biblical principles indicating sharing of possessions.

Scharper, Sally and Philip, eds. *The Gospel in Art by the Peasants of
Solentiname.* Maryknoll, New York: Orbis Books, 1984. This book shows
how the gospels can be used effectively by ordinary people.

Schmidt, Joseph F. *Praying with Thérèse of Lisieux.* Winona Minnesota: St
Mary's Press, 1992. Carefully distills Thérèse's writing, presenting her
teachings in a most helpful way.

Schreiter, Robert, C.PP.S. *Constructing Local Theologies,* New York: Orbis
Books. A systematic study of the nature and theology of indigenous
churches. An excellent read.

Scott, Foresman and Company: Glenview, Illinois, 1991, *England in
Literature.*

SECAM. *Seeking Gospel Justice in Africa.* Eldoret, Kenya: Gaba Publications,
1981.

Slattery, Hugh., msc. *HIV/AIDS, A Call to Action, Responding as Christians.*
Nairobi: Paulines Publications Africa, 2002. A thoughtful volume on
the subject of AIDS by one who is actively involved with the issue in
Southern Africa. He notes how crucial the work of small Christian com-
munites are to the solution of the problem.

Smith, Christian. *Going to the Roots.* Scottsdale: Herald Press, 1992. Smith
very knowledgeable and experienced in small Christian communities.

Snyder, Howard. *Community of the King.* Chicago: Inter-Varsity Press. 1977.
On alternative church models as agents of the kingdom. Interesting
reading about Christian community based on a practical experience in
the Irving Park Free Methodist Church in Chicago.

The African Synod. Kenya: Daughters of St Paul, 1994.

The Paulian Association. *A Storybook of Australian Small Christian Communities.*
Sydney: The Paulian Association and Communities Australia, 1998.

Torres, Sergio, Eagleson, John, eds. *The Challenge of Basic Christian
Communities.* Maryknoll, New York: Orbis Books, 1981. Reflections on
small Christian communities by some of the most eminent people in the
fields of theology and pastoral practice from the Third World. Chapter
16 has information on the use of the Bible in small communities by
Carlos Mesters, which is most enlightening.

Vanier, Jean. *Community and Growth* (Revised Edition). London: Darton,
Longman and Todd, 1989. A veritable gold-mine of reflective and practical ideas on community by the founder of L'Arche.

Veling, Terry. *Living in the Margins – Intentional Communities and the Art of*

Interpretation. New York: Crossroad, 1996. A gifted theologian sheds light on the meaning and value of intentional faith communities on the margins of parish life.

Veritas. *Come and See: A New Vision of Parish Renewal*. Dublin: Veritas Publications, 1993. An account of a parish cell system pioneered in Ballinteer, Dublin.

Weber, Hans-Ruedi. *The Book that reads me*. Geneva: WCC Publications, 1995. A worthwhile handbook for Bible study enablers.

Whitehead, Evelyn Eaton and James D. *Community of Faith: Crafting Christian Communities Today*. Mystic, Connecticut: Twenty-Third Publications, 1992. An enormously valuable book which creatively employs the insights of modern psychology and sociology to help understand the nature and dynamics of Christian community. Strong as both a theoretical analysis of community and a practical guide to life in community.

Wiltgen, Ralph, SVD. *The Rhine Flows into the Tiber*. Devon, England: Augustine Publishing Company, 1978. This book highlights the German influence at Vatican II.

Winter, Derek. *Communities of Freedom*. London: Christian Aid, 1988. A useful resource.

Wright Wendy M. *Francis de Sales, Jane de Chantal & Aelred of Rievaulx: Befriending Each Other in God*. Cincinnati, Ohio: St Anthony Messenger Press, 1996. Imaginative and bold insights.

Wuthnow, Robert. *Sharing the Journey: Support Groups and America's New Quest for Community*. The Free Press. A thought-provoking account of the new impetus towards community in, not only religious, but also civil society in the US.

Notes

NOTES ON CHAPTER ONE
1. Dom Helder Camara, *Hoping Against All Hope*, Maryknoll, New York: Orbis Books, 1964, p. 189.

NOTES ON CHAPTER TWO
2. Hugh O'Donnell, *Mrs Moody's Blues See Red*, Limerick: Salesian Press, 1980, p. 10.
3. Evelyn Eaton Whitehead & James D. Whitehead, *Community of Faith, Crafting Christian Communities Today*: Mystic, CT: XXIIIrd Publications, pp. 77-79.
4. Langdon Gilkey, *Message and Existence*, Minneapolis: Seabury Press, 1979, p. 165.
5. Ralph Hodgson, *Poems*, London: Macmillan, c. 1917.
6. Penny Lernoux, *The Cry of the People*, New York: Doubleday and Company, 1980, p. 267.
7. David J. O'Brien and Thomas Shannon (eds.), "Justice in the World," in *Renewing the Earth*, New York: Image Books, 1977, p. 391.
8. cf. *Tablet*, August 9, 1980.

NOTES ON CHAPTER THREE
9. Carlos Mesters, *The Bible and Liberation*, ed. Norman K. Gottwald, Maryknoll, New York: Orbis Books, 1983, p. 122.
10. Ibid.
11. Sally and Philip Scharper (eds), *The Gospel in Art by the Peasants of Solentiname* , Maryknoll, New York: Orbis Books, 1984, p. 32.
12. Charles de Faucauld, *Oeuvres spirituelles (Antologie)*, Paris, Seuil, 1958, p.166.
13. *Oeuvres*, St Francis de Sales, eds, Andre Ravier and Roger Devos, Paris: Bibliotheque Pleiade, Editions Gallimard, 1969, III, 260.
14. Ronald Knox, *Autobiography of a Saint, Thérèse of Lisieux, The Journey of a Soul*, London: Fontana Books, 1960, p. 228.

NOTES ON CHAPTER FOUR
15. Henri Nouwen, Modern Spiritual Masters Series, New York: Orbis Books, 1998, p. 27.
16. cf. Ronald Knox, *Autobiography of a Saint, Thérèse of Lisieux, Story of a Soul*, London: Fontana Books, 1960, pp. 179-191; also Joseph F. Schmidt, *Praying with Thérèse of Lisieux*, Winona: St Mary's Press, 1992, pp. 48-49.
17. cf. Wendy M. Wright, *Francis de Sales, Jane de Chantal & Aelred of Rievaulx, a retreat with*, Cincinnati, Ohio: St Anthony Messenger Press, 1996, p. 38.

18. Ibid, pp. 96-97.
19. Ibid, pp. 86-87.
20. John Donne, *England in Literature,* Glenview, Illinois, Scott, Foresman and Company, 1991, p.284.
21. Geffrey B. Kelly, "Bonhoeffer's 'Non-Religious' Christianity: Antecedents and Critique", *Bijdragen* 37 (1976), cf. pp. 119-123.
22. Hilaire Belloc, *Collected Verse,* Harmondsworth, Middlesex: Penguin Books, 1958 (by kind permission of the PDS Group Ltd.)
23. 'Late Fragment' from *Collected Verse* by Raymond Carver, published by Harvill Press. Used by permission of The Random House Group Limited, © Tess Gallagher.
24. William Wordsworth, *Wordsworth* (Tintern Abbey), Oxford: University Press, 1948, p. 50.

NOTES ON CHAPTER FIVE
25. Evelyn Eaton Whitehead & James D.Whitehead, *Community of Faith,* Mystic, CT: XXIIIrd Publications, cf. pp. 140-147.
26. Austin Flannery, *Vatican Council II, Evangelica Testificatio: Witness to the Gospel,* Dublin: Dominican Publications, no. 25, p. 692., Fifth Printing, 1980.
27. Jeanne Hinton, *Communities,* Guildford: Eagle, 1993, p. 39.
28. Paul VI, *Populorum Progressio (Fostering the Development of Peoples),* London: Catholic Truth Society, 1968, no. 81, p. 38.
29. Austin Flannery, *Vatican Council II. Decree on the Apostolate of Lay People,* Dublin: Dominican Publications, no. 11, p.779, Fifth Printing, 1980.
30. Segundo Galilea, *The Future of Our Past,* Notre Dame, Indiana: Ave Maria Press, 1985, p. 27.
31. Thomas Merton, *The Non-violent Alternative,* New York: Farrar, Strauss, Giroux, 1980, p. 64.

NOTES ON CHAPTER SEVEN
32. Paul VI, *Populorum Progressio (Fostering the Development of Peoples),* no. 32, p. 17.
33. Dr Hill, *Cook Book,* London, 1747.

NOTES ON CHAPTER EIGHT
34. Justice and Peace Commission of the Kenyan Bishops' Conference, *We are the Church: Lenten Campaign 1994,* Nairobi, St Joseph's Press, Kangemi, 1994, p. 3.
35. *National Catholic Reporter,* 27 October 1995, p. 2.
36. Fritz Lobinger, *Like his Brothers and Sisters,* Quezon City, Philippines: Claretian Publications, 1998.
37. *Sunday Times* (South Africa), 10 March 2002, p. 16.

NOTES ON CHAPTER NINE
38. Raymond E. Brown, *The Churches the Apostles Left Behind,* New York:

Paulist Press, 1984, p. 11.
39. Eduardo Hoornaert, *The Memory of the Christian People*, New York: Orbis Books, 1988, p. 198.
40. Michelle Connolly, Lecture, Paulian Centre, Sydney, Saturday, November 14th., 1992.
41. Bill Loader, *Colloquium*, 24/1 (1992), p. 8.
42. *New Catholic Encyclopedia*, (copyright The Catholic University of America, Washington DC, 1967), Jack Heraty & Associates, Inc., Palatine, Ill., p. 227, 1981. (CodTheod , abbreviation for *Codex Theodosianus*, ed T. Mommsen and P. Meyer, 2 v. in 3 (Berlin 1905).
43. *Small Christian Communities in the US Catholic Church: Snapshots of Great Motion – Executive Summary*, Research conducted under a grant from the Lilly Endowment, Inc., to the Institute for Ministry, Loyola University, New Orleans, Bernard J. Lee , SM, Project Director, 1999.
44. *Informe: América del Norte*, Report on US/Canadian Small Christian Communities, presented to the International Consultation on Small Christian Communities, Cochabamba, Bolivia, November, 1999.
45. *Small Christian Communities in the US Catholic Church: Snapshots of Great Motion – Executive Summary*, Research conducted under a grant from the Lilly Endowment, Inc. to the Institute for Ministry, Loyola University, New Orleans, Bernard J. Lee, SM, Project Director, 1999.
46. *Informe : América del Norte* , Report on US/Canadian Small Christian Communities, presented to the International Consultation on Small Christian Communities, Cochabamba, Bolivia, 1999.
47. Monsignor Timothy O'Brien, *Why Small Christian Communities Work*, San José: Resource Publications, 1996.
48. James O'Halloran SDB, *Small Christian Communities: A Pastoral Companion*, New York: Orbis Books, Dublin: Columba Press, 1996.
49. Bernard J. Lee SM, *The Future Church of 140 B.C.E.*, Crossroads Herder, 1995.
50. Buena Vista, *Ink*, Arvada, CO, March-April, 1997.
51. Ibid.
52. Bernard J. Lee SM, *Small Christian Communities in the U. S. Catholic Church: Snapshots of a Great Motion – Executive Summary* (Research Project), New Orleans: Institute for Ministry, Loyola University, 1999.
53. Ibid.
54. Ibid.
55. Ibid.
56. Ibid.
57. *Initiatives in Religion*, Winter, 1998.
58. Bernard J.Lee, *Small Christian Communities in the U.S. Catholic Church: Snapshots of a Great Motion – Executive Summary* (Research Project), New Orleans: Institute for Ministry, Loyola University, 1999.
59. Ibid.
60. Ibid.
61. Ibid.

62. Dr Ian M. Fraser, Address at the World Consultation on Small Christian Communities, Cochabamba, Bolivia, 1999.

63. *The Tablet*, 17 June, 2000, p. 835.

64. *Seeking Gospel Justice in Africa,* Eldoret, Kenya: Gaba Publications, 1981.

65. *AFER, Centenary of the Evangelization in Kenya*, Eldoret, Kenya: Gaba Publications, vol 32, no.4, August, 1990, pp. 186-191.

66. *The African Synod*, Kenya, Daughters of St Paul, 1994.

67. *The Tablet*: London, April 23rd, 1994, p. 500.

68. John Paul II, Post-Synodal Apostolic Exhortation, *Ecclesia in Africa (Church in Africa)*, Nairobi: Daughters of St Paul, para 89, p. 69.

69. *AMECEA Documentation Service*, Nairobi, January 28, 1985, p. 1.

70. McGarry, Cecil SJ, *What Happened at the African Synod*, Nairobi: Paulines Publications Africa, 1995, p. 146.

71. Raymond Fung, *Household of God on China's Soil*, New York: Orbis Books, 1983.

72. Joseph Prased Pinto OFM Cap., *Inculturation through Basic Communities*, Bangalore, Asian Trading Corporation, 1985, p. 176.

73. Interview, Milltown Park, Dublin, October 5th, 2001.

74. cf. *The Tablet*, London, September 15th, 2001, p. 1316.

75. cf. *The Tablet*, London, August 9th, 1980.

Index

By the same author

When the Acacia Bird Sings

James O'Halloran

'*When the Acacia Bird Sings* is a must for anyone who wishes to understand the pain of separation suffered by migrants and refugees. If ever a book should be on the national curriculum, this is it.' — Tom Hyland, 'Books of the Year', *The Irish Times*.

'The narrative is extremely well conducted and the author knows his world well. The novel will enter missionary anthologies, but why not the anthologies of literature in general?' — *Marchés Tropicaux*, France.

'A novel of stature. I read it at a sitting not because of its brevity – rather the story of the Machava family gripped me intensely. Its humane perceptions remind me of André Brink's celebrated books. Brings the open minded reader to where literature raises timely moral questions.' — *The Furrow*, Ireland.

'A harrowing narrative and an epic in the classic sense, spare and stark in its prose style. There are echoes of Antigone trying to bury her dead. Very well written.' — *Books Ireland*.

'O'Halloran's story has made me take a long look at my opinions and values. *When the Acacia Bird Sings* is one of those rare tales that does not force a falsely happy ending upon us.' — *Face Up*, for teens, Ireland.

'A moving story of the triumph of the human spirit over appalling odds. Disturbs our smugness and forces us into guilty action to help those less fortunate.' — 'Irishman's Diary', *The Irish Times*.

'Does for refugees what Alan Paton did for the victims of apartheid.' — Don Mullan, author of *Eyewitness Bloody Sunday* and *The Dublin and Monaghan Bombings*, Wolfhound Press, Ireland.

Available from your usual supplier or direct from:
The Columba Press,
55A Spruce Avenue, Stillorgan Industrial Park,
Blackrock, Co Dublin, Ireland.
E-mail: sales@columba.ie